Connectionism

CONNECTIONISM

A Hands-On Approach

Michael R. W. Dawson

Blackwell
Publishing

BLACKWELL PUBLISHING
350 Main Street, Malden, MA 02148 5020, USA
9600 Garsington Road, Oxford OX4 2DQ, UK
550 Swanston Street, Carlton, Victoria 3053, Australia

First published 2005 by Blackwell Publishing Ltd

1 2005

Library of Congress Cataloging-in-Publication Data

Dawson, Michael Robert William, 1959–
    Connectionism : a hands-on approach / Michael R.W. Dawson—1st ed.
        p. cm.
    Includes bibliographical references and index.
    ISBN-13: 978-1-4051-3074-5 (hardcover : alk. paper)
    ISBN-10: 1-4051-3074-1 (hardcover : alk. paper)
    ISBN-13: 978-1-4051-2807-0 (pbk. : alk. paper)
    ISBN-10: 1-4051-2807-0 (pbk. : alk. paper)
    1. Connectionism. I. Title.

BF311.D343 2005
153—dc22

2004028929

Set in 10/12.5 pt Dante
By Newgen Imaging Systems (P) Ltd, Chennai, India
Printed and bound in the United Kingdom
By TJ International, Padstow, Cornwall

The publisher's policy is to use permanent paper from mills that operate a sustainable forestry policy, and which has been manufactured from pulp processed using acid-free and elementary chlorine-free practices. Furthermore, the publisher ensures that the text paper and cover board have met acceptable environmental accreditation standards.

For further information
on Blackwell Publishing, visit our website:
www.blackwellpublishing.com

Contents

CHAPTER 1

Hands-On Connectionism

1.1 Connectionism in Principle and in Practice

Shortly after finishing graduate school in the late 1980s, I decided to explore in more detail the relationship between symbolic and connectionist models in cognitive science. While I had been trained in a lab that was fairly anticonnectionist (Fodor & Pylyshyn, 1988; Pylyshyn, 1991), much of my thesis research involved using parallel distributed processing (PDP) models of one sort or another (Dawson, 1991; Dawson & Pylyshyn, 1988). At a theoretical level I was interested in exploring possible compromises between these two positions.

The models that I used in my thesis research were "hardwired" in order for me to insert specific visual properties or constraints directly into my networks. So, the first step that I had to take to broaden my expertise was to learn how to train connectionist systems. To do this, I began to read the influential material of the time (McClelland & Rumelhart, 1986; Rumelhart & McClelland, 1986), and on the basis of my readings I began to convert the equations that I was seeing into working programs. Once I had replicated the work of others by developing some usable code, I built on this new expertise to develop architectures that were more original (Berkeley et al., 1995; Dawson & Schopflocher, 1992a, 1992b).

One of the things that I discovered was that my "in principle" knowledge of PDP networks that was based on equations and descriptions that I had read was quite a bit thinner than my "in practice" knowledge that I was acquiring by running the different programs that I constructed. In many cases, theoretical descriptions of connectionist models omitted to mention important practical issues that arose when the programs were created and executed. I came to the conclusion that while abstract knowledge about PDP networks is fundamentally important, particularly if one is interested in developing new learning rules or new architectures, hands-on knowledge is also necessary. You can't learn about connectionism just by reading the equations: you have to get your hands dirty and play around with some programs.

The uneasy relationship between abstract and practical knowledge haunted me when I began teaching connectionist ideas to my senior undergraduate students. One of the main themes of my foundations of cognitive science course was that there were very strong relationships between symbolic and connectionist theories (Dawson, 1998). In order to teach this theme, students were introduced to some of the basic properties of PDP models, and were given some demonstrations of connectionist networks in action. But, because of class size, students were not given the opportunity to work with these sorts of simulations on their own. When exam time rolled around, this lack of practical knowledge sometimes led to students giving answers that were a little too speculative.

I tried to deal with this problem in a fourth-year course that I developed on minds and machines. There was a good deal of abstract material in this course, because I wanted to introduce students to a variety of connectionist architectures, and I wanted to expose them to some of the basic equations that define the behavior of PDP networks. Furthermore, I wanted to develop a theoretical agenda in which I argued for a synthetic alternative to the more traditional analytic methodologies that are found in psychology and cognitive science (Dawson, 2002, 2004). However, I also tried to supplement the ease abstract ideas by providing hands-on activities to make connectionism more concrete. There were three phases of attempts to do this in the history of this course. In the first phase, I had students purchase textbooks that provided software for exploring different architectures (Caudill & Butler, 1992a, 1992b; McClelland & Rumelhart, 1988). In the second phase, because I was uncomfortable with some of the constraints that this "canned" software placed on me, I created a set of customized assignments using Microsoft Excel spreadsheets that I distributed to my students. In the third phase, I increased the flexibility of my assignments by writing my own Visual Basic programs for use in the class, where a program brought a particular PDP architecture to life, trained it to perform some problem of interest, and enabled students to examine the results by organizing them in Excel spreadsheets.

This book presents this third phase of connectionist training to the reader. It is associated with a suite of freely available programs, and other material, that can be found at http://www.bcp. psych.ualberta.ca/~mike/Book3/. Each program instantiates a particular PDP network. Chapters in this book provide a brief introduction to each network, a detailed introduction to how to use a program to explore this architecture, and a series of different exercises that are designed to highlight advantages – and disadvantages – of the network. When I teach my minds and machines course, I have students work through the exercises in this book during the term, handing in the answers to them to make up 20 percent of their grade. This provides the hands-on experience that I think that they require. The lectures focus on more abstract material, so that the exercises and the lectures complement one another to provide a balanced introduction to connectionist modeling.

1.2   The Organization of This Book

Another way in which the current book can be viewed is as a companion to *Minds and Machines: Connectionism and Psychological Modeling* (Dawson, 2004). In that book, Chapter 9 provides an introduction to the distributed associative memory, Chapter 10 introduces the perceptron, and Chapter 11 provides an overview of the multilayer perceptron. The current book can be thought of as being structured into three main sections, with each section providing exercises for exploring each of these three connectionist architectures.

1.2.1 Exploring the distributed associative memory

The first section of this book explores two different learning rules that can be used to store information in a distributed associative memory. Chapter 2 provides a brief account of the fundamental properties of this type of connectionist network, with an emphasis on Hebb-style learning. Chapter 3 gives the reader the details for installing and using a program that we call James, which is designed to implement a distributed associative memory that can be trained using either the Hebb rule or the delta rule. Chapters 4 through 8 provide a series of exercises to be done with the James program that begin by exploring conditions under which distributed associative memories work well, and that end by revealing conditions under which the performance of this kind of network is less than desirable.

1.2.2 Exploring the perceptron

The first step to overcoming the limitations of a distributed associative memory is to replace the linear activation function found in its output units with a nonlinear activation function. The result is a type of network called a perceptron, which is the focus of the second section of this book. Chapter 9 provides a brief introduction to this kind of network, focusing on three different kinds of nonlinear activation functions: the step function, the logistic equation, and the Gaussian equation. Chapter 10 supplies the details for installing and using our Rosenblatt program for exploring these three different varieties of perceptrons. The exercises in chapters 11 through 16 demonstrate the kinds of problems that these networks can and cannot solve, illustrate the potential for activation function X problem type interactions, and show how this very old architecture can still provide some interesting results of import to modern animal learning theory.

1.2.3 Exploring the multilayer perceptron

While the exercises show that the perceptron is an advance over the distributed associative memory, and that it can generate some very interesting results, it still is an architecture that is subject to some powerful limitations. In order to go beyond these limitations, additional processing units must be added to the network to mediate the signals being sent between input and output units. These additional units, called hidden units, are the hallmark of a powerful PDP architecture called the multilayer perceptron. This architecture is introduced in chapter 17, and chapter 18 describes how to use our Rumelhart program to train four different varieties of the multilayer perceptron. The exercises in the chapters that follow demonstrate the power of this kind of network, its relevance to cognitive science and psychology, and introduce some twists that include network interpretation and alternative notions of network training.

1.2.4 Personal explorations

Up to the end of chapter 26, the exercises provided in this book are designed to highlight particular points about PDP models. They provide detailed instructions, and "canned" training sets that are designed with a specific agenda in mind. However, the programs that are provided with this book are powerful enough to let the reader do more interesting activities, such as training networks on problems that the reader might be particularly interested in. The final chapter in this book provides readers with some exercises that will give them the expertise to build training sets for their own problems, and will highlight important design issues, like the encoding of input and output patterns, and so on. The programs that are associated with this book are powerful enough to cope with some challenging problems, and the reader is encouraged to use them for this purpose. Of course, after reaching this point in the book, the reader should also be in a position – after a little manual reading – to take charge of other software packages that might be more suited for the kinds of tasks that they are interested in studying.

Chapter 2

The Distributed Associative Memory

2.1 The Paired Associate Task

Mary Whiton Calkins (1863–1930) was among the first generation of women to enter psychology (Furumoto, 1980). In 1896, she published a paper in *Psychological Review* that provided the first description of the *paired associate task*. In many respects, this paradigm treats subjects in a memory experiment as if they were learning the vocabulary of a foreign language (Kintsch, 1970). Subjects learn a list of stimulus–response pairs. Sometimes this learned via the "study-test method". With this method, subjects are presented both members of the pair at the same time, and attempt to remember the association between the two. In the test phase of this method, subjects are only presented the stimulus, and must attempt to recall the associated response on their own.

Calkins' proposal for the paired associate task was inspired by the teachings of William James (1890). James' treatment of association is found in chapter 14 of his *The Principles of Psychology*, and it possesses several key elements. First, James recognized that one idea or event could be represented in the brain as a pattern of activity across a set of more than one neuron. Second, he expressed his law of habit in terms of a process that affected the ease of transit of a nerve-current through a tract: the basic idea was that neural signals would be most likely to propagate through fibres that had already been used frequently. Third, he explained succession of thoughts by hypothesizing that activity in one brain state (i.e., some set of neurons) leads to activity in some different brain state that had previously been associated with the first. "When two elementary brain-processes have been active together or in immediate succession, one of them, on reoccurring, tends to propagate its excitement into the other" (James, 1890, p. 566). Finally, James was predominately concerned with predicting which subsequent brain state would be activated by a prior brain state, given that one idea might be associated with a number of different ideas, others at different times or in different ways. James attempted to explain this kind of variation by realizing that any given neuron would be receiving signals from a number of other neurons, and that its degree of activation would depend on an entire pattern of input, and not upon an association with a single incoming signal.

After the cognitive revolution in the second half of the twentieth century, many researchers began to use computer simulations to study human memory. Some of the earliest research on connectionist models developed distributed memories capable of learning associations between pairs of input patterns (Steinbuch, 1961; Taylor, 1956), or of learning to associate an input pattern with a categorizing response (Rosenblatt, 1962; Selfridge, 1956; Widrow & Hoff, 1960). The basic structure of this kind of connectionist network, which has come to be called the *standard pattern associator* (McClelland, 1986), is essentially identical to the memory proposed by James (1890), and is ideally suited to perform the paired associate task.

2.2   The Standard Pattern Associator

The standard pattern associator is constructed from the processing units and modifiable connections defined in the generic PDP architecture (Dawson, 2004). It consists of two sets of processing units. One set (input, set A in figure 2.1) is used to represent a pattern of activity that can be described as a cue stimulus, while the other set (output, set B in figure 2.1) is used to represent a pattern of activity that will be the response stimulus. The standard pattern associator is fully connected, which means that every input unit in the network is linked, by a modifiable connection, directly to every output unit in the network.

Learning proceeds by presenting a cue stimulus and a response stimulus to the memory at the same time by activating each set of input units with the appropriate value. For example, imagine that pattern **x** is a vector made up of five different numerical values, and that pattern **y** is some other five-values vector. Assume that the association between pattern **x** and pattern **y** is to be stored in the distributed memory that is illustrated in figure 2.1. This would be accomplished by first using the five values of pattern **x** to activate input units *a* through *e* in the figure. At the same time, the five values of pattern **y** would be used to activate output units *l* through *p*. Then the network would store the association between the two patterns by using a learning rule to modify its connection weights on the basis of the different unit activities. This process can be repeated with a different set of patterns,

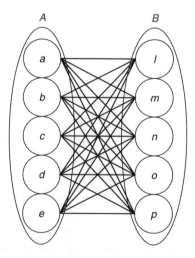

Figure 2.1   The basic structure of the distributed memory

because more than one pair of patterns can be stored in the same set of connection weights. The standard pattern associator is called a distributed memory because each association is stored throughout all the connections in the network, and because one set of connections can store several different associations.

What learning rule defines how each connection weight should be changed? One important rule is a modern reformulation of James' (1890) version of the associative law of contiguity. It begins with a proposed neurological mechanism that obeys this law: "When an axon of cell A is near enough to excite a cell B and repeatedly or persistently takes part in firing it, some growth process or metabolic change takes place in one or both cells such that A's efficiency, as one of the cells firing B, is increased" (Hebb, 1949, p. 62). Hebb's basic idea about learning was that if an input neuron and an output neuron were both active at the same time, then the synapse between them should be strengthened. His logic was that with the strengthening of the synapse, in situations in which the input neuron became active there would be an increased likelihood of the output neuron becoming active as well. This is because the output neuron would receive increased stimulation (via the reinforced synapse) from the input neuron.

In modern variations of Hebb-style learning, it is usually assumed that processor activity can be either inhibitory or excitatory. In this context, connection weight changes are not intended to increase the likelihood of activity in an output unit. Rather, the goal is to change the weight in such a way that the relationship between input and output unit activities is enhanced. In other words, if at some learning trial an input unit is in one state x, and the output unit is in some other state y, then the connection weight should be changed so that later if the input unit returns to state x, then its signal through the connection should increase the likelihood of recreating state y in the output unit.

Table 2.1 provides the four possible combinations of input unit and output unit states, as well as the desired weight change that will increase the likelihood that both states will be reproduced when the input unit's activity is set by the environment, and it sends a signal through a connection to activate the output unit (for details, see Dawson, 2004, chapter 9). Note from the table that the desired weight change is the product of the input unit and the output unit activities.

This observation provides the mathematical roots of modern Hebb-style learning. According to this learning rule, the desired change for a particular weight is the product of three different values: the activity of the input unit at one end of the connection, the activity of the output unit at the other end of the connection, and a learning rate value that is usually

Table 2.1   *The direction of weight changes that will enhance the relationship between patterns of input and output unit activities*

Activity of input unit	Activity of output unit	Direction of desired weight change
Positive	Positive	Positive
Negative	Negative	Positive
Negative	Positive	Negative
Positive	Negative	Negative

a number between 0 and 1. When these three numbers are multiplied together, the result is the desired change in weight. This result is added to the existing connection weight to store the association between pairs of units. By repeating this procedure for every connection weight in the network, the association between pairs of patterns is stored in the memory. It is assumed that before any associations are stored in the memory that all of the connection weights are initialized to a value of 0.

In order for this memory to be useful, we need to be able to retrieve information that has been stored in it. This is accomplished by presenting a cue pattern to the network by activating the input units. For example, we might present pattern **x** once again to the input units. However, during recall, we do *not* present any information to the output units. Instead, the input units send numerical signals through the weighted connections in the network, and these signals are in turn used to activate the output processors. If the memory is functioning properly, then the pattern of activation in the output units will be the pattern that was originally associated with the cue pattern. So, in our example, if pattern **x** has been presented to the input units, then the signals that these units send should cause pattern **y** to be reproduced in the output units.

The mathematics of output unit recall is very simple. Each input sends a signal, which is a numerical value. Each value is then scaled by multiplying it by the value of the weight of the connection through which the signal is being sent. Every output unit simply computes the total sum of all of the weighted signals that are being sent to it. This sum, called the net input, is the value that is used to activate the output unit.

2.3   Exploring the Distributed Associative Memory

The chapters that follow provide several different exercises for exploring the distributed associative memory. First, a program for exploring this kind of memory will be described. Second, you will see that this type of system is capable of remembering several different associations when the Hebb rule is used. Third, you will perform some exercises that illustrate some problems with the Hebb rule. Fourth, you will be introduced a new rule, the delta rule, that solves some – but not all – of these problems. This will provide the motivation for exploring a more advanced kind of connectionist network, the perceptron, later in this book.

CHAPTER 3

The James Program

3.1 Introduction

The purpose of the distributed associative memory is to learn associations between pairs of patterns. During training, a cue pattern is presented to the memory's input units, and a recall pattern is presented at the same time to the memory's output units. A learning rule is then used to modify the network's connection weights to store the association between the two patterns. Later, when training has been completed, a cue pattern is presented to the input units of the memory. This causes signals to be sent through the network's connection weights, which in turn produce activity in the network's output units. If proper learning has occurred, then the reproduced activity in the output units should be similar to, if not identical to, the recall pattern that was originally presented with the cue pattern. This kind of memory is distributed in the sense that one set of connection weights can store the associations between several different pairs of patterns.

James is a program written in Visual Basic 6.0 for the demonstration and exploration of distributed associative memory. It is designed for use on a computer based upon a Microsoft Windows operating system. A second program, JamesLite, is identical to James with the exception that it does not include the capability to save network results in Microsoft Excel workbooks. In this document, James will be the only program referred to, as the user interface for it is identical to the interface for JamesLite. A third program, JamesJava, is equivalent to JamesLite, but is written in Java. It is intended for use on alternative operating systems. All programs are distributed as freeware from the following website: http://www.bcp.psych. ualberta.ca/~mike/Book3/

3.2 Installing the Program

James is distributed from the above website as a .zip file. The following steps will result in the program being installed on your computer:

1. Download the file James.zip to your computer by going to the website, click on the program icon, and save the file in any desired location on your computer.

2. Go to the saved James.zip file on your computer, and unzip it with a program like WinZip. The result will be three different objects: setup.exe, setup.lst and James.cab.
3. Run the setup.exe program. This will call an install program that will complete the installation of the program on your computer, which will include the installation of an "Examples" folder with a few sample training files.

3.3   Teaching a Distributed Memory

3.3.1   Starting the program

The program can be started in two different ways. First, one can go into the directory in which the program was installed and double-click on the file "James.exe". Second, one can go to the start button on the computer, choose programs, scroll to the program group BCPNet, and select the program James.exe.

3.3.2   Loading a file to train a network

After the program is started, the first form that appears is used to select a file for training the distributed memory. This form is illustrated in figure 3.1. By using the left mouse button and the drive selection tool located in the upper left of the form, one can choose a computer drive

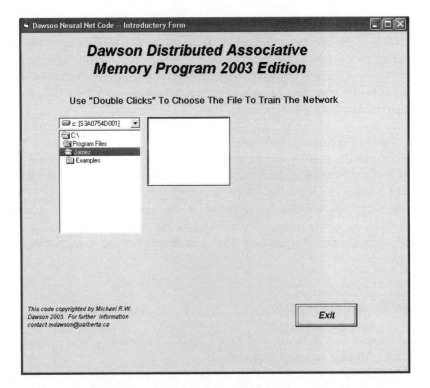

Figure 3.1   The file-reading form of the James program

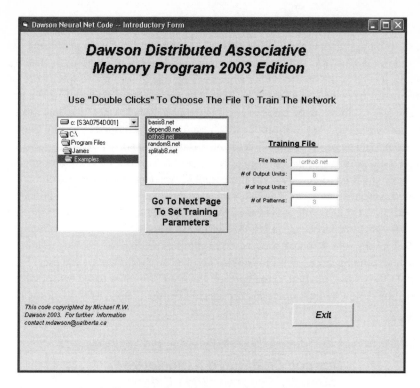

Figure 3.2   The file-reading form of the James program after a file has been read

on which directories and files are located. The available directories on the selected drive are listed in the directory selection tool that is immediately below the drive selection tool. One opens a directory by double-clicking it with the left mouse button. If the directory contains any files that end with the extension .net, then these files will be displayed in the file selection box located in the upper middle of the form. The properties of .net files are described in chapter 27. These files have a particular format that the James program is designed to read, and only files that end in this extension can be used to train the network.

One chooses a .net file by double-clicking one of the file names that is displayed in the file selection box. When this is done, the program reads the desired file, some of the file's properties are displayed, and another button appears on the form. In figure 3.2, the file "ortho8.net" has been selected (and read). On the right of the form its general properties are displayed, and the button permitting the user to proceed to the next part of the program is displayed under the file selection box. In this example, if "ortho8.net" has been selected, but is not really the file that is desired, one can simply go back to the file selection tools and choose another file. When its file name is double-clicked, the new file will be read in, and will replace the properties of the previous (undesired) file. Once the desired file has been selected, all that is required is to press the "Go To Next Page To Set Training Parameters" button with a left-click of the mouse. If instead one desires to close the program, then one can left-click the "Exit" button displayed on the bottom right of the form.

3.3.3   Setting the training parameters and training the network

When the program reads in the .net file, this only determines how many processing units are connected in the network, and defines the input and desired output patterns that are used in training. It is up to the user to define what learning rule to use, and to specify the value of the parameters to control (and stop) learning. The second form displayed by the program allows the user to choose these parameters. The paragraphs below describe how this is done. If the reader wishes to learn more about what exactly is accomplished by setting these values on this form, then he or she should look through Dawson (2004).

The second form, which is illustrated in figure 3.3, consists of a number of different tools that can be used to quickly control the kind of learning that will be carried out by the distributed associative memory. The first tool is used to choose which of two learning rules, the Hebb rule or the delta rule, will be used to modify the connection weights of the network. The default rule is the Hebb rule. A left-click of the mouse on this tool is all that is required to select the learning rule. A second tool is used to choose a method for stopping training. In the first method, training stops after a maximum number of epochs (set by the user) have been reached. In the second method, training stops when the sum of squared error (SSE) for the network drops below a minimum level (also specified by the user). A left-click of the mouse is

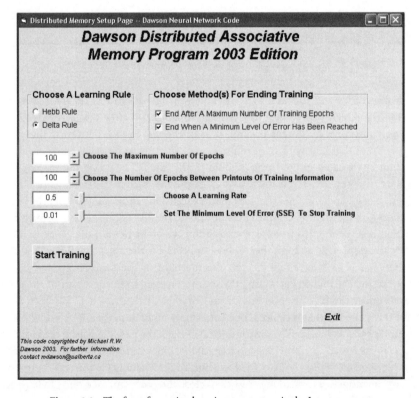

Figure 3.3   The form for setting learning parameters in the James program

used to select either of these methods; when a method has been selected, a check mark appears in the tool. Importantly, the user can select both methods to be used in the same simulation. When this is done, then the simulation will stop as soon as one of the two conditions is met.

There are two suggestions for setting this aspect of training. First, the user should always set a maximum number of epochs for training to end, just as a precautionary measure. This is why this method is selected as a default. Second, ending processing by using SSE is not recommended when the Hebb rule is being used for training, as this learning rule is not explicitly designed to minimize error.

The four remaining tools on the form are used to set numerical values that control training. The first is a tool for specifying the maximum number of training epochs by left-clicking either arrow beside the value's box. This will either increase or decrease the value of this parameter, depending upon which arrow is selected. The maximum number of training epochs can also be set directly by left-clicking the value's box with the mouse, and typing in the desired value. Note that it if the user chooses a value for this variable, then the "End After A Maximum Number Of Training Epochs" selection should also be selected. If this latter option does not have a check mark beside it, then the program will ignore this number when it is run! In other words, just changing this number is not enough to ensure that the program will use it!

The second is a tool for specifying the number of training epochs between printouts of training information. During training, the program will periodically print out information to tell the user how things are progressing. This includes information about what epoch has been reached, what the network SSE is, and the degree to which network SSE has changed since the last printout. The frequency of these printouts is controlled by the number displayed in this tool, which can be set in a fashion similar to that described for the previous tool. The default value (displayed in the figure) is 100. If this value is selected, then every 100 epochs the user will receive updates about network learning. The value selected for this parameter also defines the spacing of the x-axis of the "SSE by Epochs" plot that can be created from a form described later in this document.

The third is a tool for specifying the learning rate used by either learning rule. More details on the role of learning rate in the equations that govern this system can be found in Dawson (2004). The learning rate is used for either learning rule. In setting the learning rule, two rules of thumb should be followed. First, if the learning rate is 0, then no learning will be accomplished. Second, it would not be typical to set learning rates greater than 1, although the user is free to explore the behavior of the network when this is done. The learning rate can be set in two different ways. One is to left-click on the arrow of the slider tool that is beside the value, hold the mouse button down, and use the mouse to slide the value of the learning rate up or down. The other is to select the box in which the learning rate is displayed, and to type in the desired learning rate.

The fourth is a tool for specifying the minimum level of network error (that is, sum of squared error, or SSE) to control termination of learning. This value can be set using the same methods described for the previous tool. The default value for this parameter is 0.5. If this value is set to a smaller value, then the user is requiring the network to generate more accurate responses before learning is ended. If this value is increased, then the user is permitting the network to end training when a larger amount of error is evident in the network's responses.

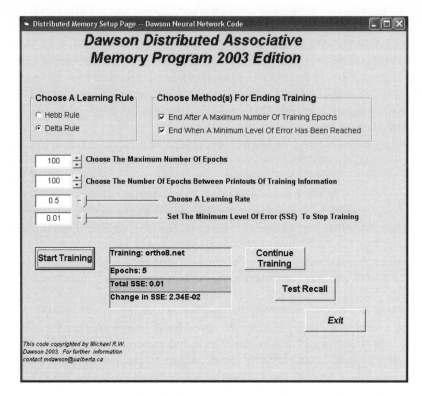

Figure 3.4   The form after training has taken place

When the delta rule is used to train the network, the smaller this value is set, the longer it will take the network to converge. It is possible to set this value to 0, and to therefore require the network to generate perfect responses. However, in some cases the network will be incapable of achieving this degree of performance (e.g., for linearly dependent training sets), and training will therefore never stop unless a maximum number of training epochs has also been selected. Note that it if the user chooses this parameter, then the "End When A Minimum Level Of Error Has Been Achieved" option should also be selected. If this latter option does not have a check mark beside it, then the program will ignore this number when it is run! In other words, just changing this number is not enough to ensure that the program will use it.

Once these tools have been used to select the desired training parameters, associations (memories) can be stored in the network by pressing the "Start Training" button with a left-click of the mouse. When this is done, new boxes appear on the form to show the user how training is proceeding, as is illustrated in figure 3.4. When training stops, two new buttons appear on the form. By pressing the "Continue Training" button, more training occurs using the settings that have already been selected on this form. By pressing the "Test Recall" button, the user moves to a new form that can be used to explore the performance of the trained network. The details of this form are described below. Of course, pressing the "Exit" button terminates the program.

3.4   Testing What the Memory Has Learned

Once training has been completed, the distributed associative memory has stored a set of associations between pairs of patterns. With the press of the "Test Recall" button of the form that has just been described, the program presents a number of options for examining the ability of the network to retrieve the information that it has stored. Some of these options involve the online examination of network responses, as well as the plotting of learning dynamics. Other options permit the user to save properties of the network in files that can be examined later. One of these file options enables the user to easily manipulate network data, or to easily move the data into another program (such as a statistical analysis tool) for more detailed analysis (e.g., factor analytic analysis of final connection weights).

The "Test Recall" causes the program to present a form to the user that permits him or her to do two general types of activities. This form is illustrated in figure 3.5. The first activity is the study or saving of network properties, which is described in more detail below. The second activity is returning to previous forms to either continue training the network on the same problem, or to read in a new problem for training and study.

For either of these activities, the user selects the specific activity to perform from either list that is illustrated in the figure on the right. Double-clicking the list item with the left mouse button results in the activity being carried out. The sections that follow first describe

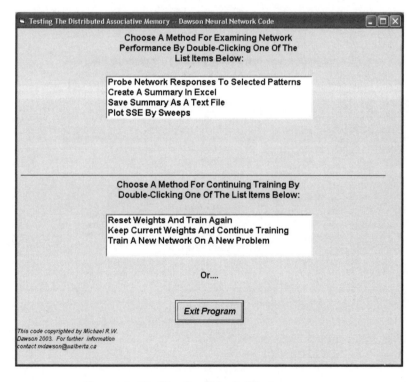

Figure 3.5   The "Test Recall" form of the James program

the different activities that are possible by selecting any one of the four actions laid out in the control box on the upper part of the form. Later sections describe the result of double-clicking any one of the three actions made available in the control box on the lower part of the form. Again, an "Exit Program" is also provided to allow the user to exit the program from this form.

3.4.1   Testing responses to individual patterns

After the network has learned some associations, it may be of interest to the user to examine the particular responses of the network to individual cue patterns in the training set. For instance, in cases where the network is not performing perfectly, it could be that it is responding correctly to some cues, but not to others. By double-clicking on the list item "Probe Network Responses To Selected Patterns", the user causes the program to provide a form that allows the network to be tested one cue pattern at a time.

The form that permits this is shown in figure 3.6. It provides a large window in which network behavior is printed. When the form is initially presented, this window is blank. Left-button mouse clicks on the arrow controls at the top of the form are used to select the number of the pattern to be presented to the network. When the desired pattern number has been selected, the "Ok" button is pressed. The cue pattern is then presented to the network, and the network's response is displayed. The display provides details about the cue pattern, the actual

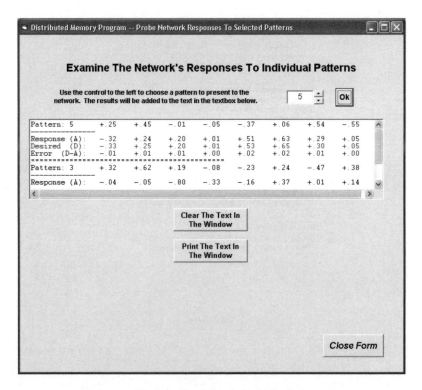

Figure 3.6   The form for testing recall of individual patterns

network response, the desired network response, and the error of the network. For instance, in the illustration, "Pattern 5" has just been selected for presentation to the network.

More than one pattern can be tested in this way. The new pattern information is always displayed on top of previous pattern information. For example, in figure 3.6, the Pattern 5 information was requested immediately after studying the network's responses to Pattern 3. One can use the two scroll bars on the window to examine all of the information that has been requested. At any point in time, one can send this information to the system's default printer by pressing the button for printing. Also, one can erase the window by pressing the button for clearing the display. When the "Close Form" button is pressed, this form closes, and the user is back to the "Test Recall" list options.

3.4.2   Plotting learning dynamics

In Dawson (2004), much of the comparison of the two learning rules for the distributed associative memory depends upon an examination of how network error changes as a function of epochs of training. If the user chooses the "Plot SSE By Sweeps" option from the list in the "Test Recall" form, then the program automatically plots this information using a bar chart, as is illustrated in figure 3.7. One can import this chart directly into a word processing document by simultaneously pressing the "Alt" and "Print Screen" keys on the keyboard (which copies the

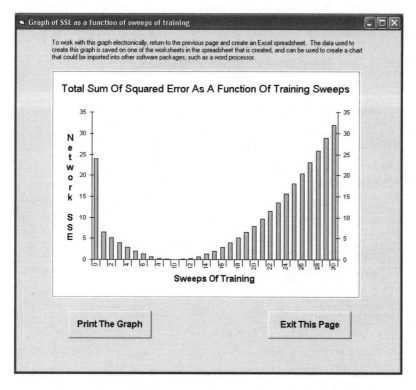

Figure 3.7   A bar chart of learning dynamics generated by the James program

active window into the clipboard), going to the document, and pasting the clipboard into the document. One can print this chart on the default printer by left-clicking the mouse over the "Print The Graph" button. A left-click of the "Exit This Page" button closes the graph, and returns the user to the page that provides the options for testing network performance.

With respect to the graph produced in this form, an example of which can be seen in figure 3.7, the SSE axis is computed automatically, and the sampling of the bars across the Sweeps axis is determined by the choice of epochs between printouts made by the user on the program's second form. If the graph doesn't look quite right, then the user might consider re-running the simulation with a different choice for epochs between printouts. If a different kind of graph is desired, then the user might wish to save the network data to file. The data used to create this graph can be saved when this is done, and imported into a different software package that can be used to create graphs of different appearance.

3.4.3   Saving results in a text file

One of the options for storing information about network performance is to save network results as a text file. The form that permits this to be done, which is shown in figure 3.8, is accessed by choosing the list item "Save Summary As A Text File" from the "Test Recall" page.

There are two sets of controls on this form. The first is a set of drive, directory, and file control boxes that are very similar to those found on the very first form seen when the program starts to

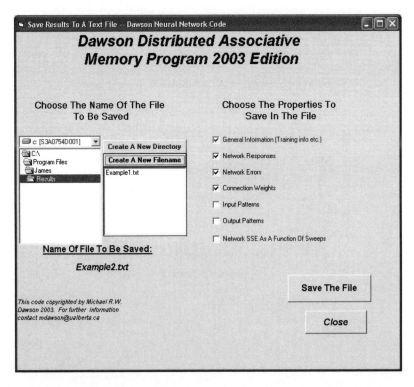

Figure 3.8   The form for saving different kinds of network information to a text file from the James program

run. One uses the drive and directory controls to navigate to a folder in which network data is to be saved. If it is necessary to create a new folder, a left-click of the mouse on the "Create A New Directory" button creates a dialog that permits the new directory to be named and created. Once the desired directory has been opened, the existing text files (.txt) in it are displayed. This is because the network data will be saved in such a file. One can overwrite an existing file by double-clicking it with the left mouse button. If a new file needs to be created, the dialog for doing so is accessed by a left-click of the mouse on the "Create A New Filename" button.

After choosing the location in which information is to be saved, the check boxes on the right of the form are set to determine what kinds of information will be saved. If a check box is not selected, then the corresponding information is simply not written to the file. To save the file, after the desired check boxes have been selected, the user left-clicks the "Save The File" button with the mouse. The form remains open after this is done, because in some instances the user might wish to save different versions of the network information in different locations. This form is closed by a left-mouse click on the "Close Button", which returns the user to the "Test Recall" form.

3.4.4   Saving results in an Excel workbook

A second method for saving network performance is to save it in a structured Microsoft Excel workbook. This option is only available in the James program, and is not part of the other programs for exploring this kind of connectionist network. It should obviously only be selected by users who also have Microsoft Excel installed on their computer. It is selected by a double-click of the "Create A Summary In Excel" list item that is offered in the "Test Recall" form.

When this item is selected, a patience-requesting message is displayed on the "Test Recall" form, and a number of different programming steps are taken to build an Excel workbook. When this is completed, the workbook is displayed as its own window, which will open on the user's computer in front of any of the James program's windows. When the workbook has been created successfully, then the user should see something similar to the screen shot that is presented in figure 3.9.

All of the possible information that could be saved in the text version of a saved network is saved on this spreadsheet. Each different class of information is saved on its own worksheet in this Excel workbook. One can view different elements of this information by using the mouse to select the desired worksheet's tab on the bottom of the worksheet. The worksheet opens (as illustrated in figure 3.9) with the "General Information" tab selected. When this workbook is open, it is running in Excel as a standalone program that is separate from the James software. One can select different tabs in the worksheet to examine network properties. For example, in figure 3.10, the "Connection Weights" tab has been selected. After examining the worksheet, the user might wish to save it to disk by using the Save File utility provided in Excel.

One problem with having this information being displayed with a completely separate program is that it begins to use up memory resources on the computer that cannot be directly controlled by either program. For instance, it is possible to leave this workbook open, and to return to the James program. However, this practice is not recommended. Instead, potential system crashes are likely to be avoided by closing the Excel workbook before returning to James. When James is returned to, the "Test Recall" form will still be displayed.

If saving Excel files from James causes system crashes, it is likely to be because of memory resource conflicts. The Excel options were built into James because they provide a convenient

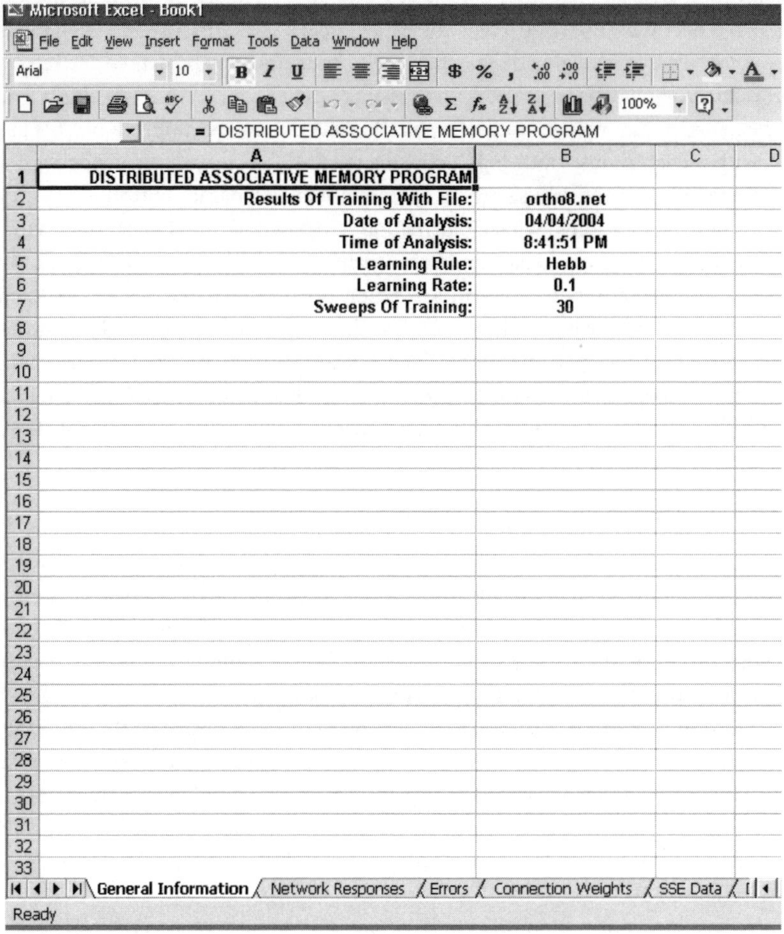

Figure 3.9   An Excel workbook created by the James program, opened to the "General Information" tab

format for working with network data after training has been accomplished. However, the Excel capability is not required for the distributed associative memory software to be used productively. If Excel problems are encountered frequently on your computer, our recommendation is to use JamesLite instead, and save network performance as text files only.

3.4.5   Leaving the "Test Recall" Form

Once the user has finished examining the performance of a trained network, the list at the bottom of the "Test Recall" form provides different options for network training. If the "Reset Weights And Train Again" option is selected, then all of the connection weights are set to zero, the network is readied for the same problem that it has just learned, and the user is returned to the form that permits training parameters to be selected. If the "Keep Current Weights And Train Again" option is selected, the network is trained on the same problem, but

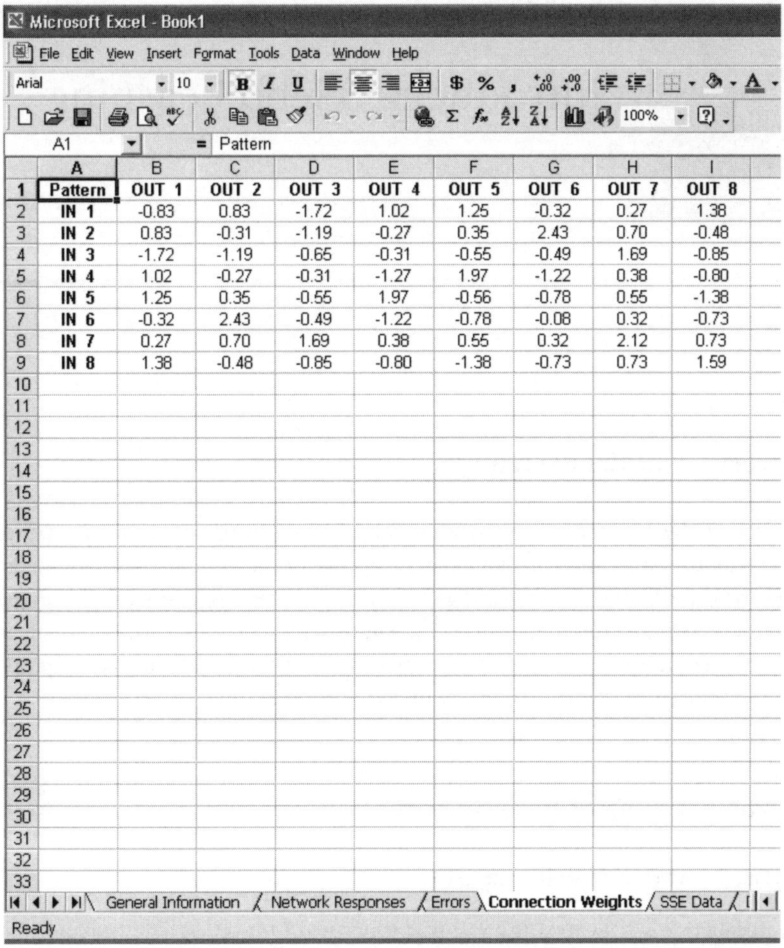

Pattern	OUT 1	OUT 2	OUT 3	OUT 4	OUT 5	OUT 6	OUT 7	OUT 8
IN 1	-0.83	0.83	-1.72	1.02	1.25	-0.32	0.27	1.38
IN 2	0.83	-0.31	-1.19	-0.27	0.35	2.43	0.70	-0.48
IN 3	-1.72	-1.19	-0.65	-0.31	-0.55	-0.49	1.69	-0.85
IN 4	1.02	-0.27	-0.31	-1.27	1.97	-1.22	0.38	-0.80
IN 5	1.25	0.35	-0.55	1.97	-0.56	-0.78	0.55	-1.38
IN 6	-0.32	2.43	-0.49	-1.22	-0.78	-0.08	0.32	-0.73
IN 7	0.27	0.70	1.69	0.38	0.55	0.32	2.12	0.73
IN 8	1.38	-0.48	-0.85	-0.80	-1.38	-0.73	0.73	1.59

Figure 3.10 An Excel workbook created by the James program, opened to the "Connection Weights" tab

the weights created from the learning that was just completed are not erased. The user is returned to the form that permits training parameters to be selected. They must be set again if settings other than the default settings are desired. If the "Train A New Network On A New Problem" option is selected, then the user is returned to the program's first form to be able to read in a new problem for training. If none of these options are desired, then the program can be closed by pressing the "Exit Program" button with a left-click of the mouse.

3.5 Using the Program

This chapter has provided an overview of the James program. The next few chapters provide some example exercises that use the program to introduce the reader to the advantages and disadvantages of the distributed associative memory.

CHAPTER 4

Introducing Hebb Learning

4.1   Overview of the Exercises

The purpose of this chapter is to provide two initial exercises that are designed to familiarize the reader with the James software. One main objective of the exercises is for you to download the James (or JamesLite) software package to your computer, install the program, and run it. This step might require examining some of the information that was provided in the previous chapter. The second main objective is to use the program to examine some of the properties of a distributed associative memory trained with the Hebb rule.

4.2   Hebb Learning of Basis Vectors

4.2.1   Basis vectors and their properties

In many instances when we measure various properties of objects, it is convenient to organize these measurements as sets of numbers. For example, in a perception study we might be interested in the RGB properties of different colors that are being presented to subjects on a monitor. For one of the colors, the red value might be 200, the green value 20, and the blue value 13. We could represent this one color as the set of numbers (200, 20, 13).

There are two very natural ways of thinking about this kind of representation. In one, the object is viewed as a point in space, and the location of this point is determined by using each number in the set as the value of one of the point's coordinates. In our example above, the point is located in a three-dimensional space, and its x-coordinate is 200, its y-coordinate is 20, and its z-coordinate is 13. In other words, the values of the different measurements that were taken can be used to position the object in space.

In the other, the object is viewed as a vector in space. A vector is a directed distance from the origin of the space. The values of the different measurements are used to determine the location of the endpoint of this vector in space. So, in our example the object could be represented as the vector $c' = [200, 20, 13]$. This vector can be considered to be the line drawn from the origin of the space at location (0, 0, 0) to the endpoint of the vector at the location (200, 20, 13).

Vector representations are useful, because instead of thinking about an object as a point in space, we might instead consider its distance or direction from the origin of the space.

Regardless of whether an object is represented as a point or as a vector, this representation is not made in a vacuum. The numbers that are used to define a point or a vector are situated in the context of a coordinate system. For instance, in the example above the representation of the object would be fixed in a three-dimensional coordinate system, where the x-axis of this system would correspond to the red value of the color, the y-axis would correspond to the green value, and the z-axis would correspond to the blue value.

The axes that define a coordinate system can themselves be represented as special vectors that are called basis vectors. In our example, the basis vector for the x-axis would be $\mathbf{x}' = [1, 0, 0]$. Similarly, the vector $\mathbf{y}' = [0, 1, 0]$ and the vector $\mathbf{z}' = [0, 0, 1]$ would represent the y-axis and the z-axis respectively. A set of basis vectors has several important properties. In particular, the set is mutually orthonormal. This means the following: first, each vector has a length of 1; second, any two vectors from the set are orthogonal to one another (i.e., when joined at their base, the angle between them would be $90°$ or $\pi/2$ radians). Because of mutual orthonormality, the correlation between any pair of basis vectors will be equal to zero, while the correlation of a basis vector with itself will be equal to 1.

4.2.2   A training set constructed from basis vectors

The purpose of exercise 4.1 is to demonstrate associative learning using the Hebb rule, using a set of basis vectors to construct the stimulus set. The basis vectors that were used defined the coordinate system for an eight-dimensional space, and are listed in table 4.1. Note that in this table, because the vectors are listed out in a row, they are all labeled as being transposed vectors with the superscript T.

In order to create a training set, a pair of basis vectors was selected, where one basis vector was the "stimulus", and the other basis was the "response". Eight different pairs of this type were created. They were $\mathbf{u}_1$ (the stimulus) paired with $\mathbf{u}_8$ (the response), $\mathbf{u}_2$ paired with

Table 4.1   *The basis vectors for an eight dimensional space, used to create an orthonormal training set*

Name	Value
$\mathbf{u}_1^T$	$[1, 0, 0, 0, 0, 0, 0, 0]$
$\mathbf{u}_2^T$	$[0, 1, 0, 0, 0, 0, 0, 0]$
$\mathbf{u}_3^T$	$[0, 0, 1, 0, 0, 0, 0, 0]$
$\mathbf{u}_4^T$	$[0, 0, 0, 1, 0, 0, 0, 0]$
$\mathbf{u}_5^T$	$[0, 0, 0, 0, 1, 0, 0, 0]$
$\mathbf{u}_6^T$	$[0, 0, 0, 0, 0, 1, 0, 0]$
$\mathbf{u}_7^T$	$[0, 0, 0, 0, 0, 0, 1, 0]$
$\mathbf{u}_8^T$	$[0, 0, 0, 0, 0, 0, 0, 1]$

$\mathbf{u}_7$, $\mathbf{u}_3$ paired with $\mathbf{u}_6$, $\mathbf{u}_4$ paired with $\mathbf{u}_5$, $\mathbf{u}_5$ paired with $\mathbf{u}_4$, $\mathbf{u}_6$ paired with $\mathbf{u}_3$, $\mathbf{u}_7$ paired with $\mathbf{u}_2$, and $\mathbf{u}_8$ paired with $\mathbf{u}_1$. After learning, when a stimulus vector was presented to the input units of the memory, the hope was that the memory would reproduce the response vector in its output units. Each basis vector was used once as a stimulus vector, and was also used once as a response vector. The complete training set is contained in the file "basis8.net" (see section 3.3.2).

4.2.3 Procedure for basis vectors

Run the James program, and load the file "basis8.net". On the setup page (see figure 3.3), choose the Hebb rule, choose to end after a maximum number of sweeps, and set this maximum number of sweeps to 10. Have the program print out every epoch by setting the sweeps between printouts value to 1. Use a learning rate of 0.1; the minimum SSE value need not be changed, because it will not be used. Start training by pressing the appropriate button. Press the test recall button. Examine learning over time by plotting the SSEs. Exit the graph, and then create an Excel spreadsheet. When the spreadsheet appears, examine the network error to each pattern, and examine the connection weights that are displayed in the spreadsheet. Close the Excel spreadsheet without saving it. Then, to proceed to exercise 4.2, tell the program to train a new network on a new problem.

Exercise 4.1

1. What is the total SSE when training ends?
2. Describe the appearance of the graph of SSE as a function of training epoch.
3. What can be said about these errors?
4. What is the relationship between the set of connection weights, and the input and output patterns whose associations are stored in the weights? (To answer this question, remember you can take a look at the set of input patterns and the set of output patterns, because this information is stored in the spreadsheet as well.)

4.3 Hebb Learning of Orthonormal, Non-Basis Vectors

4.3.1 Orthonormal vectors

In the previous exercise, we noted that the basis vectors that are used to define a coordinate system are mutually orthonormal. A basis vector is easily identified because one of its entries will have the value of 1, and all of its other entries will have the value of 0. Other vectors can easily be identified as not being basis vectors, because these vectors are constructed from numbers that are not equal to 1 or zero. However, this does not mean that this different set of vectors cannot be mutually orthonormal.

Imagine taking a set of basis vectors, like the eight that we used in exercise 4.1, and holding the entire set at the origin of the coordinate system where all of the endpoints of the eight vectors met. We could then rotate the entire coordinate system to some different orientation in space. This rotation would not change the length of any of the eight vectors, nor would it change the position of any vector in the set relative to any of the other vectors. As a result, the vectors would still be mutually orthonormal. However, because the endpoints of each vector would have been moved to some new position, the vectors would no longer be basis vectors. Because of this new position, the values for each vector would no longer be a single 1 and seven 0s. The result of performing this rotation would be the production of a set or mutually orthonormal vectors that were not basis vectors. The second exercise involves training a network with a set of patterns created from such a set of vectors.

4.3.2   The training set for exercise 4.2

The second exercise involves using the distributed memory to store associations between vectors that are mutually orthogonal, but which are not basis vectors. There are a number of different approaches that can be used to create a set of orthonormal vectors like the ones provided in table 4.2. I created this set using the mathematical programming language called Maple. First, I used Maple to create eight different randomly generated vectors for me, where each vector was composed of eight different numerical values. Then I had Maple apply the Gram-Schmidt procedure to these vectors. This procedure starts by treating one random vector as being in the orthonormal set. It then takes a second vector, examines its projections onto the first vector, and modifies the second vector to make it orthogonal to the first. It repeats this process with a third vector, making it orthogonal to the preceding two. I repeated this procedure until a set of eight mutually orthogonal vectors was created. Finally, I scaled each of the vectors produced by the Gram-Schmidt procedure so that each had a length of 1 unit.

These eight different mutually orthonormal vectors were used to create eight stimulus–response pairs in a training set whose structure was essentially the same structure as the training set used in the previous exercise. The eight stimulus–response pairs were $\mathbf{v}_1$ (the stimulus)

Table 4.2   A set of mutually orthonormal vectors, but not basis vectors, used to create a second training set

Name	Value
$\mathbf{v}_1^T$	[2.726E-01, 3.901E-01, -3.082E-01, -1.565E-01, 6.364E-01, -4.847E-01, 9.673E-02, 6.853E-02]
$\mathbf{v}_2^T$	[3.505E-01, -2.166E-01, 6.276E-02, -2.762E-01, 2.920E-01, 2.763E-01, -4.666E-01, -6.088E-01]
$\mathbf{v}_3^T$	[3.171E-01, 6.190E-01, 1.921E-01, -8.109E-02, -2.313E-01, 2.361E-01, -4.711E-01, 3.762E-01]
$\mathbf{v}_4^T$	[-3.283E-01, 2.514E-01, 2.031E-01, 1.363E-02, 5.287E-01, 6.454E-01, 2.975E-01, 5.478E-02]
$\mathbf{v}_5^T$	[2.504E-01, 4.471E-01, -8.069E-03, -5.367E-02, -3.729E-01, 6.236E-02, 5.353E-01, -5.522E-01]
$\mathbf{v}_6^T$	[-4.451E-02, -5.132E-02, -8.284E-01, -3.408E-01, -1.624E-01, 3.804E-01, 1.176E-02, 1.475E-01]
$\mathbf{v}_7^T$	[-5.174E-01, 3.655E-01, -2.902E-01, 4.328E-01, -5.472E-03, -9.601E-02, -4.129E-01, -3.839E-01]
$\mathbf{v}_8^T$	[5.119E-01, -1.354E-01, -2.290E-01, 7.656E-01, 1.062E-01, 2.421E-01, 7.246E-02, 7.728E-02]

Exercise 4.2

1. What is the total SSE when training ends?
2. How does this compare to the total SSE from exercise 4.1?
3. Describe the appearance of the graph of SSE as a function of training epoch.
4. How does this appearance compare to the graph that was obtained in exercise 4.1?
5. What can be said about network errors, and how does this relate to what was found in exercise 4.1?
6. Examine the connection weights that resulted from this training. How do they relate to the weights that were observed in exercise 4.1?
7. If one were to examine the connection weights of this network in an attempt to determine how the memory stored its knowledge, would this be a straightforward task to accomplish? If not, then speculate on what approach one might be forced to take to interpret the internal structure of this kind of network.

paired with $\mathbf{v}_8$ (the response), $\mathbf{v}_2$ paired with $\mathbf{v}_7$, $\mathbf{v}_3$ paired with $\mathbf{v}_6$, $\mathbf{v}_4$ paired with $\mathbf{v}_5$, $\mathbf{v}_5$ paired with $\mathbf{v}_4$, $\mathbf{v}_6$ paired with $\mathbf{v}_3$, $\mathbf{v}_7$ paired with $\mathbf{v}_2$, and $\mathbf{v}_8$ paired with $\mathbf{v}_1$. The entire training set can be found in the file called "ortho8.net".

4.3.3   Procedure for mutually orthonormal vectors

The purpose of the second exercise is to demonstrate associative learning, accomplished via Hebb learning, with a training set that *seems* more complicated. Load the file ortho8.net. (If you are running the program immediately after finishing exercise 4.1, make sure that you have instructed the program to train a new network on a new problem before reading this file in.) This file consists of eight pairs of vectors that are mutually orthonormal, and thus is very similar to the training set used in exercise 4.1. However, each processing unit has a negative or positive fractional value, so the patterns seem more complicated. *Use the same settings and procedures that were used in exercise 4.1 to train this network on this new problem.* After training, examine the dynamics of learning by plotting SSE as a function of training epochs. Then use the Excel spreadsheet to examine network errors, and to examine the connection weights, and to answer the questions below. Close the spreadsheet, and then exit the program.

APPENDIX TO CHAPTER 4 – CREATING MUTUALLY ORTHOGONAL VECTORS WITH MAPLE

The remainder of this chapter illustrates my session with Maple V in which I created the mutually orthogonal set of vectors. This appendix isn't mandatory reading; I'm including it because it took me some time to find a straightforward set of steps that enabled me to construct the training set that was used in exercise 4.2, and I thought that its inclusion might save time for the reader if he or she ever desired to build a similar training set.

Step 1: Use linear algebra to create eight random vectors, where each of these vectors is composed of eight entries

```
> with(linalg):
```

Construct random eight vectors.

```
> v1:=randvector(8);
  v2:=randvector(8);
  v3:=randvector(8);
  v4:=randvector(8);
  v5:=randvector(8);
  v6:=randvector(8);
  v7:=randvector(8);
  v8:=randvector(8);
```

Maple responded to these commands by creating the vectors below:

```
v1 := [49, 63, 57, -59, 45, -8, -93, 92]
v2 := [43, -62, 77, 66, 54, -5, 99, -61]
v3 := [-50, -12, -18, 31, -26, -62, 1, -47]
v4 := [-91, -47, -61, 41, -58, -90, 53, -1]
v5 := [94, 83, -86, 23, -84, 19, -50, 88]
v6 := [-53, 85, 49, 78, 17, 72, -99, -85]
v7 := [-86, 30, 80, 72, 66, -29, -91, -53]
v8 := [-19, -47, 68, -72, -87, 79, 43, -66]
```

Step 2: Use the Gram–Schmidt procedure to convert the random vectors into 8 mutually orthogonal vectors

```
> u1:=evalf(GramSchmidt([v1,v2,v3,v4,v5,v6,v7,v8])[1]);
  u2:=evalf(GramSchmidt([v1,v2,v3,v4,v5,v6,v7,v8])[2]);
  u3:=evalf(GramSchmidt([v1,v2,v3,v4,v5,v6,v7,v8])[3]);
  u4:=evalf(GramSchmidt([v1,v2,v3,v4,v5,v6,v7,v8])[4]);
  u5:=evalf(GramSchmidt([v1,v2,v3,v4,v5,v6,v7,v8])[5]);
  u6:=evalf(GramSchmidt([v1,v2,v3,v4,v5,v6,v7,v8])[6]);
  u7:=evalf(GramSchmidt([v1,v2,v3,v4,v5,v6,v7,v8])[7]);
  u8:=evalf(GramSchmidt([v1,v2,v3,v4,v5,v6,v7,v8])[8]);
```

Maple responded to the commands above by creating the eight vectors below:

```
u1 := [49., 63., 57., -59., 45., -8., -93., 92.]
u2 := [63.71069903, -35.37195839, 101.0920376, 41.06262770,
          73.02002972, -8.381338617, 59.69193858, -22.11460591]
u3 := [-24.51304229, 4.992136681, 15.27728132, 16.15431670,
          -6417551815, -65.88935866, -23.07796286, -18.21252522]
u4 := [-13.88185000, -24.49219808, -7.192072797, 1.209012101,
          -4.759984519, -30.22831583, 38.38497197, 67.89863220]
u5 := [97.98051728, 44.96037814, -35.61487742, 81.39602507,
          -57.40742939, -25.01096476, -.8424949571, 16.34520539]
```

```
u6 := [-62.26799176, 35.49640447, 30.33448329, 82.91310876,
         8.011354803, 48.86274602, -12.33370622, 31.09806856]
u7 := [2.915584575, -14.06455412, -14.19951297, 8.967455383,
         16.13506845, .3543704639, -12.44604673, 2.184020762]
u8 := [5.965161985, -52.99314568, 32.75010757, 4.767974727,
         -48.06852306, 12.84142348, -33.41694144, 6.726836847]
```

Step 3: Normalize these vectors to be of unit length

```
> A1:=u1/norm(u1,2);
  A2:=u2/norm(u2,2);
  A3:=u3/norm(u3,2);
  A4:=u4/norm(u4,2);
  A5:=u5/norm(u5,2);
  A6:=u6/norm(u6,2);
  A7:=u7/norm(u7,2);
  A8:=u8/norm(u8,2);
```

Maple responded to the commands above by creating the eight vectors below:

```
A1   :=[.2726348527,      .3505305249,      .3171466653,      -.3282746185,
         .2503789463, -.04451181268, -.5174498224, .5118858458]
A2   :=[.3901200154,      -.2165932750,      .6190173372,      .2514389764,
         .4471238827, -.05132148917, .3655119211, -.1354144677]
A3   :=[-.3081932714,      .06276425899,      .1920755185,      .2031021549,
         -.008068546796, -.8284021525, -.2901505569, -.2289792373]
A4   :=[-.1565221834,      -.2761571634,      -.08109286133,      .01363198808,
         -.05367030833, -.3408336780, .4328025170, .7655782305]
A5   :=[.6363929605,      .2920220156,      -.2313220823,      .5286750755,
         -.3728668205, -.1624486413, -.005472086440, .1061636939]
A6   :=[-.4847112732,      .2763138319,      .2361320094,      .6454185751,
         .06236260199, .3803611321, -.09600898113, .2420759684]
A7   :=[.09673077448,      -.4666217624,      -.4710993118,      .2975145745,
         .5353155181, .01175700054, -.4129243067, .07245957521]
A8   :=[.06853074133,      -.6088115575,      .3762494893,      .05477685996,
         -.5522350488, .1475286460, -.3839104078, .07728124016]
```

Is the set orthogonal? To test this, construct the orthogonal matrix A out of the eight unit-length vectors. Then, create the transpose of this matrix, and multiply the two together. If the set is orthogonal, then the identity matrix will be the result.

```
> A:=augment(A1,A2,A3,A4,A5,A6,A7,A8);
>
```

After this command, Maple constructs a matrix by pasting together the eight vectors that were just created:

```
A     :=[.2726348527,      .3901200154,      -.3081932714,      -.1565221834,
         .6363929605, -.4847112732, .09673077448 , .06853074133]
       [.3505305249,      -.2165932750,      .06276425899,      -.2761571634,
         .2920220156, .2763138319, -.4666217624, -.6088115575]
```

```
[.3171466653,       .6190173372,       .1920755185,       −.08109286133,
  −.2313220823, .2361320094, −.4710993118, .3762494893]
[−.3282746185,       .2514389764,       .2031021549,       .01363198808,
  .5286750755, .6454185751, .2975145745, .05477685996]
[.2503789463,       .4471238827,       −.008068546796,       −.05367030833,
  −.3728668205, .06236260199, .5353155181, −.5522350488]
[−.04451181268,       −.05132148917,       −.8284021525,       −.3408336780,
  −.1624486413, .3803611321, .01175700054, .1475286460]
[−.5174498224,       .3655119211,       −.2901505569,       .4328025170,
  −.005472086440, −.09600898113, −.4129243067, −.3839104078]
[.5118858458,       −.1354144677,       −.2289792373,       .7655782305,
  .1061636939, .2420759684, .07245957521, .07728124016]
```

Compute A'*A and A*A' using the commands below. To save space, I'm not including the results – but when you give Maple these last commands, the result are two identity matrices, which show that the desired mutually orthogonal set of vectors has been created.

```
> At:=transpose(A);
> evalm(At &* A);
> evalm(A &* At);
```

CHAPTER 5

Limitations of Hebb Learning

5.1 Introduction

The Hebb learning rule has enjoyed a great deal of popularity for a number of different reasons. First, the Hebb rule is an elegant statement of an important associative principle, the law of contiguity. Second, in modern cognitive science there is an increasing desire to relate properties of functional theories to neural mechanisms (Dawson, 1998). Many researchers have noted the numerous similarities between Hebb's account of learning and the biological mechanisms that govern long-term potentiation in the brain (Brown, 1990; Cotman, Monaghan, & Ganong, 1988; Martinez & Derrick, 1996). Third, even when memory systems trained by Hebb-style learning rules make mistakes, these mistakes are interesting, because they are often analogous to the kinds of errors made by human subjects in experiments on associative learning (Eich, 1982; Murdock, 1982; Murdock, 1997).

In spite of these attractions, there are some harsh limitations that are faced by a distributed associative memory that is trained by the Hebb rule (for details, see Dawson (2004)). First, the Hebb rule will modify network connections even in situations where these modifications are not required because perfect recall has already been achieved. Unfortunately, the effect of this additional learning is to introduce systematic errors in the memories that the system recalls. Second, the memory only works well when the stimuli being associated are completely uncorrelated. This chapter provides some exercises in which these sorts of limitations are explored.

5.2 The Effect of Repetition

The purpose of this exercise is to demonstrate one limit of associative learning when the Hebb rule is used.

5.2.1 Procedure

Run the James program, and load the file "ortho8.net" that was used in exercise 4.1. On the setup page, choose the Hebb rule, and choose to end after a maximum number of sweeps.

Have the program print out every epoch by setting the sweeps between printouts value to 1. Use a learning rate of 0.1; the minimum SSE value need not be changed, because it will not be used. *Importantly, set the maximum number of sweeps to 30.* When this is done, the network will have been presented each pattern three times as frequently as was the case in exercise 4.1. After the program has stopped training, examine SSE over time, and examine the network properties using Excel, in order to answer the questions below. After this examination is complete, if you are going to proceed directly to exercise 5.2, then close the spreadsheet, and instruct the program to train a new network on a new problem.

Exercise 5.1

1. What is the total SSE for the network after training has finished?
2. How does this value for SSE compare to the same value that was observed in exercise 4.1? What can one conclude from this comparison?
3. Examine how SSE for this network changed over time. Compare and contrast the performance in this simulation to that observed for the same training set in exercise 4.1. What are the implications of this comparison for Hebb rule learning?
4. Describe the kind of errors that the network made. What is the relationship between these errors and the training procedure?
5. In some sense, there is a degree of correctness in the network's responses to the stimulus vectors. In what sense are the responses correct, and in what sense are the responses incorrect?

5.3 The Effect of Correlation

5.3.1 Linearly independent vectors

In chapter 4, we used a set of mutually orthonormal vectors to create some patterns to be associated by the James program. We saw that the basis vectors that define the coordinates for a space were a special set of mutually orthonormal vectors.

Basis vectors are special because they can be used to define any vector that can be defined in the space that the basis vectors span. For example, consider the three-dimensional space of red, blue, and green color that was provided as an example in chapter 4. The basis vectors for the x-, y-, and z-axes of this space are $x' = [1, 0, 0]$, $y' = [0, 1, 0]$ and $z' = [0, 0, 1]$. Consider some object (i.e., a particular color) that is represented in this space. For instance, one object could be represented as the vector $c' = [200, 20, 13]$. This vector can be considered to be the line drawn from the origin of the space at location (0, 0, 0) to the endpoint of the vector at the location (200, 20, 13). What is the relationship between this vector and the basis vectors of the space?

In addition, basis vectors are special because they can be used to construct any vector that can be represented in the space that they span. You can create these vectors by multiplying each basis vector by some weight, and then adding all of them together to form a single vector. For example, the example vector c' is equal to the weighted sum $(200 \, x' + 20 \, y' + 13 \, z')$. Because of this, we can say that c' is linearly dependent on the basis vectors.

Basis vectors are also special because they are *linearly independent*. This means that one cannot define one of the basis vectors as a weighted sum of any of the other basis vectors. In other words, the only time that one can say that the expression $a\,\mathbf{x}' = b\,\mathbf{y}' + c\,\mathbf{z}'$ is true is when the numbers a, b, and c are all equal to 0 (Blyth & Robertson, 1986). There are no other nonzero values for a, b, and c that will make this expression true.

A set of mutually orthogonal vectors is always a linearly independent set. However, one can have a linearly independent set of vectors that is not orthogonal. This is because the definition of linear independence only focuses on whether a vector can be created by adding other vectors together. This definition is not affected by whether vectors are uncorrelated with each other (i.e., orthogonal) or not. So, it is possible to create a set of linearly independent vectors that are correlated with one another.

5.3.2   A linearly independent training set

In chapter 4, we found that the Hebb rule could be used to correctly store associations between a set of mutually orthonormal vectors. In exercise 5.2, you will be exploring the performance of the memory when this condition is relaxed to a certain extent. In this case, the patterns to be presented to the network are linearly independent, but, unlike chapter 4, they are not orthogonal to one another. How do the correlations among patterns affect performance of the memory?

Table 5.1 provides a set of linearly independent vectors, where each vector has been scaled to have a length of 1. These vectors were used to create a training set whose structure was identical to that of the training sets that were used for the exercises in chapter 4. The only differences

Table 5.1   *A set of linearly independent vectors that were used to create another training set for the distributed associative memory*

Name	Value
$\mathbf{v}_1^T$	$[-3.999E-01, -4.198E-01, -5.209E-01, -3.899E-01, 2.529E-01, -2.557E-01,$ $-1.735E-01, 3.576E-01]$
$\mathbf{v}_2^T$	$[-5.713E-01, -4.377E-01, 4.387E-02, 2.515E-01, -4.345E-01, -4.650E-01,$ $-4.554E-01, 5.662E-01]$
$\mathbf{v}_3^T$	$[3.872E-01, 3.350E-01, 5.045E-01, 4.276E-01, 5.189E-02, -2.906E-02,$ $-2.602E-01, 5.662E-01]$
$\mathbf{v}_4^T$	$[-1.904E-02, 1.742E-01, 4.387E-02, -4.213E-01, 1.297E-01, 1.337E-01,$ $6.144E-01, -1.073E-01]$
$\mathbf{v}_5^T$	$[-5.205E-01, 4.243E-01, -5.209E-01, 4.276E-01, 6.032E-01, 1.976E-01,$ $2.530E-01, 2.741E-01]$
$\mathbf{v}_6^T$	$[1.016E-01, -3.037E-01, -9.870E-02, -4.087E-01, 2.919E-01, -4.708E-01,$ $-4.843E-01, -1.192E-01]$
$\mathbf{v}_7^T$	$[-2.539E-01, 4.377E-01, 2.413E-01, 2.704E-01, 5.253E-01, -5.522E-01,$ $1.373E-01, 3.099E-01]$
$\mathbf{v}_8^T$	$[1.333E-01, -1.608E-01, 3.619E-01, 3.773E-02, 5.189E-02, 3.662E-01,$ $0.000E+00, 1.847E-01]$

are the particular values of the vectors in the table. The eight stimulus-response pairs were v_1 (the stimulus) paired with v_8 (the response), v_2 paired with v_7, v_3 paired with v_6, v_4 paired with v_5, v_5 paired with v_4, v_6 paired with v_3, v_7 paired with v_2, and v_8 paired with v_1. The entire training set can be found in the file called "independ8.net". The appendix to this chapter shows how I used Maple to create this training set and to confirm that it is linearly independent.

5.3.3   Procedure

The purpose of this exercise is to demonstrate a second limit of associative learning when the Hebb rule is used. Run the James program, and load the file "independ8.net". On the setup page, choose the Hebb rule, and choose to end after a maximum number of sweeps. Have the program print out every epoch by setting the sweeps between printouts value to 25. Use a learning rate of 0.1; the minimum SSE value need not be changed, because it will not be used. *Set the maximum number of sweeps to 500.* After the program has stopped training, examine SSE over time, and examine the network properties using Excel, in order to answer the questions below. Exit the program once the exercise has been completed, unless you are planning to proceed to the exercises presented in chapter 6.

Exercise 5.2

1. What is the total SSE for the network after training has finished?
2. Examine how SSE for this network changed over time. In general, what can be said about the performance of this network on this problem?
3. Continuing with an examination of total SSE, did this value ever decrease during training? How close did this value approach to 0? What are the implications of these observations?
4. Describe the kind of errors that the network made. Is the network generating errors to a small number of problems, or are errors for all of the training patterns uniformly large?
5. Rerun the network on the independ8.net problem, with a maximum number of sweeps set to 100, training with the Hebb rule, and printing out information every sweep. Play with the learning rate a bit, and examine the SSE curve when the program stops training. Are you able to improve the performance of the network in any significant way? What are the implications of these observations? (To answer this question, you should provide some information about what you settings you used to run the study.)

APPENDIX TO CHAPTER 5 – CREATING THE LINEARLY INDEPENDENT SET OF VECTORS

The remainder of this chapter is an appendix that demonstrates how I created the linearly independent, correlated vectors that were used in exercise 5.2. This was done with the Maple V program; in the appendix below any entry preceded by a ">" is a command that was entered into Maple.

This extract from the Maple V worksheet demonstrates a procedure for creating a set of vectors that are linearly independent, but not orthogonal to one another. The goal of this is to create a set of vectors that are correlated with one another to a random extent. When this set of vectors is used to create a training set for a distributed associative memory, the Hebb rule should be unable to learn associations without errors, but the Delta rule should be able to learn the associations perfectly if given enough stimulus presentations.

The basic idea is that if one creates a set of eight vectors randomly, then it is going to be highly likely that this is a set that is linearly independent, but not orthogonal. However, the linear independence of this set should be tested. The first half of this worksheet creates a set of random vectors, where each vector is composed of eight entries, and each vector is of unit length. The second half of this worksheet tests for linear independence, and computes the correlations between the vectors.

```
> with (linalg):
```

Step 1: Create eight random vectors

```
> v1 := randvector (8);
v2 := randvector (8);
v3 := randvector (8);
v4 := randvector (8);
v5 := randvector (8);
v6 := randvector (8);
v7 := randvector (8);
v8 := randvector (8);
```

Maple generates the following set of vectors to this command:

```
v1 := [65, 46, -24, 63, 73, 76, -68, 67]
v2 := [-38, 23, 14, 58, -92, -8, 36, -90]
v3 := [96, -19, -4, 38, -61, -58, -91, 45]
v4 := [-79, -27, 32, -24, -46, 12, 81, 63]
v5 := [-85, -36, -35, 11, 90, 31, 47, -50]
v6 := [-54, 71, -71, -17, 64, -34, 60, 99]
v7 := [48, 36, 73, -40, 49, 55, 24, 65]
v8 := [6, -65, 52, 99, -39, 49, -76, -15]
```

Step 2: Normalize these vectors to be of unit length

```
> A1 := v1/norm (v1,2);
A2 := v2/norm (v2,2);
A3 := v3/norm (v3,2);
A4 := v4/norm (v4,2);
A5 := v5/norm (v5,2);
A6 := v6/norm (v6,2);
A7 := v7/norm (v7,2);
A8 := v8/norm (v8,2);
```

Maple computes these vectors; I've deleted the output to save some space. They are given as the rows of matrix A below.

Are these vectors linearly independent? To test this, first stack them all together into a matrix:

```
> A :=evalf (augment (A1,A2,A3,A4,A5,A6,A7,A8));

A := [-.3998891869, -.4198144122, -.5209254083, -.3898600091,
        .2529429689, -.2557404853, -.1734718181, .3575802177]
      [-.5712702670, -.4376788554, .04386740280, .2515225865,
        -.4345430493, -.4649827007, -.4553635225, .5661686782]
      [ .3871942921, .3349583078, .5044751322, .4275883970,
        .05188573724, -.02906141879, -.2602077272, .5661686782]
      [-.01904234223, .1741783200, .04386740280, -.4213003324,
        .1297143431, .1336825264, .6143793556, -.1072740653]
      [-.5204906877, .4242805231, -.5209254083, .4275883970,
        .6031716954, .1976176478, .2529797347, .2741448337]
      [ .1015591585, -.3036955324, -.09870165631, -.4087242032,
        .2918572719, -.4707949844, -.4842754921, -.1191934059]
      [-.2538978964, .4376788554, .2412707154, .2703867806,
        .5253430895, -.5521669570, .1373318560, .3099028554]
      [ .1332963956, -.1607799877, .3619060731, .03772838799,
        .05188573724, .3661738767, 0, .1847497791]
```

Step 3: Test for linear independence by computing the rank of the matrix that was just created
Maple computes rank by performing Gaussian elimination on the rows of the matrix. The rank of the matrix A is the number of non zero rows in the resulting matrix. If the matrix is of full rank (i.e., rank is equal to the number of rows in the matrix) then we can be assured that the vectors are linearly independent. So, in the current example, if the value for rank is less than 8, we should go back to the start of the worksheet and compute a new set of random vectors.

```
> rank (A);
```

Maple responds to this command by generating a number for the rank of the matrix. The number that it generates is 8, indicating that our random matrix is of full rank.

Step 4: Demonstrations of correlations between vectors
Just because the vectors are linearly independent does not mean that they do not have correlations between them. The vectors were normalized to be of unit length, so that the inner product of any two vectors will be exactly equal to the Pearson correlation between them. To compute the entire set of correlations, first compute the transpose of the matrix, and then premultiply the matrix by its transpose. The result will be a correlation matrix.

```
> At:=transpose (A);
```

I've deleted the transpose from the Appendix to save space; it can easily be computed from the matrix A that was listed above. The command below takes the resulting transposed matrix, and multiplies it through the original matrix A:

```
> evalf (evalm (At &* A));
```

Table 5.2 is the correlation matrix for the set of vectors that results from the matrix multiplication command given above. I've rounded to two decimal places to make it easier to read. Note that the diagonal

Table 5.2   The correlation matrix for the set of vectors derived using the method described in this appendix

	A1	A2	A3	A4	A5	A6	A7	A8
A1	1.00	0.16	0.63	−0.14	−0.25	0.39	0.00	−0.45
A2	0.16	1.00	0.23	0.54	0.51	0.25	0.61	0.03
A3	0.63	0.23	1.00	0.31	−0.32	0.05	−0.08	0.13
A4	−0.14	0.54	0.31	1.00	0.04	0.06	−0.07	0.55
A5	−0.25	0.51	−0.32	0.04	1.00	−0.14	0.30	0.16
A6	0.39	0.25	0.05	0.06	−0.14	1.00	0.55	−0.38
A7	0.00	0.61	−0.08	−0.07	0.30	0.55	1.00	−0.36
A8	−0.45	0.03	0.13	0.5	0.16	−0.38	−0.36	1.00

is equal to 1.00, but that the off-diagonal entries are nonzero. If the set of vectors that we created was orthonormal, all of the off-diagonal entries in the matrix below would be equal to zero. So, we can now use the rows of matrix A as the set of linearly independent – but correlated – vectors for use in a training set for the distributed memory.

CHAPTER 6

Introducing the Delta Rule

6.1 Introduction

In chapter 4, we saw that the Hebb rule could be successfully used to store a number of different associations in a distributed associative memory. However, in chapter 5 we also saw that this ability depended crucially on the properties of the patterns being associated, and on how these patterns were presented to the memory. For instance, if the patterns were constructed from vectors that were mutually orthonormal, then Hebb learning succeeded. However, if the patterns were linearly independent but correlated, then Hebb learning failed. Similarly, if training proceeded until total SSE was equal to 0, then all was well with Hebb learning. However, if patterns were presented to the network after SSE had reached a value of 0, then errors were introduced into the memory, and SSE climbed with each additional pattern presentation.

6.2 The Delta Rule

The problems that were observed in chapter 5 are not necessarily problems with distributed associative memories in general. Instead, they are the result of storing associations in this memory by using the Hebb rule. Fortunately, this is not the only rule that is available. In this section, an alternative rule is briefly introduced. Later in this chapter some exercises are presented that are designed to compare the performance of this new rule, called the delta rule, to the performance that we have seen in the previous two chapters.

6.2.1 The problem of too much learning

In chapter 5, we trained the distributed associative memory with a set of orthonormal patterns, using a learning rate of 0.1. Learning was evident early in training, because the sum of squared network error – computed over all outputs and all patterns – steadily decreased, and reached a value of 0.00 by the 10th epoch. However, when patterns were presented beyond the 10th epoch, network SSE began to climb, indicating that the additional training was introducing error. Our intuitions about learning suggest that this should not happen, because we would expect that more learning should result in better performance.

Why does Hebb learning contradict these expectations? It is because Hebb learning modifies weights after each stimulus presentation, even when the weights should not be changed. In other words, Hebb learning does not use any feedback about the errors that the network is making (Dawson, 2004). As a result, it does not stop changing weights when performance has reached perfection. It continues to modify weights, and undoes the learning that it has already accomplished.

6.2.2   Error correction in associative learning

To solve the problem of too much learning, it is necessary to have a learning rule that is sensitive to the amount of error in the network's current performance. If this error is large, then large weight changes are necessary. If this error is smaller, then smaller weight changes are necessary. If this error is zero, then no weight changes are required at all.

In order for this sensitivity to be added to a learning rule, network error must be calculated before any weight changes are performed. In the distributed associative memory, this would entail presenting the stimulus member of a pattern pair first, sending signals through the existing connection weights, and producing a response in each of the network's output units. These actual responses would then be compared to the responses that are desired (i.e., compared to the cue member of the pair). One form of this comparison would be to compute a numerical value for each unit's error. This is done by subtracting the observed activity in the unit from the desired activity in the unit. More mathematical details about this computation are provided in Dawson (2004).

Once error has been computed, learning can proceed. It is essentially the same as Hebb learning, where a weight change is the result of multiplying three different numbers together. As was the case with Hebb learning, the first is the learning rate, and the second is the activity of the processing unit at the input end of the connection. The only difference between the delta rule and the Hebb rule is the third number. In the Hebb rule, it was the activity of the processing unit at the output end of the connection. In contrast, in the delta rule this third number is the error calculated for the processing unit at the output end of the connection. Once this weight change has been calculated, it is added to the existing value for the weight. This is performed for all of the weights in the network. Then another stimulus can be presented to the network.

With the delta rule, the amount of learning – that is, the degree to which a connection is modified – is proportionate to the amount of error that has been calculated, which is what we desired above. One consequence of this is that when all of the output errors reach zero, changes to the weights will not occur, even if patterns are presented. This will solve the problem of too much learning. However, error-driven learning will change the dynamics of the system. Early on, error should be high, and large weight changes will occur. But with each weight change, network performance should improve, and as a result learning will slow down. Because of this, we are not going to be 100 percent sure in advance about when a set of associations will be completely learned by the distributed memory. As a result, instead of training the memory for a pre-set number of epochs, we are more likely to train the network until total SSE reaches some acceptably low value. So, when the delta rule is used, it is important to remember to tell the program to use either criterion for stopping (i.e., total number of sweeps or minimum SSE).

6.3   The Delta Rule and the Effect of Repetition

The purpose of this exercise is to repeat an earlier study, but doing so with the delta rule instead of the Hebb rule. The issue of interest is whether the delta rule is capable of solving one of the problems with Hebb learning that was demonstrated in chapter 5.

6.3.1   Procedure

Run the James program, and load the file "ortho8.net" that was used in Exercises 4.1 and 5.1. On the setup page, *choose the "Delta Rule"*, and choose to end after a maximum number of sweeps. Have the program print out every epoch by setting the sweeps between printouts value to 1. Use a learning rate of 0.1; the minimum SSE value need not be changed, because it will not be used in this particular exercise. *Set the maximum number of sweeps to 30*. When this is done, the network is being treated exactly as it was in exercise 5.1, with the exception of the learning rule that is being used. After the program has stopped training, examine SSE over time, and examine the network properties using Excel, in order to answer the questions below. After this examination is complete, if you are going to proceed directly to exercise 6.2, then close the spreadsheet, and instruct the program to train a new network on a new problem.

Exercise 6.1

1. What is the total SSE for the network after training has finished?
2. How does this value for SSE compare to the same value that was observed in exercise 5.1? What can one conclude from this comparison?
3. Examine how SSE for this network changed over time. Compare and contrast the performance in this simulation to that observed for the same training set in exercise 5.1. What are the implications of this comparison for delta rule learning?

6.4   The Delta Rule and the Effect of Correlation

If everything went as expected in the preceding exercise, then you should have found that the delta rule solved the problem of too much learning that plagued the Hebb rule. This should not be surprising since, when the delta rule was introduced, the motivation was to find a solution to this particular problem. However, from chapter 5 it should be recalled that the Hebb rule faced another problem as well: the inability to learn associations between patterns that were linearly independent, but correlated. How does the delta rule do when faced with this second situation? The goal of exercise 6.2 is to answer this question.

6.4.1   Procedure

The purpose of this exercise is to repeat an earlier study, but doing so with the delta rule instead of the Hebb rule. The issue of interest is whether the delta rule is capable of solving the second problem with Hebb learning that was demonstrated in chapter 5. Run the James program, and load the file "independ8.net" that was used in exercise 5.2. On the setup page, *choose the "Delta Rule"*, and choose to end after a maximum number of sweeps, *and also choose to end when SSE has reached an acceptably low level*. Have the program print out every 100 epochs. Use a learning rate of 0.1; the minimum SSE value should be kept at the default level of 0.05. What this means is that when total SSE reaches 0.05 or lower, the program will stop training the network. *Set the maximum number of sweeps to 6,000.* Train the network until it converges. If it has not reached an SSE of 0.05 or smaller after 6,000 sweeps, continue training by pressing the "Continue Training" button. My experience with this problem is that you should not have to do this, because SSE will most probably reach an acceptable level after approximately 5,100 sweeps. After the program has stopped training, examine SSE over time, and examine the network properties using Excel, in order to answer the questions below.

Exercise 6.2

1. What is the total SSE for the network after training has finished?
2. How many epochs of training were required before the program stopped training the network because SSE was sufficiently low?
3. How does the value for SSE compare to the same value that was observed in exercise 5.2? What can one conclude from this comparison?
4. Examine how SSE for this network changed over time. Compare and contrast the performance in this simulation to that observed for the same training set in exercise 5.1. What are the implications of this comparison for delta rule learning?

CHAPTER 7

Distributed Networks and Human Memory

7.1 Background on the Paired Associate Paradigm

In chapter 2, we noted that the paired associates task was first seen in the literature before the end of the nineteenth century (Calkins, 1894). In this task a subject must remember a list of pairs of items. "The paired-associate list is an exact counterpart of learning foreign-language equivalents of English words, where the first member of each pair (the stimulus term) is the English word and the second member of each pair (the response term) is the foreign word" (Underwood, 1966).

In the literature on human memory, there are two general ways in which the paired associate task can be presented (Underwood, 1966). The first is called *alternate study and recall*. In this method, a subject is presented each full pair in succession, and is instructed to learn the pairs. The subject is then presented each stimulus term alone, and is instructed to generate the appropriate response term. Once this has happened, another study phase is presented, followed by recall. This can be repeated until the full list is learned. The second is called the *anticipation method*. Using this procedure, a subject is presented the first stimulus term in the list by itself, and is asked to generate the appropriate response. After a brief period (say 3 seconds) the same stimulus term is presented with its to-be-associated response term, providing feedback to the subject about the accuracy of his or her response. Then this process is repeated with the next stimulus term in the list. In both methods, the dependent measure of interest is the number of stimulus presentations that are required before a subject learns the complete list.

The paired associate task was a fundamental tool used in the early days of cognitive psychology to study associative processes in verbal learning and memory (Deese & Hulse, 1967). Because this task can be viewed as a model example of the associative process, it was used to explore such issues as whether associations develop gradually, or are learned all-or-none; and whether response–stimulus associations develop in the same fashion as stimulus–response associations. Often this could be accomplished by manipulating within-list properties of stimuli, such as stimulus or response meaningfulness (Hunt, 1959; Wimer & Lambert, 1959). The paired associate task was also instrumental for investigating the effects of interference on learning and memory. Usually this involved studying the effect that the learning of one list had on the learning of later lists, and explored relationships between lists as well (Hunt, 1959; Underwood, 1957; Underwood, Runquist, & Schulz, 1959).

As one example of the way in which the paired associate task can be used to explore a particular research topic, consider the following example. Dallett (1966) was interested in the effects of acoustic similarity on the learning of paired associates, as well as on the retention of this learning. For stimuli (i.e., for the cues in the paired associate task), he chose 12 different homophone pairs (e.g., BOAR–BORE, PROFIT–PROPHET). For responses, Dallett chose 12 different sound-alike pairs that were not homophones (e.g., CANVAS–CAMPUS, MORNING–WARNING). He used these stimuli to create two different paired associate lists for each subject. He manipulated both within-list and between-list similarity by creating different pairings of these same words. For example, he created stimuli in which there was a high degree of acoustic similarity within the same list (e.g., BOAR–CANVAS and BORE–CAMPUS were in the same list). Similarly, he created stimuli in which similarity within one list was low, but similarity between the two different lists was very high (e.g., BOAR–CANVAS might be in the first list, and BORE–CAMPUS in the second list). In general, Dallett found that learning was faster in conditions in which between-list similarity was high; within-list similarity produced much slower learning of the paired associates. However, within-list similarity resulted in much higher retention, as measured by having subjects recall what they had learned a week earlier.

Modern researchers still use the paired associate task, particularly in the fields of cognitive neuroscience and neuroscience. For instance, researchers are using modern brain imaging technologies to study brain activity during paired-associate learning (e.g., Honda et al., 1998; Poldrack et al., 2001). In general, the goal of this kind of research is to explore how different memory systems interact during this kind of learning. This type of exploration is a natural extension of early functional theories that recognized that paired associate learning was multistaged, but did not posit any underlying neural mechanisms for these stages (Underwood, Runquist, & Schulz, 1959). Similarly, different versions of the paired associate task have been developed for studying memory processes in rats. This is because there is a growing view that the "cognitive map" instantiated by the hippocampus (Dawson, Boechler, & Valsangkar-Smyth, 2000; O'Keefe & Dostrovsky, 1971; O'Keefe & Nadel, 1978) is a special case of more general hippocampal associative learning (Eichenbaum, 1992, 2000; Eichenbaum et al., 1999; Long, Mellem, & Kesner, 1998). This continued interest in the mechanisms of paired associate learning is also reflected in modern simulation studies (Kahana, 2002; Rizzuto & Kahana, 2001).

One reason for the longevity of the paired associates task is that this paradigm is very simple to administer, the data that it delivers is straightforward to score and analyze, and it is very easy to manipulate the properties of to-be-associated items to explore any number of issues concerning human memory. One of the reasons that researchers have been interested in the distributed associative memory is because many of the kinds of experiments that have been performed with human subjects can be simulated with this kind of connectionist network (Carpenter, 1989; Eich, 1982; Hinton & Anderson, 1981; Murdock, 1982, 1997; Pike, 1984).

The exercises in this chapter provide some hands-on experience with using the distributed associative memory in this fashion. In the first training set, there will be a relatively low degree of similarity between each cue–response pair. In the second training set, there will be a much higher degree of similarity between each pair. This could be plausibly argued to be a simulation of a human experiment in which the semantic or acoustic similarity of the items was being manipulated. Of course, the question of interest is whether this manipulation affects the performance of this memory. A second question of interest concerns the extent to which the performance of the distributed memory in the simulation is similar to the performance of human subjects.

Table 7.1 *Correlations between selected pairs of the vectors from table 5.1*

Cue vector	Response vector	Within-pair correlation
v_1	v_7	0.00
v_2	v_8	0.03
v_3	v_6	0.05
v_4	v_5	0.04
v_5	v_4	0.04
v_6	v_3	0.05
v_7	v_1	0.00
v_8	v_2	0.03

7.2 The Effect of Similarity on the Distributed Associative Memory

7.2.1 Constructing a low similarity training set

In the first condition of our study, we would like to create a set of cue–response vectors out of the linearly independent set that was created in chapter 5. The appendix of that chapter, in addition to showing how that set of vectors was created, also presented the correlation matrix that revealed the similarity between each pair of vectors (table 5.2). We can create a "low similarity" training set by using the information that was presented in that matrix of correlations. Table 7.1 presents a set of vector pairs such that: a) each vector is used once as a cue; b) each vector is used once as a response, and c) the correlation between each cue–response pair is as close to zero as possible. The actual values of the vectors were previously provided in chapter 5. The training set created on the basis of the table below can be found in the file called "lowsim8.net".

7.2.2 Constructing a high similarity training set

In the second condition of our study, we would like to create a set of cue–response vectors from the same set of linearly independent vectors. However, in this condition we would like to rearrange the pairings so as to try to get the within-pair correlations as high as possible, but still use each vector once as a cue and once as a response. By inspecting the correlation matrix in the appendix of chapter 5, the set of vector pairs in table 7.2 meets these criteria. The training set that corresponds to this table can be found in the file called "hisim8.net".

One thing to keep in mind about these two training sets is that there are many similarities between them, which can be considered to be controlled variables. First, the training sets are built from exactly the same vectors. Second, each vector is used just once as a cue. Third, each vector is used just once as a response. The only difference between the two training sets is the pairing of one cue vector to another. In the low similarity training set, each pair is nearly orthogonal to one another. In the high similarity training set, the correlation between each pair of vectors is substantially higher. The question is whether this manipulation will affect the ability of the distributed associative memory to learn the required associations in each training set.

Table 7.2   *Correlations between a different set of selected pairs of the vectors from table 5.1*

Cue vector	Response vector	Within-pair correlation
v_1	v_6	0.39
v_2	v_7	0.61
v_3	v_4	0.31
v_4	v_3	0.31
v_5	v_8	0.16
v_6	v_1	0.39
v_7	v_2	0.61
v_8	v_5	0.16

7.2.3   Procedure for the low-similarity condition

The purpose of this procedure is to conduct the first part of the memory study using the low-similarity training set. Run the James program, and load the file "lowsim8.net". On the setup page, choose the "Delta Rule", choose to end after a maximum number of sweeps, and also choose to end when SSE has reached an acceptably low level. Have the program print out every 100 epochs. Use a learning rate of 0.1; the minimum SSE value should be kept at the default level of 0.05. Set the maximum number of sweeps to 5,000. Train the network until it converges. If it has not reached an SSE of 0.05 or smaller after 5,000 sweeps, continue training by pressing the "Continue Training" button. After the network has successfully learned the set of associations, the number of epochs of training that were required for this to happen should be recorded as indicated in table 7.3. Then reset the network to be trained once again on this problem. Repeat this until the results from ten different network "subjects" have been produced to fill the blanks in the table. (Hint: you may not need to run all ten subjects to fill in the data matrix below – as per question 5 in the exercise below.)

7.2.4   Procedure for the high-similarity condition

The purpose of this procedure is to conduct the second part of the memory study using the high-similarity training set. Load the file "hisim8.net" into the James program, and treat it exactly in the same way as you treated the low-similarity training set in the previous procedure. In other words, on the setup page, choose the "Delta Rule", choose to end after a maximum number of sweeps, and also choose to end when SSE has reached an acceptably low level. Have the program print out every 100 epochs. Use a learning rate of 0.1; the minimum SSE value should be kept at the default level of 0.05. Set the maximum number of sweeps to 5,000. Train the network until it converges. If it has not reached an SSE of 0.05 or smaller after 5,000 sweeps, continue training by pressing the "Continue Training" button. After the network has successfully learned the set of associations, the number of epochs of training that were required for this to happen should be recorded in the table below. Then reset the network to be trained once again on this problem. Repeat this until the results from ten different network "subjects" can be recorded in your table. Once the data has been recorded, close down the program and answer the questions in exercise 7.1. (Hint: you may not need to run all ten subjects to fill in the data matrix – as per question 5 in the exercise below.)

7.2.5 The results of the experiment

Follow table 7.3 to record data for the exercise below

Table 7.3   *Table showing data to be recorded for exercise 7.1*

	Epochs to converge	
Trial	Low similarity	High similarity
1		
2		
3		
4		
5		
6		
7		
8		
9		
10		
Mean		
Variance		

Exercise 7.1

1. What are the independent and dependent variables for this experiment?
2. By examining the means in your table of data, what can be concluded about the effects of the independent variable? Use appropriate statistical tests to support this conclusion.
3. From the brief description of some of the human results for the paired associate task that was given earlier in the chapter, would you conclude that the distributed associative memory is generating human-like results, or not?
4. What is the variance of the results for each condition? Why is this the case, and what are the implications for performing this kind of experiment?
5. Speculate on how the experimental methodology in this exercise could be modified to increase the variability in each column of data. Do not feel constrained by the James program – perhaps your proposed change in methodology would require some minor modifications to the program itself.
6. When the Hebb rule is used to train this kind of memory, what is the relationship between the training of the network and the two methods used to teach paired associates to humans (i.e., the alternate study and recall method and the anticipation method)?
7. When the delta rule is used to train this kind of memory, what is the relationship between the training of the network and the two methods used to teach paired-associates to humans (i.e., the alternate study and recall method and the anticipation method)?

CHAPTER 8

Limitations of Delta Rule Learning

8.1 Introduction

In previous exercises, we have seen that the delta rule offers a great deal of improvement over Hebb rule learning. Is there anything that the delta rule cannot do? The answer to this question must be "yes", otherwise modern connectionists would not be working with more sophisticated architectures like the multilayer perceptron!. The purpose of the exercise in this chapter is to explore delta rule learning with a training set that is designed to give it problems.

8.2 The Delta Rule and Linear Dependency

8.2.1 A linearly dependent training set

In chapter 4, we found that the Hebb rule could be used to correctly store associations between a set of mutually orthonormal set of vectors. In chapter 5, we discovered that the Hebb rule could not learn associations between vectors that were linearly independent, but correlated. In chapter 6, we demonstrated that the delta rule was able to overcome this particular problem. What happens to the delta rule when the relationships between the vectors used to construct a set of paired associates are manipulated yet again? In particular, how does the delta rule respond when a training set contains some degree of linear dependence?

Table 8.1 provides a set of linearly dependent vectors, where each vector has been scaled to have a length of 1, and shows how these vectors were combined to make a training set composed of eight different pairs of stimulus and response vectors. The linear dependence in this set of vectors is not complete – some of the vectors are still linearly independent. Linear dependence was built into the set in a particular way. The first seven vectors in the table are exactly the same as the first seven vectors in the linearly independent set that was described in chapter 5. Linear dependence was built into this set by modifying only one vector, $\mathbf{v}_8{}'$, and by making this vector a linear sum of two other vectors in the table. In particular, in the table below $\mathbf{v}_8{}' = \frac{1}{2}\mathbf{v}_1{}' + \frac{1}{2}\mathbf{v}_2{}'$. Because this last vector is defined as a linear combination of two other vectors in the set, some linear dependency has been introduced. At issue is how this affects the performance of the network.

The structure of this training set is identical to that of the training sets that were used for the exercises in chapters 4, 5, and 6. The only differences are the particular values of the

Table 8.1 *Linearly dependent vectors used to create another training set*

Name	Value
v_1^T	$[-3.999E-01, -4.198E-01, -5.209E-01, -3.899E-01, 2.529E-01, -2.557E-01,$ $-1.735E-01, 3.576E-01]$
v_2^T	$[-5.713E-01, -4.377E-01, 4.387E-02, 2.515E-01, -4.345E-01, -4.650E-01,$ $-4.554E-01, 5.662E-01]$
v_3^T	$[3.872E-01, 3.350E-01, 5.045E-01, 4.276E-01, 5.189E-02, -2.906E-02,$ $-2.602E-01, 5.662E-01]$
v_4^T	$[-1.904E-02, 1.742E-01, 4.387E-02, -4.213E-01, 1.297E-01, 1.337E-01, 6.144E-01,$ $-1.073E-01]$
v_5^T	$[-5.205E-01, 4.243E-01, -5.209E-01, 4.276E-01, 6.032E-01, 1.976E-01, 2.530E-01, 2.741E-01]$
v_6^T	$[1.016E-01, -3.037E-01, -9.870E-02, -4.087E-01, 2.919E-01, -4.708E-01,$ $-4.843E-01, -1.192E-01]$
v_7^T	$[-2.539E-01, 4.377E-01, 2.413E-01, 2.704E-01, 5.253E-01, -5.522E-01, 1.373E-01, 3.099E-01]$
v_8^T	$[-4.856E-01, -4.287E-01, -2.385E-01, -6.917E-02, -9.080E-02, -3.604E-01,$ $-3.144E-01, 4.619E-01]$

vectors in the table. The eight stimulus–response pairs were v_1 (the stimulus) paired with v_8 (the response), v_2 paired with v_7, v_3 paired with v_6, v_4 paired with v_5, v_5 paired with v_4, v_6 paired with v_3, v_7 paired with v_2, and v_8 paired with v_1. The training set constructed from these vectors is stored in the file "depend8.net".

8.2.2 Procedure

Run the James program, and load the file "depend8.net". On the setup page, *choose the Delta rule,* and choose to end after a maximum number of sweeps, *and also choose to end when SSE has reached an acceptably low level.* Have the program print out every 100 epochs. Use a learning rate of 0.1; the minimum SSE value should be kept at the default level of 0.05. What this means is that when total SSE reaches 0.05 or lower, the program will stop training the network. *Set the maximum number of sweeps to 5,000.* After the program has stopped training, examine SSE over time, and examine the network properties using Excel, in order to answer the questions below.

Exercise 8.1

1. What is the total SSE for the network after training has finished?
2. How many epochs of training occurred before the program stopped training the network?
3. Examine how SSE for this network changed over time. In general, what can be said about the performance of this network on this problem?
4. Describe the kind of errors that the network made, if any. Is the network generating errors to a small number of problems, or are errors for all of the training patterns uniformly large? Relate the properties of any observed errors to what you know about the structure of the training set.
5. Rerun the network on the depend8.net problem, with a maximum number of sweeps set to 5,000, training with the delta rule, and printing out information every 100 sweeps. Play with the learning rate a bit, and examine total SSE when the program stops training. Are you able to improve the performance of the network in any significant way? What are the implications of these observations? (To answer this question, you should provide some information about the settings that you used to run the study.)

CHAPTER 9

The Perceptron

9.1 Introduction

At this point in the book, we have completed all of the exercises that we are going to do with the James program. These exercises have shown that distributed associative memories are capable of storing several different pairs of associations in the same set of connection weights. However, we have also seen that these memories are limited in power. These limitations have led researchers to propose alternative connectionist architectures that are intended to be more powerful than the memories that we have been studying to this point. One of these architectures is the perceptron (Rosenblatt, 1962), and this chapter provides a brief introduction to it. A more detailed introduction to the perceptron as an elaboration of the distributed associative memory can be found in Dawson (2004).

9.2 The Limits of Distributed Associative Memories, and Beyond

Why are distributed associative memories subject to the limitations that we have discovered in the previous exercises? One possible answer to this question is that even the delta rule is not powerful enough to learn all of the associations of interest to us. However, this turns out not to be the problem. All of the learning rules that we will encounter in this chapter, and in later chapters of this book, are very similar – if not identical – to the delta rule.

A second possibility is that the basic building blocks that make up the distributed associative memory are not powerful enough. In the sections that follow, we will explore this possibility in more detail by focusing upon one architectural property, the activation function used by the output units of the distributed associative memory. We will briefly describe this function, consider its potential weakness, and propose some alternatives to it that will be incorporated into our next type of connectionist model.

9.2.1 Linear activation functions

Recall that the output units in the distributed associative memory compute their net input by adding up the weighted signals that are being sent to them by the input units through the network's connections. After net input is computed, its value is used as the activity of the output units in order to represent a memory's response to some cue pattern.

In a more general account of output unit processing, it is useful to consider an output unit as computing two different mathematical equations. The first is the net input function, which is the equation used to compute the signal that enters the output unit. In all of the networks that we will consider in this book, the net input equation is a simple sum. The second equation is the activation function, and it is used to convert the net input that has been computed into some level of internal activity in the unit. There are many different kinds of activation functions that can be found in modern connectionist networks (Duch & Jankowski, 1999). The activation function that is used by the output units in the distributed associative memory is particularly weak, and one way in which the power of such a memory could be extended would be to replace this function with one that is more powerful.

In the simulations that we have been conducting upto this point in the book, the identity function is used to compute the activity of an output unit. In other words, the output unit's activity is exactly equal to its net input. Unfortunately, the identity function implements a particularly weak relationship between net input and activity, and this weak relationship is to the detriment of the distributed associative memory. When net input is small, output activity is small. When net input is medium, output activity is medium. When net input is large, output activity is large. In short, when the identity function is used to determine unit activity, the relationship between net input and output unit activity is linear.

Many researchers would argue that connectionist models are important because they are biologically inspired, and would also claim that the processing units in such models are analogous to neurons in the brain. Interestingly, in the behavior of a neuron, there is *not* a linear relationship between net input and activity. When net input is small, a neuron's activity is small in the sense that it does not generate an action potential. As net input gradually increases, the neuron's activity does not change – it would still fail to generate an action potential. It is only when the net input becomes sufficiently large – when it exceeds some threshold – that an action potential is generated. In short, in neurons there is a nonlinear relationship between net input and activation. In order to increase the power of the distributed memory, this kind of nonlinearity has to be introduced into the output units by replacing the identity function with some other, nonlinear, activation function.

9.2.2 Nonlinear activation functions

In general terms, neurons process information by detecting weak electrical signals, called graded potentials, that stimulate, and travel through, their dendrites. If enough of these weak graded potentials arrive at the cell body of the neuron at the same time, then their cumulative effect disrupts the resting electrical state of the neuron. This results in a massive depolarization of the membrane of the neuron's axon, called an action potential, which travels along the axon to eventually stimulate some other neuron.

While graded potentials gradually decrease in intensity over time and distance, an action potential does not. An action potential is an electrical signal of constant intensity. The fact that neurons generate action potentials of fixed intensity is one of the fundamental discoveries of neuroscience, and has been called the all-or-none law. "The all-or-none law guarantees that once an action potential is generated it is always full size, minimizing the possibility that information will be lost along the way" (Levitan & Kaczmarek, 1991).

McCulloch and Pitts (1943) realized that the all-or-none law enabled them to ignore the detailed biology of neural function, and allowed them to instead describe neurons as devices that made true or false logical assertions about input information. "The all-or-none law of nervous activity is sufficient to ensure that the activity of any neuron may be represented as a proposition. Physiological relations existing among nervous activities correspond, of course, to relations among the propositions; and the utility of the representation depends upon the identity of these relations with those of the logical propositions. To each reaction of any neuron there is a corresponding assertion of a simple proposition" (McCulloch & Pitts, 1988).

In order to define connectionist processing units in a fashion consistent with the logical view of McCulloch and Pitts (1943), we need to define an activation function that has two different (but related) properties. First, the function has to implement a nonlinear relationship between net input and activation. Second, the function has to implement some maximum and minimum levels of activity that can be logically interpreted as a "true" or "false" response to a proposition. Many different activation functions meet these two requirements. In our exploration of the perceptron, we will be concerned with three of these, which are all illustrated in figure 9.1, which also includes the linear activation function (figure 9.1a) for comparison. These three functions are the step function (figure 9.1b), the logistic function (figure 9.1c), and the Gaussian function (figure 9.1d). The sections that follow briefly describe each of these activation functions.

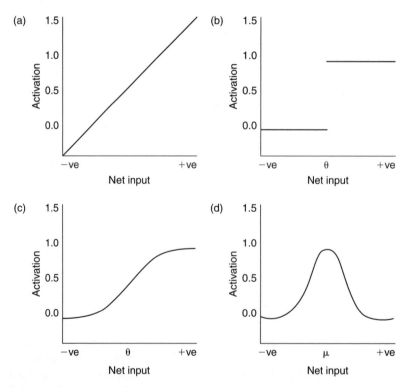

Figure 9.1   Four different activation functions: (a) a linear function; (b) a step function; (c) a logistic function; (d) a Gaussian function

9.2.3   The step function

The first nonlinear activation function to consider is called the step function. It was the activation function that was originally used to model the all-or-none law in artificial neural networks (McCulloch & Pitts, 1943), and was also the activation function that was used in the original perceptron architecture (Rosenblatt, 1962).

With the step function, a processing unit is considered to be in one of only two possible states: on or off. We will be representing the on state with an activation value of 1, and the off state with an activation value of 0. However, sometimes in the literature one might find that the off state is represented with an activation value of -1.

A unit's net input is converted into one of these two activation values by comparing the net input to some threshold value θ. If the net input is less than or equal to θ, then the unit's activity is assigned a value of 0. If the net input is greater than θ, then the unit's activity is assigned a value of 1. Note with this activation function that the relationship between net input and activity is clearly nonlinear (i.e., compare figure 9.1a to figure 9.1b). Also note that this activation function implements the all-or-none law, because no matter how high above θ becomes the net input, the resulting unit activation is always equal to 1.

9.2.4   The logistic function

The second nonlinear activation function that we will be using in the perceptron is called the logistic function. It is a continuous approximation of the step function (see figure 9.1c); its continuous nature permits calculus to be used to derive learning rules for perceptrons and multilayer perceptrons (Rumelhart, Hinton, & Williams, 1986a). Units that use this type of activation function are sometimes called *integration devices* (Ballard, 1986).

The logistic function converts net input into activation according to the following equation: $f(net_i) = 1 / (1 + \exp(-net_i + \theta_j))$. In this equation, the activity of output unit i is represented as $f(net_i)$, the net input of this unit is represented as net_i, and the bias of this unit is represented as θ_j. The bias of a unit that uses the logistic function is analogous to the threshold of a unit that uses the step function. Bias is the value of net input that produces an activation value of 0.50.

9.2.5   The Gaussian function

Both the step function and the logistic function are monotonic, in the sense that increases in net input never result in decreases in either of these activation functions. This is consistent with the behavior of some, but not all, neurons. Some neurons – such as the cone receptors in the retina – have nonmonotonic activation profiles. What this means is that they are tuned to respond to a narrow range of net input values (Ballard, 1986), and can therefore be called *value units*. If the net input is below this range, the unit will not respond. However, if the net input is above this range, the unit will also not respond. Another way to describe this nonmonotonicity is to say that the unit has two thresholds: a lower threshold for turning on, and an upper threshold for turning off.

The Gaussian function is an equation that implements this particular form of nonmonotonicity, as is illustrated in figure 9.1d. It was originally proposed in a network architecture that represented an elaboration of the multilayered perceptrons that were proposed in the 1980s (Dawson & Schopflocher, 1992b). The equation for the Gaussian is: $G(net_i) = \exp(-\pi(net_i - \mu_j)^2$. In this equation, the activity of output unit i is represented as $G(net_i)$, the net input of this unit is represented as net_i, and the bias of this unit is represented as μ_j. The value μ is similar to a threshold, in the sense that it indicates the net input value to which the unit is tuned. However, it is not a threshold. Instead, it is the value of the net input that results in the unit generating a maximum activity of 1. When net input becomes moderately smaller than μ, or moderately larger than μ, then unit activity drops off significantly, falling asymptotically to a value of 0.

The fact that the Gaussian function can be described as having an upper and lower threshold produces some interesting changes to the behavior of perceptrons built from value units. Value units can solve some problems that cannot be solved by perceptrons built from integration devices. However, integration devices can solve some problems that pose problems to value units. We will be exploring these sorts of issues in the upcoming exercises.

9.3   Properties of the Perceptron

9.3.1   What do perceptrons do?

The perceptron is very similar to the distributed associated memory. It too consists of a bank of input units, a bank of one or more output units, and a set of modifiable connections that link every input unit to every output unit. A learning rule is used to modify the connection weights in order to train the perceptron to create an association between an input pattern and an output pattern. The only crucial difference between the two architectures is the fact that the output units in a perceptron use a nonlinear activation function. As was discussed earlier, the purpose of the nonlinear activation function is to model the all-or-none law governing the generation of action potentials.

The similarity between the two architectures is emphasized in figure 9.2, which illustrates the basic architecture of a perceptron. This figure renders the perceptron as if it were a distributed memory of the type that we have studied with the James program. The only difference between the two types of networks is the activation function of the output units. This difference has been added to the figure by drawing a step function inside each of the output units in the figure.

The nonlinear activation function in the output units of a perceptron leads to a slight difference in interpreting the kind of task that a perceptron should be trained to perform. The output units of a perceptron are trained to generate a response that will be interpreted as being either on or off. This means that the output units can be assigned a logical interpretation, in the sense of McCulloch and Pitts. As a result, while a perceptron can be viewed as a kind of associative memory, the kinds of associations that it learns to make will usually be interpreted in a different fashion than were the associations that were described in previous chapters. The logical nature of an output unit's activity means that a perceptron is usually described as a device that makes decisions – it classifies input patterns. The nonlinear activation function in a perceptron is used to assign input patterns to a particular category, where this assignment is all or none.

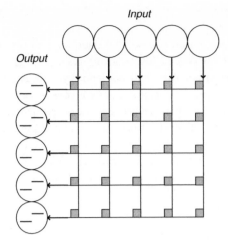

Figure 9.2   A nonlinear associative memory. This system is identical to the one illustrated in figure 2.1, with the exception that the activation function in the output units is a step function

For example, consider a simple kind of problem called the majority problem. In a majority problem, a perceptron would have N input units, and a single output unit. If the majority of the input units were turned on, then the output unit of the perceptron would be trained to turn on to those patterns. If less than the majority of the input units were turned on, then the output unit of the perceptron would be trained to turn off. Imagine that N was equal to 5. In this case, whenever three, four, or five of the input units were activated, then the perceptron would be trained to turn on. If zero, one, or two of the input units were activated, then the perceptron would be trained to turn off. Thus while it is perfectly legitimate to view the perceptron as learning to associate one kind of response with some inputs, and a different kind of response with others, more specifically we can say that the perceptron has learned to decide that some patterns have the majority of their input units turned on, while others do not. Our account of the perceptron as a pattern classifier is almost completely due to the fact that it uses a nonlinear activation function that is binary in nature.

9.3.2   The basic architecture

The basic architecture of a perceptron was illustrated above in figure 9.2. It consists of a bank of two or more input units, a bank of one or more output units, and a set of connection weights that link input units directly to output units. Each connection weight is associated with a weight, and associations between inputs and outputs are stored in this architecture by using a learning rule to modify these weights.

The input units in a perceptron are identical in nature to the input units for the distributed associative memory. The input units are used to represent patterns that are to be presented as stimuli to the perceptron. The activities of the input units can either be binary or continuous, depending on the desired interpretation of what each input unit represents. Input unit activities can be used to represent features that are either very simple or very complicated, depending on the problem to be presented to the network. As an example of a simple input, an input unit could be turned on or off to represent whether some simple stimulus was present or absent in the environment.

The output units in a perceptron represent an elaboration of the output units in a distributed associative memory. The two are identical with respect to their net input function. The output units in a perceptron calculate their net input by summing the signal being sent by each input unit after the signal has been scaled by a connection weight. As we have been emphasizing in this chapter, the difference between the output units in the two different kinds of networks is with respect to the activation function that is used to convert net input into internal activity. One consequence of using nonlinear activation functions in the output units is that we have to pay attention to the kind of learning rule that is used to modify connection weights. Three different learning rules will be explored, one for each of the three different activation functions that were described earlier.

9.3.3   The Rosenblatt learning rule

In the original description of the perceptron architecture, Rosenblatt (1962) developed a learning rule that could be used when output units used the step function. The logic of this learning rule is that connection weight modifications are contingent upon network performance. Let us define the error of some output unit j as the value $(t_j - a_j)$, where t_j is the desired or target value of the output, and a_j is the actual activity that the output unit generates. In calculating $(t_j - a_j)$ there are three possible outcomes. First, the value of $(t_j - a_j)$ could be equal to 0. In this case, the output unit has generated the correct response to an input pattern and no connection weight changes are required. Second, the value of $(t_j - a_j)$ could be equal to 1. In this case, the output unit has generated an error by turning off when it was desired that the unit actually turn on. In order to deal with this situation, it is necessary to increase the net input to the output unit. This could be accomplished by increasing the size of the connection weights. Third, the value of $(t_j - a_j)$ could be equal to -1. In this case, the output unit has made an error by turning on when it should have turned off. The remedy for this problem would be to decrease the unit's net input by subtracting from the values of the connection weights.

An examination of the three possible values for error, and of the resulting change that these values imply for connection weights, indicates that the delta rule that we saw used in the distributed associative memory can also be used for the perceptron. Rosenblatt (1962) proposed that the desired change to the weight connecting input unit i to output unit j can be expressed as: $\Delta w_{ij} = \eta(t_j - a_j) a_i$. In this equation, η is a learning rate that will ordinarily range between 0 and 1, $(t_j - a_j)$ is the error calculated for output unit j, under the assumption that a_j is calculated using the step function, and a_i is the activity of input unit i.

An output unit that uses the step function can be described as a classifier that makes a single straight cut through a pattern space. Each input pattern is represented as a point in that pattern space, with the position of each point being defined by the activity of each input unit. The input unit activities are used to define coordinates in the pattern space. Patterns that fall on one side of the cut the output unit makes will result in the output unit turning off. Patterns that fall on the other side of the cut will result in the output unit turning on. When a perceptron's weights are trained using the delta rule, the result is that the cut through pattern space made by the output unit is rotated. However, to solve some problems we also need to be able to translate this cut through space instead of just rotating it. In order to translate the cut, we need to be able to modify the threshold θ_j of the output unit. This can easily be done by assuming that the threshold is the value of the connection weight that comes from an additional input unit that is always on. With this interpretation, the desired change in the threshold θ_j of some output unit j can be defined as: $\Delta\theta_j = \eta(t_j - a_j)\, 1$.

The delta rule, when applied to a perceptron, is very powerful. Rosenblatt (1962) used it to derive his famous perceptron convergence theorem. This theorem proved that if a solution to a pattern classification problem could be represented in the connection weights of a perceptron, then the delta rule was guaranteed to find a set of connection weights that solved the problem. For our purposes, the fact that the delta rule can be used to train a perceptron also provides additional evidence about the similarity between perceptrons and distributed associative memories.

9.3.4   The gradient descent rule

Rumelhart, Hinton, and Williams (1986a, 1986b) defined the total error for a network whose output units are integration devices as the sum of squared error, E, where the squared error is totaled over every output unit and every pattern in the training set: $E = \frac{1}{2} \sum\sum (t_{jp} - a_{jp})^2$. In this equation, t_{jp} represents the target activity for output unit j when it is presented pattern p, and a_{jp} represents the observed activity for output unit j when it is presented pattern p. The first summation (i.e., the second Σ in the equation) is performed over the total number of patterns in the training set, and the second summation (i.e., the first Σ in the equation) is performed over the total number of output units in the perceptron.

With network error defined as above, and with the logistic equation serving as a continuous approximation of the step function, Rumelhart, Hinton, and Williams (1986a, 1986b) were in a position to use calculus to determine how a weight should be altered in order to decrease error. They derived equations that determined how a change in a weight changed the net input to an output unit, how the resulting change in net input affected the output unit's activity, and how altering the output unit's activity affected error as defined above. They then used these equations to define how to change a weight, when a given pattern has been presented, in order to have the maximum effect of learning. This definition was a new statement of the error for an output unit j, which we will represent as δ_j. They found that the fastest way to decrease network error was to take the error that was used in the delta rule, and to multiply this error by the first derivative of the logistic equation, $f'(net_j)$. The first derivative of the logistic equation is equal to the value $a_j(1 - a_j)$. So, the new equation for output unit error became: $\delta_j = (t_j - a_j)\, f'(net_j) = (t_j - a_j)\, a_j(1 - a_j)$.

A new learning rule for a perceptron that uses the logistic activation function can be defined by inserting this new error term into the delta rule equation. This results in what we will call the gradient descent rule for training a perceptron: $\Delta w_{ij} = \eta\delta_j\, a_i = \eta\,(t_j - a_j)\, a_j \times (1 - a_j)\, a_i$.

As was the case with the delta rule, the bias of the logistic can also be modified by the learning rule. To do this, the bias is treated as if it were equal to the weight of a connection between the output unit and an additional input unit that is always activated with a value of 1 for every training pattern in the training set. With this assumption, the gradient descent rule for modifying bias can be stated as: $\Delta\theta_j = \eta\,\delta_j\,1 = \eta\,(t_j - a_j)\,a_j\,(1 - a_j)\,1$.

What is the purpose of multiplying the output unit's error value by the derivative of the activation function before modifying the weight? At any point in time during learning, a perceptron can be represented as a single point or location on a surface. The coordinates of the location are given by the current values of all of the perceptron's weights (and of its bias). Each point on this surface has a height, which is equal to the value of total network error. One can think about learning as a process that moves the perceptron along this error surface, always seeking a minimum error value. Every time that the perceptron changes its connection weights, it takes a step "downhill" on the error surface, moving to a location that has lower height (i.e., a lower error value). The size of the step that is taken is determined by the size of the learning rate. The direction in which the step is taken is dictated by the error calculated for an output unit. In order to minimize total network error as quickly as possible, it is desirable that at each step the perceptron move in the direction that is the steepest "downhill". The first derivative of the activation function is the part of the equation that determines the direction from the current location on the space that has the steepest downhill slope. By multiplying output unit error by the derivative, the network is permitted to take the shortest "diagonal" path along the error surface.

9.3.5   The Dawson–Schopflocher rule

How would one train a perceptron whose output units are value units? The first plausible approach would be to adopt the gradient descent rule. To do this, one would define a new error term by taking the gradient descent rule described in section 9.3.4 and replacing the first derivative of the logistic ($f'(net_j)$) with the first derivative of the Gaussian ($G'(net_j)$), which is equal to $-2\pi(net_j)G(net_j) = -2\pi(net_j)\,(\exp(-\pi(net_i - \mu_j)^2))$. However, Dawson and Schopflocher (1992b) found that when they did this, learning was very inconsistent. In some cases, training proceeded very quickly. However, in the majority of cases, the network did not learn to solve the problem. Instead, its connection weights were changed in such a way that the network learned to turn off to all of the training patterns by moving all of the net inputs into one of the tails of the Gaussian function.

To correct this problem, Dawson and Schopflocher (1992b) elaborated the equation for total network error by adding a heuristic component to it. This heuristic component was designed to keep some of the net inputs in the middle of the Gaussian function. It was a statement that asserted that when the desired activation value for output unit j was 1, the error term should include an attempt to minimize the difference between the net input to the unit net_j and the unit's mean μ_j. Their elaborated expression for total network error was: $E = \frac{1}{2}\Sigma\Sigma(t_{pj} - a_{pj})^2 + \frac{1}{2}\Sigma\Sigma\,t_{pj}\,(net_{pj} - \mu_j)^2$.

After defining this elaborated error term, Dawson and Schopflocher (1992b) used calculus to determine what kind of weight change was required to decrease total network error. As was the case for the derivation of the gradient descent rule, this resulted in a new expression for output unit error to be included in an expression that was similar to the delta rule. However, because their elaborated error expression had two components, Dawson and Schopflocher found that the error for an output value unit also had two components.

The first component was identical to the expression in the gradient descent rule that defined the term δ_{pj}, with the exception that it used the first derivative of the Gaussian instead of the logistic: $\delta_{pj} = (t_{pj} - a_{pj}) G' (net_{pj}) = (t_{pj} - a_{pj}) (-2\pi (net_{pj}) (\exp(-\pi (net_{pj} - \mu_{pj})^2)))$.

The second component was represented with the term ϵ_j, and was the part of output unit error that was related to the heuristic information that Dawson and Schopflocher (1992b) added to the equation for total network error. The equation for this error term was: $\epsilon_{pj} = t_{pj} (net_{pj} - \mu_j)$.

The complete expression for an output unit's error was found to be the difference between these two expressions of error, and Dawson and Schopflocher discovered that a learning rule for a network of value units was defined by a gradient descent rule that used this more complex measure of output unit error: $\Delta w_{ij} = \eta (\delta_j - \epsilon_j) a_i$.

Similarly, Dawson and Schopflocher (1992b) that the mean of an output unit's Gaussian could also be trained. This was done by assuming that the value j was the weight from an additional input unit that was always turned on. This assumption results in a learning expression very similar to the ones that were provided earlier for training the threshold of a step function or the bias of a logistic function: $\Delta\mu = \eta (\delta_j - \epsilon_j)$.

In summary, Dawson and Schopflocher (1992b) demonstrated that a perceptron with output units that used the Gaussian activation function could be trained with a variant of the gradient descent rule that was derived for integration devices. The learning rule that they developed differed from the more traditional gradient descent rule in only two ways. First, it used the first derivative of the Gaussian equation. Second, it used an elaborated expression for output unit error, which included a heuristic component that is not found in the traditional gradient descent rule.

9.4   What Comes Next

In this chapter, we have introduced the notion of a perceptron as being an elaboration of the distributed associative memory that was explored in the first chapters of this book. We have also described three different versions of the perceptron: one that uses the delta rule to train output units that use the step activation function, one that uses the gradient descent rule to train output units that are integration devices, and one that uses a modified gradient descent rule to train output units that are value units.

In the chapters that follow, we will be exploring the advantages and disadvantages of these three variations on the generic perceptron architecture. We will be performing a number of exercises that illustrate the kinds of problems that these networks can solve, as well as the kinds of problems that pose difficulty for these networks. We will also be exploring how the perceptron can be used to explore some issues that are current in the animal learning literature. All of these explorations will be conducted with a new program, called Rosenblatt. General instructions for installing and using this program are provided in chapter 10.

CHAPTER 10

The Rosenblatt Program

10.1 Introduction

Rosenblatt is a program written in Visual Basic 6.0 for the demonstration and exploration of perceptrons. It is designed for use on a computer running a Microsoft Windows operating system. A second program, RosenblattLite, is identical to Rosenblatt with the exception that it does not include the capability to save network results in Microsoft Excel workbooks. A third program, RosenblattJava, is identical to RosenblattLite, but is written in Java so that it can be used on computers that do not use the Windows operating system. In this chapter, Rosenblatt will be the only program referred to, as the user interface for it is identical to the interface for the other two programs. All programs are distributed as freeware from the following website: http://www.bcp.psych.ualberta.ca/~mike/Book3/.

The current program explores pattern classification with three different versions of the perceptron. In the first, the Rosenblatt training rule – which is equivalent to the delta rule that was introduced with the James program in chapter 3 – is used to train a perceptron with a threshold activation function. In the second, gradient descent is used to train a perceptron that uses a logistic activation function as a continuous approximation of the threshold activation function. In the third, a variation of the gradient descent rule is used to train a perceptron that uses a Gaussian activation function in its output units. This last function means that the output units in essence have two different thresholds, instead of one. These variations of the perceptron are described in more detail in chapter 10 of Dawson (2004).

10.2 Installing the Program

Rosenblatt is distributed from the above website as a .zip file. The following steps will result in the program being installed on your computer:

1. Download the file Rosenblatt.zip to your computer by going to the website, click on the program icon, and save the file in any desired location on your computer.
2. Go to the saved Rosenblatt.zip file on your computer, and unzip it with a program like WinZip. The result will be three different objects: setup.exe, setup.lst and Rosenblatt.cab.

3. Run the setup.exe program. This will call an Install program that will complete the installation of the program on your computer, which will include the installation of an "Examples" folder with a few sample training files.

10.3   Training a Perceptron

10.3.1   Starting the program

The program can be started in two different ways. First, one can go into the directory in which the program was installed and double-click on the file "Rosenblatt.exe". Second, one can go to the start button on the computer, choose programs, scroll to the program group BCPNet, and select the program Rosenblatt.exe.

10.3.2   Loading a file to train a network

After the program is started, the first form that appears is used to select a file for training the distributed memory. This form is illustrated in figure 10.1. By using the left mouse button and the drive selection tool located in the upper left of the form, one can choose a computer drive on which directories and files are located. The available directories on the selected drive are listed in the directory selection tool that is immediately below the drive selection tool.

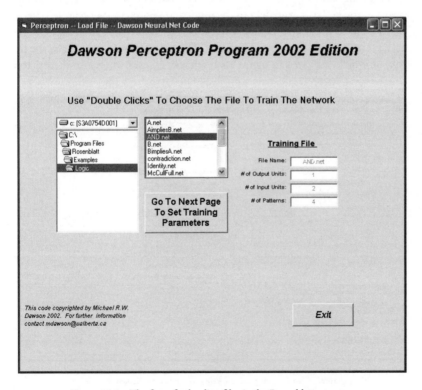

Figure 10.1   The form for loading files in the Rosenblatt program

One opens a directory by double-clicking it with the left mouse button. If the directory contains any files that end with the extension .net, then these files will be displayed in the file selection box located in the upper middle of the form. The properties of .net files are described later in this book. These files have a particular format that the Rosenblatt program is designed to read, and only files that end in this extension can be used to train the network.

One chooses a .net file by double-clicking one of the file names displayed in the file selection box. When this is done, the program reads the desired file, some of the file's properties are displayed, and another button appears on the form. In figure 10.1, the file "AND.net" has been selected (and read). On the right of the form its general properties are displayed, and the button permitting the user to proceed to the next part of the program is displayed under the file selection box.

In this example, if "AND.net" has been selected, but is not the file that is desired, one can simply go back to the file selection tools and choose another file. When its file name is double-clicked, the new file will be read in, and will replace the properties of the previous (undesired) file.

Once the desired file has been selected, all that is required is to press the "Go To Next Page To Set Training Parameters" button with a left-click of the mouse. If instead one desires to close the program, then one can left-click the "Exit" button displayed on the bottom right of the form.

10.3.3   Setting the training parameters and training the network

When the program reads in the .net file, this only determines how many processing units are connected in the network, and defines the input and desired output patterns that are used in training. It is up to the user to define what learning rule to use, and to specify the value of the parameters to control (and stop) learning. The second form displayed by the program, an example of which is shown in figure 10.2, allows the user to choose these parameters.

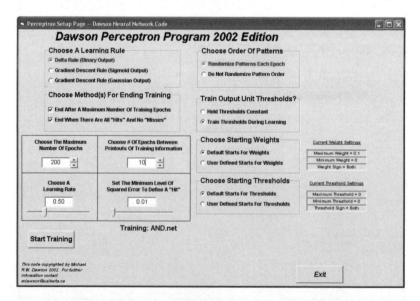

Figure 10.2   The form for setting parameters in the Rosenblatt program

This section describes how this is done. If the reader wishes to learn more about what exactly is accomplished by setting these values on this form, then he or she should look through chapter 10 of Dawson (2004).

The second form consists of a number of different tools that can be used to quickly control the kind of learning that will be carried out by the distributed associative memory. The first tool is used to choose which of three learning rules is to be used to train the perceptron. This choice also determines what activation function is being used in the perceptron's output units. The default rule is the delta rule. When this rule is selected, the activation function is a step function. An output unit will generate a response of 1 when its net input is greater than a threshold, and a response of 0 otherwise. The second rule is a gradient descent rule for training output units with a continuous activation function, which in this case is the logistic equation. The derivative of the logistic equation is used to speed learning up by scaling the error term. The third rule is a gradient descent rule for training output units that employ a Gaussian activation function (i.e., value units). This rule is based on Dawson and Schopflocher's (1992b) modification of gradient descent training, which uses an elaborated error term. It too scales error with the derivative of the activation function to speed learning up. A left-click of the mouse on this tool is all that is required to select which of the three learning rules will be used.

A second tool is used to choose a method for stopping training. In the first method, training stops after a maximum number of epochs (this value is set by the user). In the second method, training stops when there is a "hit" for every pattern and every output unit. This means that when each output is generating an acceptably accurate response for each pattern, training will stop. A left-click of the mouse is used to select either of these methods; when a method has been selected, a check mark appears in the tool. Importantly, the user can select both methods to be used in the same simulation. When this is done, then the simulation will stop as soon as one of the two conditions is met. This is the default situation, and it is recommended.

A third tool determines the order in which patterns will be trained. The program is epoch-based, which means that each epoch or "sweep" of training involves presenting every pattern once to the perceptron. When a pattern is presented, output unit error is used to modify the weight values. One can have the program present patterns in a random order each epoch, which is the recommended practice. However, if pattern order is being manipulated, you can turn this option off with a left-click of the mouse. When this is done, the patterns will always be presented in the order in which they are listed in the .net file that has been input.

A fourth tool determines whether the thresholds of the units (i.e., the threshold for the binary activation function, the bias for the logistic function, or the value of mu for the Gaussian function) should be trained. The default is to train the thresholds, because this permits the output units to "translate" their "cuts" through pattern space. However, in some situations it may be required to hold this value constant, which can be done with a left-click of the mouse button.

A fifth tool is used to determine the starting values of the connection weights, which are randomly selected from a distribution. In the default situation, the maximum value of a weight is 0.1, the minimum value is 0, and the sign option is "both", which means that negative and positive weights are possible. These defaults are displayed to the right of the weight-start tool.

With these default values, weights will be randomly selected from a rectangular distribution that ranges from −0.1 to +0.1. However, in some cases it may be desirable to explore different starting states. This can be accomplished by left-clicking the "User Defined Starts For Weights" option. When this option is selected, a new form appears, as is shown in figure 10.3. This form is used to set the minimum (absolute) value for a weight, the maximum (absolute) value for a weight, and the desired sign for the weight (positive, negative, or either). When the desired settings have been selected, the "Use These Settings" button will select them, and close the form. If it is decided that the default settings are desired, then this can be accomplished by using the "Use Default Settings" button. Whatever settings have been selected will be updated on the right of the settings form.

A sixth tool is used to determine the starting values of the randomly selected thresholds for the output units. The default is to assign every output unit a threshold of 0, regardless of which activation function has been selected. If different randomly selected starts are desired, then a left-click of the "User Defined Starts For Thresholds" option will reveal a form similar to the one shown in figure 10.3. The settings can be changed in the same way as on the form described above for manipulating the starting parameters for the weights.

The four remaining tools on the form are used to set numerical values that control training. The first is a tool for specifying the maximum number of training epochs by left-clicking either arrow beside the value's box. This will either increase or decrease the value of this parameter, depending upon which arrow is selected. The maximum number of training epochs can also be set directly by left-clicking the value's box with the mouse, and typing in the

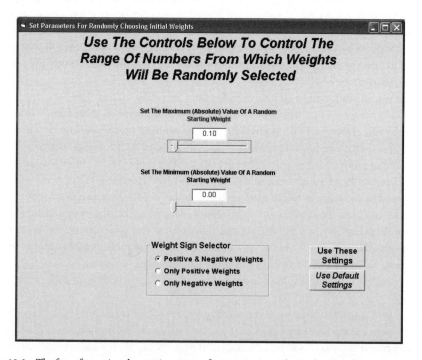

Figure 10.3 The form for setting the starting states of connection weights in the Rosenblatt program

desired value. Note that if the user chooses a value for this variable, then the "End After A Maximum Number Of Training Epochs" selection should also be selected. If this latter option does not have a check mark beside it, then the program will ignore this number when it is run! The default value (shown in figure 10.2) is 200.

The second is a tool for specifying the number of training epochs between printouts of training information. During training, the program will periodically print out information to tell the user how things are progressing. This includes information about what epoch has been reached, what the network SSE is, and the degree to which network SSE has changed since the last printout. The frequency of these printouts is controlled by the number displayed in this tool, which can be set in a fashion similar to that described for the previous tool. The default value (displayed in figure 10.2) is 10. If this value is selected, then every 100 epochs the user will receive updates about network learning. The value selected for this parameter also defines the spacing of the x-axis of the SSE plots that can be created from a form described later in this chapter.

The third is a tool for specifying the learning rate. More details on the role of learning rate in the equations can be found in chapter 10 of *Minds and Machines: Connectionism and Psychological Modeling* (Dawson, 2004). The learning rate is used for all three learning rules. In setting the learning rate, two rules of thumb should be followed. First, if the learning rate is 0, then no learning will be accomplished. Second, it would not be typical to set learning rates greater than 1, although the user is free to explore the behavior of the network when this is done. The learning rate can be set in two different ways. One is to left-click on the arrow of the slider tool that is beside the value, hold the mouse button down, and use the mouse to slide the value of the learning rate up or down. The other is to select the box in which the learning rate is displayed, and to type in the desired learning rate. The default learning rate is 0.5. For some problems, when the Gaussian activation function is used, it may be desirable to speed learning up by *decreasing* this value to 0.1 or even to 0.01. For the other activation functions, the speed of learning can usually be increased by increasing the learning rate, provided that the learning rate is kept smaller than 1.0.

The fourth is a tool for specifying the minimum level of error (that is, SSE) to define a "hit". The default value for this setting is 0.01. With this setting, this means that if the desired value of an output unit is 1.00, then if the unit generates activity of 0.9 or higher, a "hit" will have occurred. This is because $1.00 - 0.9 = 0.1$, and the square of 0.1 is 0.01. Similarly, if the unit generates activity of 0.1 or smaller for a desired output of 0.00, then a "hit" will have occurred. If a more conservative definition of "hit" is desired, then this tool should be used to make the minimum SSE value smaller. If a more liberal definition is required, then this value should be made larger. The smaller the value, the longer it will take learning to occur. However, if this value is too large, learning will end quickly, but the perceptron's responses to stimuli will not be very accurate.

Once these tools have been used to select the desired training parameters, associations (memories) can be stored in the network by pressing the "Start Training" button with a left-click of the mouse. When this is done, new boxes appear on the form to show the user how training is proceeding (see figure 10.4). When training stops, two new buttons appear on the form. By pressing the "Continue Training" button, more training occurs using the settings that have already been selected on this form. By pressing the "Test Recall" button, the user

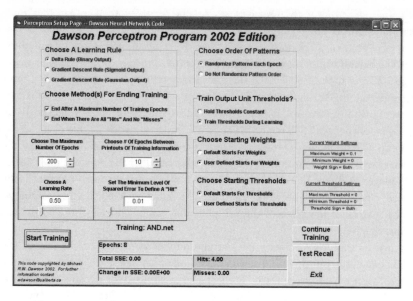

Figure 10.4   The appearance of the form after a network has converged to a solution to a problem

moves to a new form that can be used to explore the performance of the trained network. The details of this form are described below. Of course, pressing the "Exit" button terminates the program. Note that as training proceeds, information about the number of sweeps, the total network SSE, and the number of hits and misses is displayed. In figure 10.4, training stopped after 9 epochs because SSE had dropped to zero, and there were 4 hits and 0 misses on the training patterns.

10.4   Testing What the Memory Has Learned

Once training has been completed, the perceptron has learned to classify a set of input patterns. With the press of the "Test Recall" button of the form that has just been described, the program presents a number of options for examining the ability of the network to retrieve the information that it has stored. Some of these options involve the online examination of network responses, as well as the plotting of learning dynamics. Other options permit the user to save properties of the network in files that can be examined later. One of these file options enables the user to easily manipulate network data, or to easily move the data into another program (such as a statistical analysis tool) for more detailed analysis (e.g., factor analytic analysis of final connection weights).

The user selects the specific activity to perform from either list that is illustrated in figure 10.5. Double-clicking the list item with the left mouse button results in the activity being carried out. The sections that follow first describe the different activities that are possible by selecting any one of the four actions laid out in the control box on the upper part of the form. Later sections describe the result of double-clicking any one of the actions made

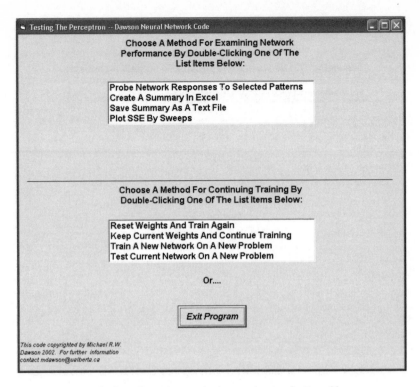

Figure 10.5 The form for testing a trained network using the Rosenblatt program

available in the control box on the lower part of the form. Again, an "Exit Program" button is also provided to allow the user to exit the program from this form.

10.4.1   Testing responses to individual patterns

After the network has learned some classifications, it may be of interest to the user to examine the particular responses of the network to individual cue patterns in the training set. For instance, in cases where the network is not performing perfectly, it could be that it is responding correctly to some cues, but not to others, rather than responding inaccurately to all of the stimuli. By double-clicking on the list item "Probe Network Responses To Selected Patterns", the user causes the program to provide a form that allows the network to be tested one cue pattern at a time.

The form that permits this is depicted in figure 10.6. It provides a window in which network behavior is printed. When the form is initially presented, this window is blank. Left-button mouse clicks on the arrow controls at the top of the form are used to select the number of the pattern to be presented to the network. When the desired pattern number has been selected, the "Ok" button is pressed. The cue pattern is then presented to the network, and the network's response is displayed. The display provides details about the cue pattern, the actual network response, the desired network response, and the error of the network. For instance, in the figure 10.6, Pattern 4 has just been presented to the network.

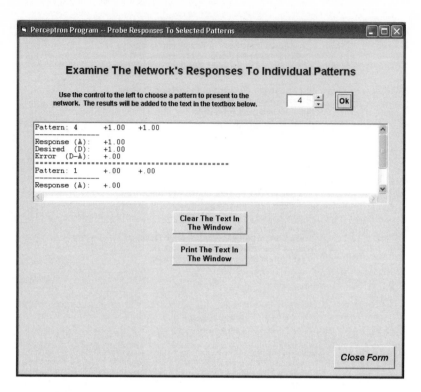

Figure 10.6   The form for presenting individual patterns to a trained perceptron using the Rosenblatt program

More than one pattern can be tested in this way. The new pattern information is always displayed on top of previous pattern information. One can use the two scroll bars on the window to examine all of the information that has been requested. At any point in time, one can send this information to the system's default printer by pressing the button for printing. Also, one can erase the window by pressing the button for clearing the display. When the "Close Form" button is pressed, this form closes, and the user is back to the "Test Network" list options.

10.4.2   Plotting learning dynamics

A comparison of the three learning rules for the perceptron might require examining how network error changes as a function of epochs of training. If the user chooses the "Plot SSE By Sweeps" option from the list in the network testing form, then the program automatically plots this information using a bar chart. An example chart is provided in figure 10.7. One can import this chart directly into a word processing document by simultaneously pressing the "Alt" and "Print Screen" keys on the keyboard (which copies the active window into the clipboard), going to the document, and pasting the clipboard into the document. One can print this chart on the default printer by left-clicking the mouse over the "Print The Graph" button. A left-click of the "Exit This Page" button closes the graph, and returns the user to the page that provides the options for testing network performance.

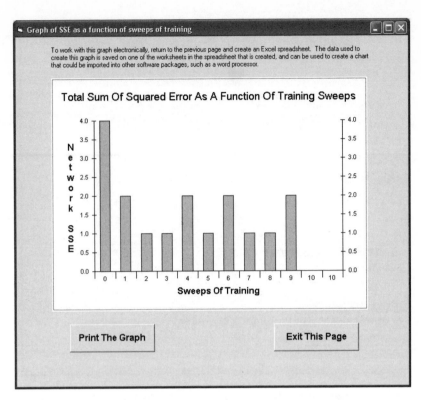

Figure 10.7 The form for plotting learning dynamics (squared error as a function of training) using the Rosenblatt program

With respect to the graph produced in this form, the SSE axis is computed automatically, and the sampling of the bars across the Sweeps axis is determined by the choice of epochs between printouts made by the user on the program's second form. If the graph doesn't look quite right, then the user might consider re-running the simulation with a different choice for epochs between printouts. If a different kind of graph is desired, then the user might wish to save the network data to file. The data used to create this graph can be saved when this is done, and imported into a different software package that can be used to create graphs of different appearance.

10.4.3 Saving results in a text file

One of the options for storing information about network performance is to save network results as a text file. The form that permits this to be done, illustrated in figure 10.8, is accessed by choosing the list item "Save Summary As A Text File" from the "Test Network" page.

There are two sets of controls on this form. The first is a group of drive, directory, and file control boxes that are very similar to those found on the very first form seen when the program starts to run. One uses the drive and directory controls to navigate to a folder in which network data is to be saved. If it is necessary to create a new folder, a left-click of the mouse

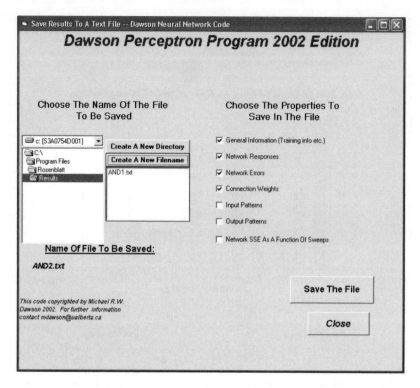

Figure 10.8   The form for saving network results as a text file

on the "Create A New Directory" button creates a dialog that permits the new directory to be named and created. Once the desired directory has been opened, the existing text files (.txt) in it are displayed. This is because the network data will be saved in such a file. One can overwrite an existing file by double-clicking it with the left mouse button. If a new file needs to be created, the dialog for doing so is accessed by a left-click of the mouse on the "Create A New Filename" button.

After choosing the location in which information is to be saved, the check boxes on the right of the form are set to determine what kinds of information will be saved. If a check box is not selected, then the corresponding information is simply not written to the file. To save the file, after the desired check boxes have been selected, the user left-clicks the "Save The File" button with the mouse. The form remains open after this is done, because in some instances the user might wish to save different versions of the network information in different locations. This form is closed by a left-mouse click on the "Close Button", which returns the user to the "Test Network" form.

10.4.4   Saving results in an excel workbook

A second method for saving network performance is to save it in a structured Microsoft Excel workbook. This option is only available in the Rosenblatt program, and is not available in

RosenblattLite or in RosenblattJava. It should obviously only be selected by users who also have Microsoft Excel installed on their computers. It is selected by a double-click of the "Create A Summary In Excel" list item that is offered in the "Test Network" form.

When this item is selected, a patience-requesting message is displayed on the "Test Network" form, and a number of different programming steps are taken to build an Excel workbook. When this is completed, the workbook is displayed as its own window, which will open on the user's computer in front of any of the Rosenblatt program's windows. When the workbook has been created successfully, then the user should see something similar to the screen shot that is presented in figure 10.9.

All of the possible information that could be saved in the text version of a saved network is saved on this spreadsheet. Each different class of information is saved on its own worksheet in this Excel workbook. One can view different elements of this information by using the mouse to select the desired worksheet's tab on the bottom of the worksheet. The worksheet opens (as illustrated in the figure) with the "General Information" tab selected.

When this workbook is open, it is running in Excel as a standalone program that is separate from the Rosenblatt software. One can select different tabs in the worksheet to examine network properties. For example, in figure 10.10, the "Connection Weights" tab has been

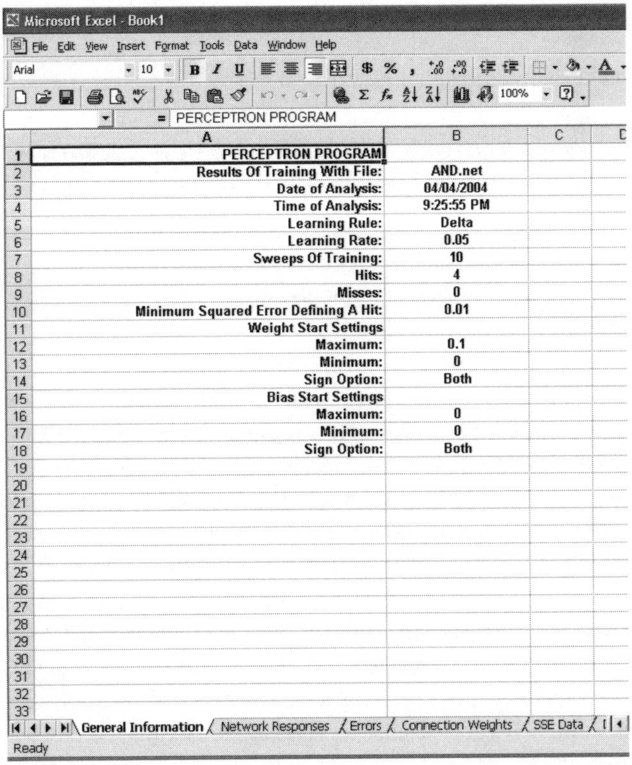

Figure 10.9 Network results displayed in an Excel workbook, opened to the "General Information" tab

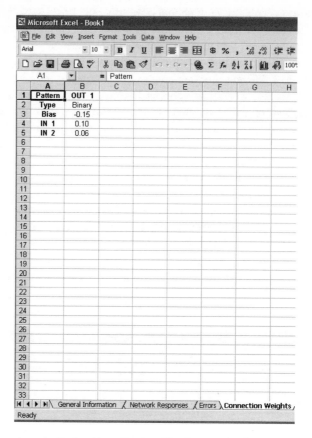

Figure 10.10   Network results displayed in an Excel workbook, opened to the "Connection Weights" tab

selected. After examining the worksheet, the user might wish to save it to disk. This is done by using the Save File utility provided by Excel.

One problem with having this information being displayed with a completely separate program is that it begins to use up memory resources on the computer that cannot be directly controlled by either program. For instance, it is possible to leave this workbook open, and to return to the Rosenblatt program. However, this practice is not recommended. Instead, potential system crashes are likely to be avoided by closing the Excel workbook before returning to Rosenblatt. When Rosenblatt is returned to, the "Test Network" form will still be displayed.

If saving Excel files from Rosenblatt causes system crashes, it is likely to be because of memory resource conflicts. The Excel options were built into Rosenblatt because they provide a convenient format for working with network data after training has been accomplished. The Excel data can also be easily copied and pasted into statistical packages like Systat. However, the Excel capability is not required for the distributed associative memory software to be used productively. If Excel problems are encountered frequently on your computer, our recommendation is to use RosenblattLite instead, and save network performance as text files only.

10.4.5   Leaving the "Test Network" form

Once the user has finished examining the performance of a trained network, the list at the bottom of the "Test Network" form provides different options for network training. If the "Reset Weights And Train Again" option is selected, then all of the connection weights are randomized, the network is readied for training on the same problem that it has just learned, and the user is returned to the form that permits training parameters to be selected. If the "Keep Current Weights And Train Again" option is selected, the network is trained on the same problem, but the weights created from the learning that was just completed are not erased. The user is returned to the form that permits training parameters to be selected. They must be set again if settings other than the default settings are desired. If the "Train A New Network On A New Problem" option is selected, then the user is returned to the program's first form to be able to read in a new problem for training. If the "Train The Current Network On A New Problem" option is selected, then the user can read in a new problem, but it will be presented to the network with the weights preserved from the previous training. This option can be used to study the effect of pre-training on learning a new problem. If none of these options are desired, then the program can be closed by pressing the "Exit Program" button with a left-click of the mouse.

CHAPTER 11

Perceptrons and Logic Gates

11.1 Introduction

The translation of neural function into the operations of a two-valued logic was a critical step in the development of artificial neural networks, because it permitted McCulloch and Pitts to develop proofs about the potential power of their models (McCulloch & Pitts, 1943). However, one limitation of the McCulloch–Pitts architecture was that their networks did not learn. Is it possible to use a general learning rule and, using a set of stimulus–response examples, teach a network how to compute basic logical operations? The exercises in this chapter begin to explore this possibility.

11.2 Boolean Algebra

11.2.1 The work of Boole

In his obituary for George Boole (1815–1864), the Reverend Robert Hartley wrote "the facts of his personal history are few and simple, but they serve to illustrate how a man of humble origin, with very slender aids from without, may, by the force of genius and the labor of research, rise to a position of great eminence" (Boole, 1952, p. 426). Boole, who was self taught, made enormous contributions to the fields of logic and probability. Interestingly, for a period that began not long after his death, Boole's work was largely forgotten. However, early in the twentieth century it reemerged, in a modified format, as a central component in the development of modern computers.

Boole's major work was his monograph entitled *An investigation of the laws of thought, on which are founded the mathematical theories of logic and probabilities* (Boole, 1854). Boole's pioneering achievement in this book was the translation of basic logical operations into the operations of common algebra, with the goal of using mathematical operations to advance logical theory. He wrote that his intent was "to investigate the fundamental laws of those operations of the mind by which reasoning is performed; to give expression to them in the symbolical language of a Calculus, and upon this foundation to establish the science of Logic and construct its method; to make that method itself the basis of a general method for the application of the mathematical doctrine of Probabilities; and, finally, to collect from the various elements of truth brought to view in the course of these inquiries some probable intimations concerning the nature and constitution of the human mind" (p. 1).

In order to use mental operations to inspire his formal account, Boole (1854) took language as his starting point. "That language is an instrument of human reason, and not merely a medium for the expression of thought, is a truth generally admitted" (p. 26). Boole observed that the fundamental elements of language are signs or symbols. From this he went on to hypothesize that all the operations of language could be formalized from three basic components. The first were literal symbols (X, Y, etc.) that represented things (or sets of things). The second were signs ($+$, $-$, $\times$) representing operations by which new concepts of things could be created by combining existing symbols for things. The third was the sign of identity ($=$), which foreshadowed Boole's mathematical goal (i.e., the development of expressions that equated some strings of symbols with others).

After proposing these building blocks, Boole (1854) developed basic algebraic laws for relating them. Imagine that the symbol X represents some set of objects, and that the symbol Y represents a different set of objects. Boole's basic law was $X^2 = X$, which indicates that Boole used multiplication to define the intersection of sets. Using Boole's own example, if X represents "all objects that are white", and if Y represents "all objects that are sheep", then XY represents "all objects that are white sheep".

Why did Boole (1854) choose multiplication to represent intersection? "His system is completely interpretable as an algebra in which the 'elective symbols' are restricted to the numbers 0 and 1" (Lewis & Langford, 1959, p. 13). Boole's "fundamental law of thought" $X^2 = X$ (Boole, 1854, p. 54) is only algebraically true if one substitutes either the number 0 or the number 1 for the symbol X. "Thus it is a consequence of the fact that the fundamental equation of thought is of the second degree, that we perform the operation of analysis and classification, by division into pairs of opposites, or as it is technically said, by dichotomy" (p. 55). This dichotomous view of mental operations would later prove central to the definition of digital circuits.

With dichotomy being a natural consequence of his fundamental law of thought, Boole (1854) went on to provide precise definitions of two special symbols, *0* and *1*. In modern terms, *0* is equivalent to the empty set, and *1* is equivalent to the universal set (i.e., the set of all possible sets). With this modern context in mind, it is clear why Boole wrote that "whatever class of objects is represented by the symbol X, the contrary class will be represented by $1 - X$" (p. 53). From this Boole's definition of what we call the null set was possible: $X - X^2 = 0$, or more frequently $X(1 - X) = 0$.

In these definitions of the symbols *0* and *1* Boole (1854) uses algebraic operators other than multiplication. Boole used the algebraic sign "$+$" to represent the aggregation of sets, which was intended to be equivalent in meaning to the word "or". Boole used the algebraic sign "$-$" to represent the opposite of aggregation, which he termed exception. So, to represent the phrase "all sheep except those that are white" with our two example sets above, we would use expression $Y - XY$.

What was Boole's (1854) goal in creating a notation in which linguistic or logical expressions could be acted upon algebraically? What Boole desired was a system in which one could start with some given information, and then derive valid new information by applying algebraic operators. In this system, the given information would be expressed as equations involving symbols representing sets. "We may in fact lay aside the logical interpretation of the symbols in the given equation; convert them into quantitative symbols, susceptible only of the values 0 and 1; perform upon them as such all of the requisite processes of solution; and finally restore to them their logical interpretation" (p. 76). In short, Boole proposed an approach in which logical expressions would be converted into numbers, new numerical statements would be derived via algebra, and then new, valid logical expressions would appear when these resultant numerical statements were converted back into logical expressions.

Boole's (1854) work was pioneering because it represented "for the first time that a complete and workable calculus is achieved, and that operations of the mathematical type are systematically and successfully applied to logic" (Lewis & Langford, 1959, p. 9). Boole's formalism was the basis for future developments of symbolic logic. "It is not to be denied that Boole's system is consistent and perfect within itself. It is, perhaps, one of the most marvelous and admirable pieces of reasoning ever put together" (Jevons, 1971, p. 67).

11.2.2   Modern Boolean algebra and Shannon's work

While Boole's (1854) algebra was pioneering and revolutionary, one of the reasons that it inspired future developments in symbolic logic was because Boole's system was cumbersome, idiosyncratic, and in some instances mysterious. "The quasi-mathematical methods of Dr. Boole especially are so mystical and abstruse, that they appear to pass beyond the comprehension and criticism of most other writers, and are calmly ignored" (Jevons, 1971, p. 84).

For example, consider the aggregation of terms in Boole's (1854) system. There are some expressions of aggregation that are likely to be seen as algebraic expressions, but which are not logically interpretable. One example of such an expression is $1 + X$, which Boole (1854, p. 55) deemed uninterpretable "because we cannot conceive of the addition of any class X to the universe 1". The expression $X + Y$ only yields a logical interpretation in the event that X and Y are disjoint sets, that is – in Boole's notation – only when $XY = 0$. If X and Y share some elements, then the expression makes algebraic sense, but has no corresponding logical interpretation. In other words, if one were to translate a Boolean expression of aggregation $X + Y$ into common language, it would read X or Y but not both. Because of Boole's interpretation of "or", an expression like $X + X$ in algebra would have no corresponding logical interpretation.

Modifications of Boole's (1854) approach were intended to tighten the relationship between algebraic expressions and logical interpretation in such a way that every algebraic expression could be assigned an interpretation. One of the major modifications that was adopted by nearly all subsequent researchers was a broadening of the common interpretation of "or" to mean "either one, or the other, or both". "Thus what is the same as A or A is the same as A, a self-evident truth" (Jevons, 1971, p. 25). This led to another fundamental law, which Jevons called the law of unity: $X + X = X$. The law of unity was uninterpretable in Boole's original system, but leads to several advantages in later symbolic logics. Other modifications included the elimination of the operations of subtraction and division, as well as the inclusion of a new relation $X \subset Y$ to indicate that one set was a proper subset of another. The modern version of Boolean algebra is represented in a formalization worked out by Ernst Schröder in 1890 (Lewis & Langford, 1959).

Boolean algebra was originally developed to be applied to sets of objects. However, it is equally applicable to assertable statements (Lewis & Langford, 1959). For instance, let A be the set of instances in which some statement a can be said to be true, and let B be the set of instances in which some statement b can be said to be true. The algebraic expression AB would therefore represent the set of instances in which both a and b are true. Similarly, the algebraic expression $A \subset B$ would represent the subset of instances that could be stated as "if a is true then b is true".

This interpretation of Boolean algebra can be further restricted so that it applies specifically to propositions (Lewis & Langford, 1959). A proposition is an assertable statement that can only be true or false. To make this restriction explicit in Boolean algebra, one must add the assumption that "for every element a, either $a = 0$ or $a = 1$" (p. 79). This assumption is a very particular interpretation of Boole's (1854) emphasis on the dichotomous nature of thought, and leads to a modern version of Boolean algebra that is called the two-valued algebra. As we have already seen, the two-valued algebra was used as the formalism to provide a logical description of neurons, under the assumption that the neurons adopt the all-or-none law (McCulloch & Pitts, 1943).

The two-valued algebra was also a fundamental tool in the development of modern computers. A masters student at MIT named Claude Shannon realized that this algebra could be used to describe switching circuits (Shannon, 1938, 1949). In Shannon's use of the algebra, the symbol X represented a contact on a relay or a switch, and the symbol $\sim X$ represented a break contact on a relay or switch. The series connection of two switches X and Y was represented by the expression $X + Y$, and the parallel connection of these two switches was represented by the expression XY. A closed circuit was represented by the constant 0, and an open circuit was represented by the constant 1. Some of the modern variations of the two-valued algebra – such as Jevon's (1971) law of unity – meant that it could be used to simplify expressions far easier than could other algebras when they were applied to switching circuits. One could describe a circuit algebraically, and then manipulate this description to derive other equivalent circuits. One advantage of this is that the algebra could be used to derive simpler circuits.

A second advantage of Shannon's (1938) approach was that one could describe simple switching circuits – in particular, circuits in which there were two input lines and one output line – as a logic gate. Each input line represented a variable, which could be either true (i.e., 3 volts) or false (i.e., 0.5 volts). The logic gate combined these two inputs in a fashion that could be described in terms of one operator in the two-valued logic, and output a signal that could be interpreted as either being true or false. Table 11.1 illustrates four such logic gates for the two inputs A and B. One is an AND gate, one is an OR gate, one inverts the signal from A, and one inverts the signal from B.

A functionally complete set of gates is a set of logic gates that can be used to construct other circuits for computing any function in the two-valued algebra. The three types of logic gates represented in table 11.1 (AND, OR, INVERT) represent a functionally complete set of gates.

Table 11.1   *The responses of four different logic gates (AND, OR, INVERT A, INVERT B) to the possible states of two input variables (A, B)*

Inputs		Logic gates and their outputs			
A	B	AND	OR	INVERT A	INVERT B
False	False	False	False	True	True
False	True	False	True	True	False
True	False	False	True	False	True
True	True	True	True	False	False

11.3   Perceptrons and Two-Valued Algebra

The purpose of the exercises in this chapter is to provide an introduction to training percep-trons using the Rosenblatt program. This will be accomplished by training a perceptron to compute the truth table for the four logic gates in table 11.1 given. The perceptron that will be trained will have two input units, one for the variable *A*, the other for *B*. If a variable is true, then its input unit will be activated with a value of 1. If a variable is false, then its input unit will be activated with a value of 0. There will be four different training patterns that will be presented to the perceptron, one for each possible combination of the values of *A* and *B* (i.e., one for each row in the table).

The perceptron that will be trained will have four different output units. The output unit will be trained to generate an activation of 1 when its logical combination of *A* and *B* is true, and to generate an activation of 0 when its logical combination of *A* and *B* is false, as indicated in table 11.1. The first output unit will be trained to compute AND, the second to compute OR, the third to compute ~*A* (i.e., to invert *A*), and the fourth to compute ~*B*.

In our previous exercises that used the James program, when network error was used as a criterion to stop training, we did this by having training stop when the total sum of squared error for the network dropped below some minimum value. In the Rosenblatt program, a different approach is used. In the spirit of two-valued logic, when one pattern is presented to the network, each output unit is either going to be right or it is going to be wrong. When an output unit is right, we will count it as a "hit". When an output unit is wrong, we will count it as a "miss". The maximum number of hits that are possible for a training set is equal to the total number of training patterns times the total number of output units. For example, the network that we will be training below has four different training patterns, and four different output units. So, we will want training to stop when there are 16 hits (and 0 misses).

How is a hit defined? For each pattern presented during a training epoch, we will compute the squared difference between the desired activity of an output unit and its actual activity. When this squared difference is smaller than a minimum value that will be set before training, we will count a hit. Otherwise, we will count a miss. The default setting for this minimum value is 0.01. What this means is that if the desired output activity for a unit is 1, if it generates a value higher than 0.9 then it will count as a hit. This is because $(1 - 0.9)^2 = 0.1^2 = 0.01$, which is our mini-mum value. Using similar logic, if the desired output activity for a unit is 0, if it generates a value smaller than 0.1 then it will count as a hit. Otherwise, it will count as a miss. If for some reason we want to increase the accuracy of what a network learns, we can do this by decreasing this hit criterion. For instance, by setting it to 0.0025, the network will have to generate activity higher than 0.95 to turn "on", and lower than 0.05 to turn "off". If for some reason we want a more liberal definition of a hit, then we can do this by increasing this criterion value.

11.3.1 Procedure for the Delta Rule

Install and run the Rosenblatt program, referring back to chapter 10 if necessary. Load the file "Boole4.net". On the setup page, choose "Delta Rule", and keep the remaining settings at their default values:

- End after a maximum number of training epochs
- End when there are all "hits" and no "misses"
- Randomize patterns each epoch
- Train thresholds during learning
- Default starts for weights
- Default starts for thresholds
- Maximum number of epochs = 1,000
- Number of epochs between printouts = 100
- Learning rate = 0.5
- Minimum level of squared error to define a "hit" = 0.01

Press the "Start Training" button to begin training. When the network converges to a solution to the problem, press the "Test Recall" button. Then, have the program build an Excel spreadsheet to summarize the results. This spreadsheet will contain all of the information required to answer the following questions. If you are using a version of the Rosenblatt program that does not use Excel, then save the results of training to a file that you can examine later to answer the questions.

Exercise 11.1

1. What is the total SSE for the network after training has finished?
2. How many epochs of training occurred before the program stopped training the network?
3. When the delta rule is used in the Rosenblatt program, the step activation function is being used in the output units. The unit will only turn on when its net input (i.e., the incoming signals from the inputs added to the bias) equals 0. Armed with this knowledge, look at the two connection weights that feed into the first output unit, and look at the bias of this output unit. Explain how this output unit computes the AND of *A* and *B*.
4. Look at the two connection weights that feed into the second output unit, and look at the bias of this output unit. How does this unit compute the OR of *A* and *B*?
5. Look at the two connection weights that feed into the third output unit, and look at the bias of this output unit. Explain how this output unit INVERTS the signal from *A*.
6. Look at the two connection weights that feed into the fourth output unit, and look at the bias of this output unit. How does this output unit INVERT the signal from *B*?

11.3.2 Procedure for the Gradient Descent Rule

Run the Rosenblatt program once again on the file "Boole4.net". On the setup page, choose "Gradient Descent Rule (Sigmoid Output)", and keep the remaining settings at their default values, which should be the same as in the previous exercise:

- End after a maximum number of training epochs
- End when there are all "hits" and no "misses"
- Randomize patterns each epoch
- Train thresholds during learning
- Default starts for weights
- Default starts for thresholds
- Maximum number of epochs = 1,000
- Number of epochs between printouts = 100
- Learning rate = 0.5
- Minimum level of squared error to define a "hit" = 0.01

Press the "Start Training" button to begin training. If the network has not converged to a solution after 1,000 epochs, press the "Continue Training" button. When the network converges to a solution to the problem, press the "Test Recall" button. Then, have the program build an Excel spreadsheet to summarize the results. This spreadsheet will contain all of the information required to answer the following questions. If you are using a version of the Rosenblatt program that does not use Excel, then save the results of training to a file that you can examine later to answer the questions.

Exercise 11.2

1. What is the total SSE for the network after training has finished?
2. How many epochs of training occurred before the program stopped training the network?
3. How do your answers to questions 1 and 2 above compare to your answers to questions 1 and 2 in exercise 11.1? If the answers are different, provide a brief explanation of why this is to be expected.
4. When the gradient descent rule is used in the Rosenblatt program, the logistic activation function is being used in the output units. Armed with this knowledge, look at the two connection weights that feed into the first output unit, and look at the bias of this output unit. (Again, a unit's net input is the sum of the weighted signals coming from the inputs plus the unit's bias.) Explain how this output unit computes the AND of *A* and *B*. How does this explanation compare to the explanation of AND that you provided for the perceptron that was trained with the delta rule?
5. Look at the two connection weights that feed into the second output unit, and look at the bias of this output unit. Explain how this output unit computes the OR of *A*

and **B**. How does this explanation compare to the explanation of OR that you provided for the perceptron that was trained with the delta rule?

6. Look at the two connection weights that feed into the third output unit, and look at the bias of this output unit. Explain how this output unit INVERTS the signal from *A*. How does this explanation compare to the explanation of INVERT that you provided for the perceptron that was trained with the delta rule?

11.3.3 Procedure for exploring bias

Run the Rosenblatt program once again on the file "Boole4.net". On the setup page, choose "Delta Rule", and *set the option to hold thresholds constant during training*. Keep the remaining settings at their default values, which should be the same as in the previous exercise, with the exception of holding thresholds constant:

- End after a maximum number of training epochs
- End when there are all "hits" and no "misses"
- Randomize patterns each epoch
- *Hold thresholds constant during learning*
- Default starts for weights
- Default starts for thresholds
- Maximum number of epochs = 1,000
- Number of epochs between printouts = 100
- Learning rate = 0.5
- Minimum level of squared error to define a "hit" = 0.01

Press the "Start Training" button to begin training. If the network has not converged to a solution after 1,000 epochs, press the "Continue Training" button. If the network has not solved the problem after 3,000 sweeps, then do not train any further. You should observe that the network generates only 13 hits, and 3 misses, after this amount of training, and that network performance will not improve. Have the program build an Excel spreadsheet to summarize the results. This spreadsheet will contain all of the information required to answer the following questions. If you are using a version of the Rosenblatt program that does not use Excel, then save the results of training to a file that you can examine later to answer the questions.

Exercise 11.3

1. What is the total SSE for the network after training has finished?
2. How many epochs of training occurred before the program stopped training the network?

3. Examine the responses of the network to each pattern, and the errors computed for each output unit for each pattern. In what way is the network behaving correctly? In what way is the network making mistakes?

4. With the default settings, and with thresholds held constant during training, every output unit always has a threshold of 0. Armed with this knowledge, examine the connection weights that feed into any output unit that is generating errors. Explain why any errors are being made.

5. Given your answer to question 4, speculate on the role of the threshold in the perceptron, and speculate on why it might be important to let the learning rule train thresholds in addition to training the connection weights.

CHAPTER 12

Performing More Logic With Perceptrons

12.1 Two-Valued Algebra and Pattern Spaces

Chapter 11 provided a brief introduction to two-valued algebra, culminating in the presentation of a functionally complete set of logic gates (AND, OR, INVERT). A moment's reflection, though, reveals that there must be many more logic gates that can be expressed for a two-valued algebra, and that this functionally complete set is merely a sample of a larger set of primitive logic gates.

In the two-valued algebra, a logic gate is an operator that combines the values of two input variables, and makes some resulting judgment. The input values of two variables A and B can only be one of two values, true or false. This means that, in the two-valued algebra, a logic gate can be only be presented one of four possible stimulus patterns: $(\sim A, \sim B)$, $(A, \sim B)$, $(\sim A, B)$, or (A, B). The response of the logic gate when presented one of these patterns can also only be true or false. By looking at the pattern of responses that a logic gate makes to the set of four possible stimuli, one can determine what relationship between A and B is being computed. For instance, if the logic gate responds "true" to the stimulus (A, B) and "false" to the other three stimuli, then it must be computing the AND relationship (or, in some of the historic notation seen in chapter 11 (Boole, 1854), it must be computing AB).

How many different logic gates can be defined for the two-valued algebra? The answer to this question is the number of different patterns of responses that can be generated to the set of four stimuli. Given that the output of a logic gate must be binary (i.e., true or false), and that there are four different stimulus patterns that must be responded to, the number of different patterns of responses that can be generated is 2^4, or 16. Therefore the two-valued algebra must consist of 16 different primitive logical operations. The first of these operations is CONTRADICTION, where the logic gate generates a "false" response to each of the four stimuli. The last of these operations is TAUTOLOGY, where the logic gate generates a "true" response to each of the four stimuli. The other 14 possible logic gates generate "false" to some of the stimuli, and "true" to the others. The complete set of logic gates is provided in the table later in this section.

For the purposes of the exercises in the current chapter, it will be convenient to think of these logical operators from a slightly different perspective. Imagine a logic gate to be a perceptron with two input units (one for *A* and one for *B*) and one output unit (for computing the relationship between *A* and *B*). As was the case in chapter 11, let an input activation value of 1 represent "true", and a value of 0 represent "false". So, when this perceptron is being trained, it will be presented four different sets of numbers as inputs: (0, 0), (1, 0), (0, 1), and (1,1). In chapter 4 we saw that in some instances it is useful to represent sets of numbers as points.

Figure 12.1 shows a graph in which each of these four patterns involved in the two-valued algebra is represented as a point in a two-dimensional space, where the x-axis represents the value of *A*, and the y-axis represents the value of *B*. We will call this the *pattern space* for the two-valued algebra. In processing this pattern space to perform two-valued logic, a perceptron must learn to carve the space into different decision regions (Lippmann, 1989). For example, one straight cut through this pattern space will separate it into two regions. If the point representing a pattern falls in one region of a pattern space so divided, then the point will be classified as being "true" (i.e., the perceptron would turn its output unit on to this pattern). If the point falls in the other region of the pattern space, then the point will be classified as being "false" (i.e., the perceptron would turn its output unit off to this pattern). Clearly there must be 16 different ways in which the pattern space for two-valued algebra can be carved up to separate true points from false points. Figure 12.1 illustrates three of these, for AND, OR, and INVERT. In these examples, a straight line is drawn to represent the straight cut that separates the space into decision regions, false points are represented as outline squares, and true points are represented as solid squares.

Given that there are 16 different primitive operations in the two-valued algebra, it is not surprising that in logical formalisms each operation is represented with its own notation. Table 12.1 represents the output responses of each of the 16 operations to each of the four possible input patterns; the first column in this table provides a traditional logical notation for

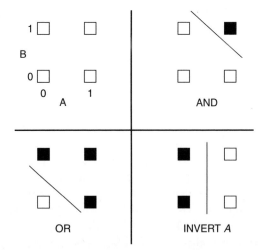

Figure 12.1   A pattern space for two binary input variables (upper left), and the carving of this space into decision regions for three different logical operators (AND, OR, INVERT *A*). In these latter three diagrams, a filled square is a pattern that the logical operator would turn "on" to

Table 12.1 *Responses of 16 logical operators to the possible states of two different input variables*

	Inputs	Pattern 1	Pattern 2	Pattern 3	Pattern 4
	A	False	False	True	True
	B	False	True	False	True

Logic gates (Standard notation)	Logic gates (Jots notation)	Output 1	Output 2	Output 3	Output 4
Contradiction	*A* ⬚⬚ *B*	False	False	False	False
~*A* ∧ ~*B*	*A* ⬚⬚ *B*	True	False	False	False
~*A* ∧ *B*	*A* ⬚⬚ *B*	False	True	False	False
~*A*	*A* ⬚⬚ *B*	True	True	False	False
A ∧ ~*B*	*A* ⬚⬚ *B*	False	False	True	False
~*B*	*A* ⬚⬚ *B*	True	False	True	False
A ⊗ *B*	*A* ⬚⬚ *B*	False	True	True	False
~(*A* ∧ *B*)	*A* ⬚⬚ *B*	True	True	True	False
A ∧ *B*	*A* ⬚⬚ *B*	False	False	False	True
~(*A* ⊗ *B*)	*A* ⬚⬚ *B*	True	False	False	True
B	*A* ⬚⬚ *B*	False	True	False	True
A ⊃ *B*	*A* ⬚⬚ *B*	True	True	False	True
A	*A* ⬚⬚ *B*	False	False	True	True
B ⊃ *A*	*A* ⬚⬚ *B*	True	False	True	True
A ∨ *B*	*A* ⬚⬚ *B*	False	True	True	True
Tautology	*A* ⬚⬚ *B*	True	True	True	True

these operations (Mendelson, 1970). A second notational approach is to represent each operation with its own graphical symbol (a "jot"), which is occasionally seen in the literature (McCulloch, 1988). For example, McCulloch would represent tautology as *A* ⬚ *B*. I have developed my own system of jots for these 16 operations, where the appearance of each jot is modeled after the appearance of the pattern space as drawn in figure 12.1. My system is provided in the second column of table 12.1; to see how it works, one need only compare the jot for AND (⬚), OR (⬚) or INVERT (⬚) to the pattern space drawings in figure 12.1. This notational system may be convenient to use when considering answers to the questions below. The appendix to this chapter provides some information about obtaining the font set that I created for this jot notation.

12.2   Perceptrons and Linear Separability

12.2.1   Linear separability

If you examine the 16 jots in table 12.1, then you should see that they fall into different classes. Twelve of the jots have a single line in them that separates outline squares from solid squares. Two of the jots have no line in them, because all of the squares in the jot are of the same type. However, we could easily add a single line to these jots (outside of the four points that the jot illustrates), so one could argue that these two jots are just special cases that belong to the same set as the 12 that we have already discussed. The remaining two jots have two lines in them to separate the two types of squares, and because of this stand out as being different.

Each of the jots used in the table above is based upon a plot of a pattern space, such as those that were described in section 12.1. The differences between jots that we have just seen reflects an important property of the different ways in which the pattern space for two-valued algebra can be carved into decision regions. Fourteen of these carved pattern spaces (including the pattern spaces for CONTRADICTION and TAUTOLOGY) are said to be *linearly separable*. In a linearly separable pattern space, all of the points that belong to one class can be separated from all of the points that belong to the other class by carving a single, straight cut through the pattern space. If a pattern space is *linearly nonseparable*, then it is impossible to separate one set of points from the other using a single straight cut. The two jots that stand out as being different from the other 14 are different because they represent two operations in the two-valued algebra that are linearly nonseparable.

The exercise below is an extension of the exercises that were performed in chapter 11. Its primary goal is to explore the ability of perceptrons to learn more logical operations than just the four that were taught in exercise 11.1. As was the case in this previous exercise, you will train a perceptron with two input units to represent the four possible stimuli in the two-valued logic. However, instead of only having four output units, you will be working with a perceptron that has 16 output units. Each output unit corresponds to one of the logical operations in table 12.1; output unit 1 corresponds to the first logical operation in the table, output unit 2 corresponds to the second logical operation in the table, and so on.

12.2.2   Procedure

Using the Rosenblatt program, load the file "Boole 16.net". This file represents table 12.1 in a format that can be processed by the perceptron architecture. On the setup page, choose "Delta Rule", and keep the remaining settings at their default values, with the exception that the learning rate can be reduced to a value of 0.1:

- End after a maximum number of training epochs
- End when there are all "hits" and no "misses"
- Randomize patterns each epoch
- Train thresholds during learning
- Default starts for weights
- Default starts for thresholds
- Maximum number of epochs = 1,000
- Number of epochs between printouts = 100
- *Learning rate = 0.1*
- Minimum level of squared error to define a "hit" = 0.01

Press the "Start Training" button to begin training. *The network will not converge to a solution in which the number of misses drops to 0.* Keep training the network until there are 60 hits and 4 misses. Then, have the program build an Excel spreadsheet to summarize the results.

This spreadsheet will contain all of the information required to answer the following questions. If you are using a version of the Rosenblatt program that does not use Excel, then save the results of training to a file that you can examine later to answer the questions.

Exercise 12.1

1. Examine the responses of the network to the training set, as well as the errors computed for each output unit and each training pattern. What logical operations are causing the perceptron difficulty? (Note: if an output unit is generating three correct responses for a logical operation, but is generating an error for the fourth response, then we will say that this operation is posing a problem, simply because the output unit has failed to respond correctly to all of the input patterns.)

2. Focus on the errors being made by the perceptron in more detail. For each output unit that is making at least one error, describe the output unit's response to each of the four input patterns.

3. For each output unit that is making at least one error, examine the threshold for that unit as well as the two connection weights that are feeding into that unit. Use this information, in the context of your description of responses in question 2, to explain why the output unit is not responding correctly. (Remember – if you used the delta rule, then the output units are using the step activation function.)

4 On the basis of your answer to question 3, is it possible in principle for these incorrect output units to eventually learn to respond correctly, or are they doomed to eternal failure? If you think that they cannot learn to respond correctly, then explain this belief. If you think that they can respond correctly, then explain why, and return to the program to try to validate this belief empirically. (Hint: I don't recommend this latter approach!)

APPENDIX TO CHAPTER 12: THE DAWSONJOTS FONT

The DawsonJots font was created with Macromedia Fontographer 4.1 for Windows. Versions of the font files are available for download from the site that provides web support for this book.

CHAPTER 13

Value Units and Linear Nonseparability

13.1 Linear Separability and Its Implications

The main implication from exercise 12.1 is that perceptrons that use the step activation function are unable to learn to solve linearly nonseparable problems. This will also be the case for perceptrons that use the logistic function, because the logistic is best thought of as a continuous approximation of the step function. While we have demonstrated this limitation empirically in chapter 12, proofs of this limitation also exist (Minsky & Papert, 1988). These proofs are elegant formalizations of some of the intuitions that you explored when answering questions 3 and 4 of exercise 12.1. Many researchers have claimed that the original publication of such proofs in 1969 led to the near extinction of research on artificial neural networks (Medler, 1998). Minsky and Papert (1988, p. xii) have a slightly different view of this history: "One popular version is that the publication of our book so discouraged research on learning in network machines that a promising line of research was interrupted. Our version is that progress had already come to a virtual halt because of the lack of adequate basic theories". It is certainly the case that perceptrons are unable to represent solutions to some problems that seem very elementary to us, and as a result this restricts our interest in perceptrons as models in psychology and cognitive science. However, the specific problems that perceptrons have depend crucially on their activation function. We'll begin to explore this issue in this chapter by considering how value units cope with the logic problems that were posing difficulties for the network in chapter 12.

13.1.1 Why typical perceptrons can't solve nonseparable problems

Why can't perceptrons that use the step activation function solve linearly nonseparable problems? One answer to this question comes from considering a perceptron to be a tool for a geometric projection. In the case of the two-valued algebra, the connection weights of a perceptron are used to project a two-dimensional representation of the pattern space onto a one-dimensional representation. That is, the connection weights convert the (x, y) coordinates of a pattern in a two-dimensional plane into a single number (the net input) that is the coordinate of the point on a one-dimensional number line. The threshold of the perceptron represents a divider on this number line. If a net input falls on one side of this divider, then the pattern that generates this net input is false. If the net input falls on the other side of this divider, then the pattern is true. However, when a perceptron projects a linearly nonseparable logic problem onto this one-dimensional line, the single divider cannot separate all of the false patterns from all of the true patterns. In order to do this, the perceptron would need two dividers. However, it only has one, because its output unit only has one threshold – in the typical architecture (Rosenblatt, 1962).

13.1.2 What value units have to offer

When the perceptron architecture was introduced in chapter 9, one of the points that was stressed was that different activation functions could be used in the output units. One of these activation functions was the Gaussian that was used to create networks of value units (Dawson & Schopflocher, 1992b). Value units are of particular interest in the context of learning the linearly nonseparable operations of the two-valued algebra because they can be described as if they have two thresholds, a lower threshold and an upper threshold. If the net input of a pattern falls between the two thresholds, then the unit's activation will be high. If the net input falls below the lower threshold, or above the upper threshold, then the unit's activation will be low. It would seem that this kind of activation function is ideally suited to deal with the linearly nonseparable problems that posed challenges to the perceptron that was studied in chapter 12. The purpose of the next exercise is to generate some data that is relevant to this hypothesis.

13.2 Value Units and the Exclusive-Or Relation

One of the logical operations that was shown to be problematic for a perceptron that used the step function was exclusive-or (XOR, or $A \otimes B$, or A ⧆ B). In the following exercise, we will train a perceptron with two input units and only one output unit. The output unit is intended to compute XOR, and differs from the perceptron investigated in chapter 12 by being a value unit. The issue of interest is whether this change affects the ability of the perceptron to compute this logical relation.

13.2.1 Procedure for XOR

Using the Rosenblatt program, load the file "XOR.net". On the setup page, choose "Gradient Descent Rule (Gaussian Output)", and keep the remaining settings at their default values:

- End after a maximum number of training epochs
- End when there are all "hits" and no "misses"
- Randomize patterns each epoch
- Train thresholds during learning
- Default starts for weights
- Default starts for thresholds
- Maximum number of epochs $= 1,000$

- Number of epochs between printouts = 100
- Learning rate = 0.1
- Minimum level of squared error to define a "hit" = 0.01

Press the "Start Training" button to begin training. Keep training the network until it generates 4 hits and 0 misses. Then, have the program build an Excel spreadsheet to summarize the results. This spreadsheet will contain all of the information required to answer the following questions. If you are using a version of the Rosenblatt program that does not use Excel, then save the results of training to a file that you can examine later to answer the questions.

Exercise 13.1

1. What was the sum of squared error at the end of training?
2. How many epochs of training were required before the program stopped training the network?
3. Given your answers to questions 1 and 2, what are the implications of this particular network for the claim that perceptrons are unable to represent solutions to linearly nonseparable problems?
4. Remembering that this network uses the Gaussian equation described in chapter 9, and that the bias or threshold of the output unit is equal to the value of μ in the equation, examine the two connection weights that feed into the output unit, as well as the bias of the unit. How does this perceptron compute this particular logical operation? (Again, keep in mind that if the net input to the unit – total incoming signal including the bias – is equal to 0, then the unit's activity will be equal to 1.)

13.3   Value Units and Connectedness

In their detailed analysis of the limitations of perceptrons, one of the geometric properties studied intensively by Minsky and Papert (1988) was connectedness. "We chose to investigate connectedness because of a belief that this predicate is nonlocal in some very deep sense; therefore it should present a serious challenge to any basically local, parallel type of computation" (p. 70).

One of their more straightforward treatments of connectedness involved proving that a limited order perceptron could not learn to correctly classify the four figures illustrated in figure 13.1, where the two figures on the left are connected, and the two figures on the right are not connected (Minsky & Papert, 1988, pp. 12–14). For our purposes, a limited order perceptron is one in which no single connection carries information about all of the elements that make up a stimulus pattern.

In order to create a training set that includes these four figures, we need to find some way in which they can be represented by a perceptron. One approach to doing this is presented in figure 13.2. The building blocks for the four figures above are four short, vertical line segments and three long, horizontal line segments. Figure 13.2 illustrates how each of these components

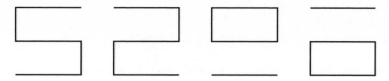

Figure 13.1 Four different patterns used by Minsky and Papert (1988) to examine the ability of perceptrons to detect connectedness: the first two figures are connected, the remaining two figures are not connected

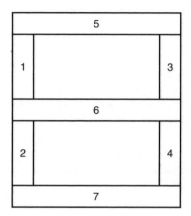

Figure 13.2 An array of seven elongated processing units that can be used to represent any of the figures in figure 13.1

can be represented with a single input unit. If a component is part of the figure, then the input unit that corresponds to the component is given a value of 1. If the component is not part of the figure, then its input unit is given a value of 0. With this kind of representation, each of the paterns in figure 13.1 can be presented to a perceptron by turning five of the input units on, and two of the input units off. As can be seen from figure 13.2, for any of the four patterns, the first four input units will indicate the states of the vertical line segments, and the final three input units will indicate the states of the horizontal line segments.

13.3.1   Procedure for connectedness

Using the Rosenblatt program, load the file "Minsky.net". On the setup page, choose the Gradient Descent Rule (Gaussian output), and keep the remaining settings at their default values:

- End after a maximum number of training epochs
- End when there are all "hits" and no "misses"
- Randomize patterns each epoch
- Train thresholds during learning
- Default starts for weights
- Default starts for thresholds
- Maximum number of epochs = 1,000

- Number of epochs between printouts = 100
- Learning rate = 0.1
- Minimum level of squared error to define a "hit" = 0.01

Press the "Start Training" button to begin training. Keep training the network until it generates all hits and no misses. Then, have the program build an Excel spreadsheet to summarize the results. This spreadsheet will contain all of the information required to answer the following questions. If you are using a version of the Rosenblatt program that does not use Excel, then save the results of training to a file that you can examine later to answer the questions.

Exercise 13.2

1. What was the sum of squared error at the end of training?
2. How many epochs of training were required before the program stopped training the network?
3. Given your answers to questions 1 and 2, what are the implications of this particular network for the claim that perceptrons are unable to represent solutions to linearly nonseparable problems?
4. Remembering that this network uses the Gaussian equation described in chapter 9, and that the bias or threshold of the output unit is equal to the value of μ in the equation, examine the two connection weights that feed into the output unit, as well as the bias of the unit. How does this perceptron compute this particular predicate?
5. Many would argue – legitimately – that this exercise is just a parlour trick. To get a sense of what I mean by this, answer the following question: what is the relationship between how this network solves the connectedness problem and how the previous perceptron solved the XOR problem? To answer this question, you should have already generated answers to question 4 in both this exercise and in the previous one.

CHAPTER 14

Network By Problem Type Interactions

14.1 All Networks Were Not Created Equally

14.1.1 Different activation functions carve pattern spaces in different ways

In chapter 12, we found that a typical perceptron that used the step function in its output units was able to compute most, but not all, of the primitive logical operations in the two-valued algebra. In chapter 13, we saw that an atypical perceptron that used an output value unit was able to compute one logical operation, exclusive-or, that could not be represented by the chapter 12 network.

Why do the two types of perceptrons have different representational capabilities? The answer to this question is because the activation function of any output unit in a perceptron can be viewed as a device that carves a pattern space into decision regions. The particular activation function in an output unit carves a pattern space in a specific manner. One can change the capabilities of a perceptron by changing the activation function, because this will alter the partitioning of the pattern space.

When a step function or logistic function is used in the output unit, then we will call the output unit an integration device. An integration device makes a single straight cut through a pattern space, where the orientation of this cut is controlled by the connection weights, and the threshold determines the lateral position of the cut. Because an integration device behaves in this manner, it is capable of representing the solution to any linearly separable problem, as we saw demonstrated in chapter 12. However, problems that are not linearly separable cannot be solved by means of a single straight slice through the space. As a result, they are beyond the capacity of an integration device.

In contrast, when the Gaussian function is used in the output unit, then we will call it a value unit. Unlike an integration device, a value unit makes two parallel straight cuts through a pattern space, where the space between the two cuts is fairly narrow. As two parallel cuts are required to solve a linearly nonseparable problem like exclusive-or, value units can be used in perceptrons to solve this kind of problem. This was the central point from the exercises in chapter 13.

14.1.2 All networks are not all-powerful

Many years ago, I was involved in writing a manuscript that highlighted some of the problems facing connectionist contributions to cognitive science (Dawson & Shamanski, 1994). One of the themes of this paper was that connectionist technology was dominating research, which was detrimental to the field. What we were concerned about was the fact that a great deal of connectionist research seemed to be focusing on advancing connectionist architectures, with each new type of network being argued as being better than its predecessors. We felt that this was a problem because it distracted researchers from exploring older – but still interesting – architectures in more detail, particularly from the perspective of contributions to cognitive science. (For one example of this approach, see the work on the distributed associative memory reported in Dawson & Schopflocher, 1992a.) We also felt that this was a problem because while a network might be better than its predecessors on some problems, it would likely have more trouble on others. In short, we expected that there should be network type by problem type interactions. As a result, the choice of network architecture would depend upon the problems to be solved.

For example, consider how a single value unit carves a pattern space into decision regions. It is obvious why this type of partitioning is advantageous for solving problems like exclusive-or. But take a look at the remaining jots presented in table 12. Are there any required partitionings of the pattern spaces for two-valued algebra that are going to cause difficulty for the value unit? The purpose of the exercise in this chapter is to empirically determine whether this is the case by training a perceptron built from value units on the 16 logical operations that were studied with a different perceptron back in chapter 12.

14.2 Value Units and the Two-Valued Algebra

14.2.1 Overview

The exercise below is an extension of the simulation that was performed in chapter 12. As was the case in that previous exercise, you will train a perceptron with two input units to represent the four possible stimuli in the two-valued logic. You will also be working with a perceptron that has 16 output units. Each output unit corresponds to one of the logical operations in table 12.1; output unit 1 corresponds to the first logical operation in the table, output unit 2 corresponds to the second logical operation in the table, and so on. The difference in this exercise is that all of the output units in this exercise will be value units. The goal of this exercise is to determine whether the value unit architecture can represent solutions to all of the logical operations or not.

14.2.2 Procedure

Using the Rosenblatt program, load the file "Boole16.net". This file represents table 12.1 in a format that can be processed by the perceptron architecture. On the setup page, *choose the gradient descent rule with the Gaussian activation function*, and keep the remaining settings at their default values:

- End after a maximum number of training epochs
- End when there are all "hits" and no "misses"
- Randomize patterns each epoch
- Train thresholds during learning
- Default starts for weights
- Default starts for thresholds
- Maximum number of epochs = 1,000
- Number of epochs between printouts = 100
- Learning rate = 0.1
- Minimum level of squared error to define a "hit" = 0.01

Press the "Start Training" button to begin training. *The network is not expected to converge to a solution in which the number of misses drops to 0.* Keep training the network until there are only 10 to 12 misses. Then, have the program build an Excel spreadsheet to summarize the results. This spreadsheet will contain all of the information required to answer the following questions. If you are using a version of the Rosenblatt program that does not use Excel, then save the results of training to a file that you can examine later to answer the questions.

Exercise 14.1

1. Examine the responses of the network to the training set, as well as the errors computed for each output unit and each training pattern. Your network should be having difficulties with four of the logical operations. What logical operations are causing the perceptron difficulty? (Note: if an output unit is generating three correct responses for a logical operation, but is generating an error for the fourth response, then we will say that this operation is posing a problem, simply because the output unit has failed to respond correctly to all of the input patterns.)

2. Focus on the errors being made by the perceptron in more detail. For each output unit that is making at least one error, describe the output unit's response to each of the four input patterns.

3. For each output unit that is making at least one error, examine the threshold for that unit as well as the two connection weights that are feeding into that unit. Use this information, in the context of your description of responses in question 2, to explain why the output unit is not responding correctly. (Remember – if you used the delta rule, then the output units are using the step activation function.)

4. On the basis of your answer to question 3, is it possible in principle for these incorrect output units to eventually learn to respond correctly, or are they doomed to eternal failure?

5. Compare the difficulties that you found for this network with the difficulties that you found for the network in chapter 12. Are they the same? If not, then why not? What are the implications of this comparison for choosing a perceptron to solve a particular pattern classification problem?

CHAPTER 15

Perceptrons and Generalization

15.1 Background

In many applied instances, researchers are interested in how what a perceptron learns on some patterns affects its performance on other patterns that it has not yet seen. For instance, if one were training a perceptron to perform some sort of medical diagnosis, the key issue would not be how well the perceptron performed on the training set, but would rather be how well the perceptron performed on new patients. This performance is called *generalization*.

In some instances, it is expected that a perceptron will generalize very well. For instance, for any linearly separable problem, all a perceptron needs to do is to use a small training set to find the right location to carve a pattern space. Once this location has been correctly determined, the perceptron should perform properly for all of the instances of the problem – especially the ones that it has not seen.

However, in some cases the training set used to provide the initial instruction for the perceptron may not be adequate, and as a result the perceptron may not perform perfectly on all of the new patterns. This, however, does not mean that the initial training was in vain. It is also possible that the perceptron learned some important information about the problem that would give it a head start on learning how to respond to new instances. In this case, if training was continued using the new patterns, then we might predict that new learning will be faster than if the initial training had not been conducted. This is called *savings*.

The purpose of the exercise in this chapter is to explore generalization and savings in a perceptron that is being trained to deal with a fairly large (but linearly separable) problem. One of the main objectives of this exercise is to show how the Rosenblatt program is flexible enough to be used to carry out this kind of experiment without requiring additional code to be written. This experience will be used in the next chapter as well, when some modern issues in animal learning theory are investigated with the Rosenblatt program.

15.2 Generalization and Savings for the 9-Majority Problem

15.2.1 Training sets

In the exercises below, we will be working with a number of different training sets that are all constructed from the 9-majority problem. The full problem is in the file "9maj.net". This problem consists of the 512 possible different binary input patterns that can be represented using the nine input units in the perceptron. There is a single output unit that is trained to make a majority judgment for each pattern. If a pattern has five or more input units turned on, then the output unit is trained to turn on. This is because this pattern has a majority of its input units activated. If four or fewer input unitss are turned on, then the output unit is trained to turn off, because the pattern does not have a majority of its input units activated. In this problem, 256 of the patterns require the output unit to turn on, and the remaining 256 require the output unit to turn off. In spite of the size of the 9-majority problem, it is still linearly separable.

We will also be working with three different subsets of the 9-majority problem. I created each of these different training sets by randomly taking some patterns from the full problem, and using randomly selected subsets to create a smaller training set. The file "9maj25.net" is a random sample of 128 different patterns, representing 25% of the full training set. This training set consists of 66 patterns to which the output unit will be turned on, and 62 to which the output unit will be turned off. The file "9maj50.net" is a random sample of 256 different patterns, representing 50% of the full training set. This training set consists of 130 patterns to which the output unit will be turned on, and 126 to which the output unit will be turned off. The file "9maj75.net" is a random sample of 384 different patterns, representing 75% of the full training set. This training set consists of 188 patterns to which the output unit will be turned on, and 196 to which the output unit will be turned off.

15.2.2   Procedure for the control condition

The purpose of the control condition is to provide some baseline information about how the perceptron learns the full 9-majority problem. Using the Rosenblatt program, load the file "9maj.net". (This is a large file; if it is causing your computer difficulties, use the full 7-majority problem instead, found as the file "7maj.net".) On the setup page, choose the delta rule, and keep the remaining settings at their default values:

- End after a maximum number of training epochs
- End when there are all "hits" and no "misses"
- Randomize patterns each epoch
- Train thresholds during learning
- Default starts for weights
- Default starts for thresholds
- Maximum number of epochs = 1,000
- Number of epochs between printouts = 100
- Learning rate = 0.50
- Minimum level of squared error to define a "hit" = 0.01

Press the "Start Training" button to begin training. Keep training the network until there are 512 hits and 0 misses. Follow table 15.1 to record the number of sweeps required for the network to converge to this solution to the problem. Then, press the "Start Training" button again. This will reset the network, and train it on the problem again. When this network converges, record the number of sweeps that were required in a similar table. Keep on repeating this procedure until

Table 15.1   *Data to be recorded for the control condition*

"Subject"	First training file	Sweeps to converge
1	9maj.net	
2	9maj.net	
3	9maj.net	
4	9maj.net	
5	9maj.net	
6	9maj.net	
7	9maj.net	
8	9maj.net	
9	9maj.net	
10	9maj.net	

the data from ten different networks ("subjects") has been collected. After the 10th network converges, record the number of sweeps, and then press the "Test Recall" button. Choose the option to train a new network on a new problem, and move on to the instructions in the next section.

15.2.3   Procedure for the first experimental condition

In the first experimental condition, a perceptron will be trained on a randomly selected 25% of the training patterns. After it converges, the full 9-majority problem will be read in, and the performance of the existing network on the full problem will be examined. This will test generalization of the network. Then, if the network is not responding correctly to all of the problems, it will be trained further on the full problem. This will allow us to explore savings in network training.

Using the Rosenblatt program, load the file "9maj25.net". (If you are examining 7-majority, load the file "7maj25.net" instead.) On the setup page, choose the delta rule, and keep the remaining settings at their default values, which will be identical to those used above. Press the "Start Training" button to begin training. Keep training the network until there are 128 hits and 0 misses. Record the number of sweeps required for the network to converge to this solution to the problem as indicated by table 15.2. Then, press the "Test Recall" button. From the bottom set of options, choose "Test Current Network On A New Problem". This will load in a new problem, but maintain the connection weights that have just been trained. Use the form that opens to read in the file "9maj.net". Once this file has been read, you should still see the options for testing the network. Choose "Create A Summary In Excel". *This will test the existing network's performance on the new file.* When it opens, examine the "General Information" page in the spreadsheet. Because you are using the delta rule, the number of misses will be equal to the sum of squared error (SSE) of the network on the new problem. Record this information in the "SSE Before Training" column of your table. Exit the spreadsheet – you will not need to save it. If there are 0 misses, then no further training is required. If there is at least one miss, though, choose the "Keep Current Weights And Continue Training" option. You will return to the form that permits you to train the perceptron. Press the "Continue Training" button. When the network converges, record the number of epochs required in the second "Sweeps To Converge" column. Then, add up the two "Sweeps To Converge" entries and record the sum in the "Total Sweeps" column.

To continue to the next "subject" in this experiment, press the "Test Recall" button, and choose the "Train A New Network On A New Problem" option. Load the "9maj25.net" file into the problem, and repeat the above procedure. Continue to do this until the data from ten different "subjects" have been collected and table 15.2 can be completed.

15.2.4   Procedure for the second experimental condition

The second experimental condition is a replication of the first, with the exception that the file "9maj50.net" is used as the first training file. (If you are examining 7-majority, load the file "7maj50.net" instead.) Taking this difference into account, repeat the procedure from section 15.2.3 until table 15.3 can be filled in.

Table 15.2   *Data to be collected for the first experimental condition*

"Subject"	First file	Sweeps to converge	Second file	SSE before training	Sweeps to converge	Total sweeps
1	9maj25.net		9maj.net			
2	9maj25.net		9maj.net			
3	9maj25.net		9maj.net			
4	9maj25.net		9maj.net			
5	9maj25.net		9maj.net			
6	9maj25.net		9maj.net			
7	9maj25.net		9maj.net			
8	9maj25.net		9maj.net			
9	9maj25.net		9maj.net			
10	9maj25.net		9maj.net			

Table 15.3   *Data to be collected for the second experimental condition*

"Subject"	First file	Sweeps to converge	Second file	SSE before training	Sweeps to converge	Total sweeps
1	9maj50.net		9maj.net			
2	9maj50.net		9maj.net			
3	9maj50.net		9maj.net			
4	9maj50.net		9maj.net			
5	9maj50.net		9maj.net			
6	9maj50.net		9maj.net			
7	9maj50.net		9maj.net			
8	9maj50.net		9maj.net			
9	9maj50.net		9maj.net			
10	9maj50.net		9maj.net			

Table 15.4   *Data to be collected for the third experimental condition*

"Subject"	First file	Sweeps to converge	Second file	SSE before training	Sweeps to converge	Total sweeps
1	9maj75.net		9maj.net			
2	9maj75.net		9maj.net			
3	9maj75.net		9maj.net			
4	9maj75.net		9maj.net			
5	9maj75.net		9maj.net			
6	9maj75.net		9maj.net			
7	9maj75.net		9maj.net			
8	9maj75.net		9maj.net			
9	9maj75.net		9maj.net			
10	9maj75.net		9maj.net			

15.2.5   Procedure for the third experimental condition

The third experimental condition is a replication of the first, with the exception that the file "9maj75.net" is used as the first training file. (If you are examining 7-majority, load the file "7maj75.net" instead.) Taking this difference into account, repeat the procedure from section 15.2.3 until table 15.4 can be filled in.

Exercise 15.1

1. For each of the three experimental conditions, what is the average of the "SSE Before Training" column? In general, what does this tell us about the ability of a perceptron to generalize what it has learned to new instances of the majority problem?

2. Does the amount of experience that a perceptron has affect its ability to generalize? (To answer this question, you need to compare the three "SSE Before Training" columns. Appropriate statistical tests are the best option for this question. You can compute independent t-tests between each pair of columns, or you can compute a one-way ANOVA using all three columns as the values to be tested.)

3. If you found that some of the networks in the three experimental conditions had errors before their second round of training, then answer this question. (Otherwise, answer it by simply saying N/A.) Examine the three "Total Sweeps" columns for the experimental conditions, and compare them to the "Sweeps To Converge" column obtained in the control condition. (This is best done with appropriate statistical tests, like a one-way ANOVA or a set of independent t-tests on all possible pairs of columns.) Is there any advantage to training a perceptron on some of the problems before training it on the complete set?

CHAPTER 16

Animal Learning Theory and Perceptrons

16.1 Discrimination Learning

In recent years, a number of researchers have incorporated artificial neural networks into studies of animal learning (Gallistel, 1990; Hawkins & Bower, 1989; Kehoe, 1988; Kruschke, 1992, 1993; Pearce, 1997; Shanks, 1995; Sutton & Barto, 1998). One reason for this is because there are strong similarities between connectionist models and mathematical models of learning. For example, the delta rule that we have used to train both the distributed associative memory and the perceptron has been proven to be formally equivalent to the Rescorla–Wagner formalization of animal learning (Sutton & Barto, 1981). A second reason for this is because many learning researchers harbor the hope that connectionist models can provide implementational accounts of learning (e.g., Shanks, 1995, chapter 4).

One type of learning that has been studied with connectionist networks is called *discrimination learning*. In discrimination learning, an animal is trained to make a response to one stimulus, and to not make the response to a different stimulus. This learning requires that the animal discriminate between the two different stimuli. For example, an animal might be presented two different sounds, such as a pure tone (stimulus A) and white noise (stimulus B), and the trained to press a bar when stimulus A is heard, but not when stimulus B is heard. For learning theorists, this kind of training would be represented as [A+, B−]. Discrimination learning could be accomplished in a perceptron as follows: first, the perceptron would have two input units, one to represent the presence or absence of stimulus A, the other to represent the presence or absence of stimulus B. Second, a learning rule would be used to train the perceptron to turn on to stimulus A, and to turn off to stimulus B.

Discrimination learning is of interest to modern researchers because it can be used to study how animals learn to respond to combinations of stimuli. One learning paradigm that focuses upon stimulus combinations is the *patterning experiment*. In a patterning experiment, an animal learns to respond in one fashion to a single stimulus, and to respond in the opposite fashion when stimuli are combined. In *positive patterning*, the animal is trained not to respond to single stimuli and to respond to their conjunction [A−, B−, AB+]. In *negative patterning*, the animal is trained to respond to single stimuli, and not to respond to their conjunction [A+, B+, AB−].

16.1.1 Perceptrons and patterning

One of the themes of connectionist models of patterning is that the perceptron is not a powerful enough model on its own to do the job. The reason for this is that patterning experiments are assumed to be linearly nonseparable, and negative patterning is equivalent to the logical operation XOR. "This is not a problem that is unique to this particular theory. There has been other attempts to develop a single layer learning networks, and it has long been appreciated that they are unable to solve negative patterning discriminations, or, as it is more generally known, the *exclusive-or* problem" (Pearce, 1997, p. 131). Similarly, Shanks (1995, p. 127) writes "people have no difficulty learning nonlinearly-separable classifications which the delta rule model we have been considering would be unable to master." As a result, researchers have been interested in exploring extensions to the perceptron that will enable it to serve as a model for patterning.

Consider a patterning experiment that involves the presence or absence of two different stimuli, A and B. A traditional perceptron model for this type of experiment would use one output unit to perform the learned judgment, and two input units that would be used to represent the presence or absence of each stimulus. This perceptron is shown on the left in figure 16.1. In learning theory terms, it is an instance of one approach to patterning, called the configural approach. "According to this view, subjects represent compound stimuli holistically and as being different from but similar to their components" (Delamater, Sosa, & Koch, 1999, p. 98). The basic perceptron model is configural in the sense that the net input to the output unit is a holistic representation that would have to distinguish compound stimuli from their components. However, as we have seen, this configural theory is assumed to be an inadequate account of patterning.

A second approach is called the *elemental approach*. The elemental approach attempts to use a perceptron to solve the patterning problem by elaborating the input pattern. In particular, an additional input unit is used to represent the presence of conjoined stimuli. So, when both A and B are present, their two input units would be turned on, but so too would be the third input unit for the conjoint stimulus AB. This elaborated perceptron is shown on the right of figure 16.1. The logic of this approach is that there is something unique in the conjunction of stimuli, and this uniqueness can serve by itself as an additional conditioned stimulus or cue. "Configural theories are based on the assumption that conditioning with a compound results

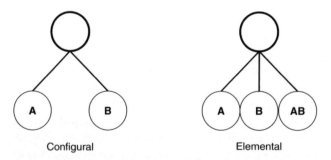

Configural Elemental

Figure 16.1 Perceptrons that could be created for two different approaches to discrimination learning

in a unitary representation of the compound entering into a single association with the reinforcer" (Pearce & Boulton, 2001, p. 119).

16.1.2 Patterning and a multilayer perceptron: a case study

A third approach to elaborating the perceptron for patterning experiments is to abandon the traditional perceptron altogether, and replace it with the multilayer perceptron that is introduced in chapter 17. This has been called the multilayer approach (Dawson, 2004). "According to this approach, it is assumed that conditioned stimulus representations change during conditioning, and that configural and/or elemental solutions develop according to the nature of the task" (Delamater, Sosa, & Koch, 1999, p. 98). In a multilayer perceptron, a layer of hidden units would be added to either of the perceptrons illustrated above, and would serve to transform the input patterns before they were processed by the output unit. Such a system "assumes that these 'unique cues' or 'configural stimuli' are not present from the outset of training but rather are themselves the product of learning" (Delamater, Sosa, & Koch, 1999, p. 98).

Delamater, Sosa, and Koch (1999) used this type of network in a study of the effect on patterning of representations that emerged in the intermediate layers of processors during a pre-training period. Their network had six different input units. Four of these were used to encode the presence of four different stimuli (A, B, C, or D). The other two were used to represent stimulus type. Both stimuli A and B were of type X. So, whenever either of these two stimuli was presented to the network, the input unit representing type X was also turned on. Similarly, stimuli C and D were of type Y; this was represented by also activating the sixth input unit whenever C or D was presented to the network. The network also had one output unit and four intermediate or 'hidden' units; all of these units employed the logistic activation function.

In the first phase of their experiment, the network was trained, using four different input patterns, to make discriminations between the four different individual stimuli (AX+, BX−, CY+, DY−). In other words, it was reinforced (i.e., trained to activate) to stimuli A and C, and not reinforced (i.e., trained to turn off) to stimuli B and D. Once a network had learned to make these discriminations, it was placed in one of four different post-training conditions, each of which involved training the network with three different input patterns.

Two of these conditions required the network to undergo a period of positive patterning. In one, this positive patterning involved the stimuli that had been previously reinforced in the pre-training (AX−, CY−, AXCY+). In the other, positive patterning was based on the stimuli that had not been previously reinforced (BX−, DY−, BXDY+). Delamater, Sosa, and Koch (1999) found that learning in the first condition was much faster than learning in the second condition. Previous reinforcement produced internal representations that aided later positive patterning.

The other two post-training conditions in their study involved negative patterning. In one, the negative patterning was based on the previously reinforced stimuli (AX+, CY+, AXCY−). In the other, it was based on the stimuli that had not been previously reinforced (BX+, DY+, BXDY−). Delamater, Sosa, and Koch (1999) found that learning in the first condition was slower than learning in the second. Previous reinforcement resulted in internal representations that hindered later negative patterning.

What was particularly interesting about the Delamater, Sosa, and Koch (1999) study was that after examining the performance of their networks, they proceeded to conduct a parallel animal learning study to determine whether pre-training affected animal patterning in the same way that it affected network patterning. In a pre-training phase, Sprague-Dawley rats learned to discriminate between two different sounds (tone vs. white noise) and between two different visual stimuli (steady light vs. flashing light). The rats then underwent a post-training patterning phase, in which they were placed in either a negative or a positive patterning paradigm, which involved either the stimuli that had been reinforced in the pre-training phase or the stimuli that had not been reinforced.

The results of the Delamater, Sosa, and Koch (1999) animal study were quite different from the predictions made on the basis of the performance of their PDP network. First, for the rats there was strong evidence that previous reinforcement of stimuli aided negative patterning – a result that was completely opposite to the prediction made by the network. Second, there was at best weak evidence that previous reinforcement aided positive patterning. "The present data suggest that if changes in the internal representations of stimuli occur throughout training, they do not do so in the manner anticipated by the standard multi-layered network" (p. 108).

16.2   Linearly Separable Versions of Patterning

16.2.1   Patterning simulations in principle and in practice

In principle, it cannot be denied that negative patterning and positive patterning are both linearly nonseparable problems. Negative patterning is logically equivalent to the A $\veebar$ B operation in the two-valued algebra. Positive patterning is logically equivalent to the A $\barwedge$ B operation in the two-valued algebra. As such, it is impossible for traditional perceptrons to represent solutions to these two types of patterning experiments in the animal learning literature.

In practice, however, things are quite different. When patterning experiments are studied by animal learning theorists who use connectionist simulations, the stimulus set that is presented is *not* linearly nonseparable. This is because these researchers fail to include all four input patterns that are required to define responses that are logically equivalent to A $\veebar$ B or to A $\barwedge$ B. Instead, it is typical that only three input stimuli are used. As a result, the stimuli that are presented in these learning experiments represent a linearly separable problem.

For example, consider table 16.1. It represents the stimuli that were actually used by Delamater, Sosa, and Koch (1999) in the study that was reviewed above. It also shows the set of stimuli that should have been used had these researchers been intent on studying patterning problems that were linearly nonseparable. Note that the difference between the two sets of stimuli is that in the latter a fourth input pattern has been added. In order to make the stimulus set logically correct, the fourth pattern involves training the network to make a response to the absence of stimuli. For example, the stimulus ~(AXCY)− means "train the network not to respond when A, X, C, and Y are all absent".

Table 16.1 presents two different options to animal learning researchers. On the one hand, if they are serious about defining patterning problems as being linearly nonseparable, then their simulation studies and their animal studies must use stimulus sets that are logically correct. This means, for instance, that positive patterning studies of animals would have to include counterintuitive conditions like ~(AXCY)+, which may not be desirable. On the other hand, if they are serious in declaring that the actual stimuli in the table above represent

Table 16.1 *The training stimuli used by Delamater, Sosa, and Koch (1999), and a revised set of training stimuli to make the original stimuli logically complete*

Post-training condition	Actual stimuli	Desired logical relation	Logically correct stimuli
Previously reinforced, positive patterning	AX− CY− AXCY+	A ⊠ B	AX− CY− AXCY+ ~(AXCY)+
Previously reinforced, negative patterning	AX+ CY+ AXCY−	A ⊠ B	AX+ CY+ AXCY− ~(AXCY)−
Not previously reinforced, positive patterning	BX− DY− BXDY+	A ⊠ B	BX− DY− BXDY+ ~(BXDY)+
Not previously reinforced, negative patterning	BX+ DY+ BXDY−	A ⊠ B	BX+ DY+ BXDY− ~(BXDY)−

their definition of patterning, then they should use much simpler models of this kind of learning. In particular, multilayered networks of the type used by Delamater, Sosa, and Koch (1999) are far too powerful, because a perceptron is capable of learning to respond correctly to any of these four sets of three input patterns.

The exercises that follow explore this second option by replicating the simulation study of Delamater, Sosa, and Koch (1999) using perceptrons instead of using a much more complex multilayered network.

16.2.2 Architecture and training sets

The two exercises below both use a perceptron to replicate the simulation study of Delamater, Sosa, and Koch (1999). The perceptron has six input units, each one for representing the presence or absence of six different stimuli (A, B, C, D, X, Y). As was the case in the original study, the stimuli X and Y are used to separate the four other stimuli (A and B, C and D) into two different classes. The perceptron has a single output unit, and (by definition) no hidden units are included in the network. In the first exercise, the output unit of the perceptron is an integration device. In the second exercise, the output unit is a value unit. There are two separate issues to explore in both exercises. First, is the perceptron capable of learning all of the regularities that were required of the multilayer network in the original study? Second, if so, then does the performance of the perceptron resemble the animal results that were briefly described earlier?

There are five training sets that are required to carry out the simulations in this chapter. The first is the file "pretrain.net", which represents the pre-training stimulus set used by Delamater, Sosa, and Koch (1999) in a format that can be read by the Rosenblatt program. It consists of four different training patterns that a perceptron must learn to discriminate before entering the second phase of the study. The remaining four files represent the patterning stimuli in the second column of table 16.1. The file "PRpos.net" holds the stimuli for the previously reinforced/positive patterning condition. The file "PRneg.net" holds the stimuli for the previously reinforced/negative patterning condition. The file "NPRpos.net" holds the stimuli for the not previously reinforced/positive patterning condition. The file "NPRneg.net" holds the stimuli for the not previously reinforced/negative patterning condition. Each of these four files consists of three different patterns to which a perceptron must learn to respond after it has completed the pre-training phase of the simulation study. One question of interest concerns the effect of the pre-training on the amount of training that is required for a network to converge on one of these four post-training stimulus sets.

16.2.3 Procedure for study 1: integration device perceptron

Basically, you will be performing the following general steps using the Rosenblatt program, steps which you should be familiar with now that you have completed the simulations from chapter 15:

- Train a network to convergence using the file pre-train.net
- Keep the weights that result, and read in one of the four files described above
- Continue training the network on the new file until it converges
- Record the number of sweeps required for this second convergence to occur following the style of table 16.2
- Reset the network, and repeat this process
- Your study will involve five separate runs on each of the cells given above, resulting in 20 separate simulations

The detailed instructions for doing this study are as follows: Run the Rosenblatt program, and load the file "pretrain.net". Choose the option to train with the gradient descent rule (logistic output), so that the output unit will be an integration device. Use the default settings that accompany this learning rule:

- End after a maximum number of training epochs
- End when there are all "hits" and no "misses"
- Randomize patterns each epoch
- Train thresholds during learning
- Default starts for weights
- Default starts for thresholds
- Maximum number of epochs = 1,000
- Number of epochs between printouts = 100
- Learning rate = 0.50
- Minimum level of squared error to define a "hit" = 0.01

Press the "Start Training" button, and train the network until it converges on a solution to the problem (i.e., 4 hits and 0 misses). Then, press the "Test Recall" button, and choose "Test Current Network On A New Problem". Read in one of the post-training condition files. For instance, to start filling in your table 16.2, read in the file "PRpos.net". Then choose the option to "Keep Current Weights And Continue Training", and press the "Continue Training" button. *Make sure that you do not press the "Start Training" button, which will reset all the weights, and erase all of the pre-training effects!* When the network converges, record the number of sweeps required in your table.

Once this is done, you are ready to replicate this procedure to run another "subject" in your experiment. Press the "Test Recall" button, and then choose to "Train A New Network On A New Problem". Have the program load in the pretraining file "pretrain.net" once again, and repeat the procedure that was described above. When five simulations using the file "PRpos.net" have been completed, continue this process, but use another one of the post-training files. Complete this process until all of the cells in table 16.2 can be filled in with data from the appropriate kind of "subject".

16.2.4 Procedure for study 2: value unit perceptron

This study is essentially the same as the one that you just carried out, with one exception. Run the Rosenblatt program, and load the file "pretrain.net". Choose the option to train with the gradient descent rule (Gaussian output), so that the output unit will be value unit. (This is the only difference between the studies!) Use the default settings that accompany this learning rule:

- End after a maximum number of training epochs
- End when there are all "hits" and no "misses"

Table 16.2 *Data to be obtained and recorded from study 1*

	Positive patterning	**Negative patterning**
	File: PRpos.net	**File: PRneg.net**
	Sweeps:	Sweeps:
Previously reinforced	Sweeps:	Sweeps:
	Sweeps:	Sweeps:
	Sweeps:	Sweeps:
	Sweeps:	Sweeps:
	Average:	*Average:*
	File: NPRpos.net	**File: NPRneg.net**
	Sweeps:	Sweeps:
Not previously reinforced	Sweeps:	Sweeps:
	Sweeps:	Sweeps:
	Sweeps:	Sweeps:
	Sweeps:	Sweeps:
	Average:	*Average:*

Exercise 16.1

1. Examine the results recorded in your table. Is it possible for perceptrons to provide potential models of patterning? Why are you in a position to make this claim?
2. Are your results consistent with those of the model that was created by Delamater, Sosa, and Koch (1999)? Make sure that you describe how your results are consistent or inconsistent, in qualitative terms – a yes or no answer will not suffice! (You will have to consult section 16.1.2 to answer this question.)
3. Are your results consistent with those of the animal data that was collected by Delamater, Sosa, and Koch (1999)? Make sure that you describe how your results are consistent or inconsistent, in qualitative terms – a yes or no answer will not suffice! (You will have to consult section 16.1.2 to answer this question.)

- Randomize patterns each epoch
- Train thresholds during learning
- Default starts for weights
- Default starts for thresholds
- Maximum number of epochs = 1,000
- Number of epochs between printouts = 100
- Learning rate = 0.10
- Minimum level of squared error to define a "hit" = 0.01

Repeat the same procedure that you used in the previous exercise to compile the data required to complete table 16.3.

Table 16.3   Data to be obtained and recorded from study 2

	Positive patterning	**Negative patterning**
Previously reinforced	**File: PRpos.net**	**File: PRneg.net**
	Sweeps:	Sweeps:
	Sweeps:	Sweeps:
	Sweeps:	Sweeps:
	Sweeps:	Sweeps:
	Sweeps:	Sweeps:
	Average:	*Average:*
Not previously reinforced	**File: NPRpos.net**	**File: NPRneg.net**
	Sweeps:	Sweeps:
	Sweeps:	Sweeps:
	Sweeps:	Sweeps:
	Sweeps:	Sweeps:
	Sweeps:	Sweeps:
	Average:	*Average:*

Exercise 16.2

1. Examine the results recorded in your table. Is it possible for perceptrons to provide potential models of patterning? Why are you in a position to make this claim?

2. Are your results consistent with those of the model that was created by Delamater, Sosa, and Koch (1999)? Make sure that you describe how your results are consistent or inconsistent, in qualitative terms – a yes or no answer will not suffice! (You will have to consult section 16.1.2 to answer this question.)

3. Are your results consistent with those of the animal data that was collected by Delamater, Sosa, and Koch (1999)? Make sure that you describe how your results are consistent or inconsistent, in qualitative terms – a yes or no answer will not suffice! (You will have to consult section 16.1.2 to answer this question.)

4. On the basis of the answers to the six preceding questions in this chapter, what are the implications of these results for using perceptrons to study patterning in experiments on animal learning?

CHAPTER 17

The Multilayer Perceptron

17.1 Creating Sequences of Logical Operations

In the exercises in preceding chapters, we have explored some variations of the perceptron, and have demonstrated that this particular architecture is perhaps more interesting and more relevant than one might expect after reading many introductory accounts of connectionism. Nevertheless, it is still the case that perceptrons are limited in the sense that they are unable to represent the solution to many different problems in their connection weights. For example, neither an integration device perceptron nor a value unit perceptron is capable of representing all of the operations in the two-valued algebra.

Much of the modern interest in artificial neural networks has arisen because researchers have gone beyond the perceptron by developing rules for training networks that have one or more layers of intermediate processors between their input and output units. These networks are extremely powerful, and are capable of representing solutions to problems that are beyond the ability of the perceptron. The purpose of this chapter is to provide a brief introduction to the multilayer perceptron. For the reader interested in a more detailed treatment of this architecture, a number of other resources are available (De Wilde, 1997; Freeman, 1994; Hertz, Krogh, & Palmer, 1991; Kasabov, 1996; Pao, 1989; Ripley, 1996; Rojas, 1996; Shepherd, 1997; Zurada, 1992).

17.1.1 The implications of the functional completeness of logical operations

Chapter 11 provided a brief introduction to the two-valued algebra. This algebra includes 16 different logical operations that can be computed over the possible binary values of two input variables. However, if one were interested in translating this logic into electronic operations in order to build working logical devices (Shannon, 1938), then not all sixteen logical operations need to be defined as primitives. This is because some subsets of all of the possible logical relations are functionally complete, which means one can combine a small set of primitive operations into a more complicated circuit in order to compute other relations that are part of the two-valued algebra.

For example, figure 17.1 illustrates a circuit whose only components are INVERT, AND, and OR gates. The circuit takes as input the values (true or false) of two signals, *A* and *B*. However, the arrangement of the logic gates in this circuit is such that the output of the circuit is another operation in the two-valued algebra, the exclusive-or of *A* and *B*.

17.1.2   Sequences of logical operations and neural networks

One important feature of the figure 17.1 circuit in comparison to the perceptrons that we have already seen is that it is multilayered. *A* and *B* can be viewed as being equivalent to input units, and the OR gate is equivalent to an output unit. The remaining four gates can also be viewed as being processing units, but they would never be found in a simple perceptron. This is because they are neither input nor output units. Because they have no direct contact with the environment, but instead only receive and send signals to other processors, they can be called hidden units. The presence of hidden units is a characteristic that is true of most modern connectionist simulations.

The use of multiple layers of processing units that have nonlinear activation functions is the source of a tremendous amount of computational power. In cognitive science, one issue at the computational level of analysis is the computational or representational power of an information processing system (Dawson, 1998). Most cognitive scientists would agree that in order for an information processor to be of interest, it must have the same computational power as a universal Turing machine. Some of the earliest modern artificial neural networks were described as circuits similar in spirit to the one above, where the 14 linearly separable operations of the two-valued algebra were used to define 14 primitive types of processing units (units that were equivalent to logic gates) (McCulloch & Pitts, 1943). McCulloch and Pitts were able to prove that one could construct a network from these building blocks that was equivalent in power to a universal Turing machine, and therefore far more powerful than the perceptrons that we have been exploring. They did this by showing how one could construct the machine head of such a Turing machine in the form of a network of their processors. "This is of interest as affording a psychological justification of the Turing definition of computability and its equivalents, Church's λ-definability and Kleene's primitive recursiveness: If any number can be computed by an organism, it is computable by these definitions" (McCulloch & Pitts, 1988, p. 35).

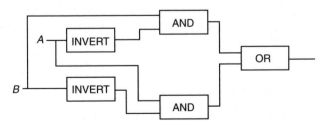

Figure 17.1   An XOR circuit constructed only from INVERT, AND, and OR logic gates

17.2 Multilayer Perceptrons and the Credit Assignment Problem

17.2.1 The credit assignment problem for multilayer networks

It has been known since at least the first half of the twentieth century that multiple layers of nonlinear processors can provide enormous computational power (McCulloch & Pitts, 1943; Shannon, 1938). Why, then, was so much research in the 1950s and 1960s devoted to exploring learning in much less powerful networks, such as the perceptron (Rosenblatt, 1962)? The reason is that researchers could build powerful multilayer systems, like McCulloch–Pitts networks, but such networks could not be taught. Learning rules like the delta rule developed by Rosenblatt were capable of training networks that had no hidden units. However, as soon as one or more layers of hidden units were desired, there was no known method for adjusting the weights of the connections that were deep inside the network.

Why is it difficult to train multilayer networks? Recall that any of the learning rules that we have been using to train perceptrons use the product of three different numbers to modify a connection weight: the learning rate, the activity at the input end of the connection, and the error at the output end of the connection (Dawson, 2004). The problem with training a multilayer network is that we do not know the value of all three of these numbers for all of the connections in the network.

In particular, the problem is that we are missing the error values required to update some of the connections. We know how to define error for an output unit, because it is equal to the difference between the actual response of the output unit and the desired response. As a result, we can modify all of the connection weights that feed directly into an output unit. (Regarding the other two numbers that are required, we ourselves set the learning rate, and the signal at the input end of any of these connections will be the activity of a hidden unit.) However, we run into a problem when we attempt to modify any connection weight that feeds into a hidden unit. This is because we do not have an error value to use for a hidden unit. This error value is unknown because we do not have any idea about what the desired response for a hidden unit should be.

The absence of hidden unit error is an example of the *credit assignment problem* (Minsky, 1963). "In playing a complex game such as chess or checkers, or in writing a computer program, one has a definite success criterion – the game is won or lost. But in the course of play, each ultimate success (or failure) is associated with a vast number of internal decisions. If the run is successful, how can we assign credit for the success among the multitude of decisions?" (p. 432). The version of this problem that faced neural network researchers prior to the 1980s was that they could not assign the appropriate "credit" – that is, the appropriate blame – to each hidden unit for its contribution to output unit error. In connectionist networks, the inability to assign such credit translated into an inability to train any of the weights that feed into a layer of hidden units.

17.2.2 The generalized delta rule

Many researchers believe that Minsky and Papert's publication of the first edition of *Perceptrons* in 1969 led to the near extinction of "old connectionism" (Papert, 1988). A dramatic rebirth of artificial neural network research, in the form of "new connectionism", occurred in the mid-1980s. One of the driving forces behind this renaissance was significant progress in connectionist learning algorithms. In particular, a solution to the credit assignment problem was discovered, allowing researchers to train multilayer networks.

Rumelhart, Hinton, and Williams (1986a, 1986b) were able to solve the credit assignment problem after they decided to use the logistic equation to approximate the step function that was used in older connectionist architectures such as McCulloch–Pitts networks and perceptrons. This allowed them to use calculus to determine the effect of weight changes on a measure of the error of a network's responses to training patterns (Dawson, 2004). One consequence of this approach was that they were able to improve the delta rule by using the derivative of the logistic activation function to define a gradient descent algorithm. We have already used this approach in our gradient descent training of the perceptron. A second consequence was that they also were able to determine how network error could be altered by changes in weights that fed into a hidden unit. In essence, their equations defined hidden unit error. They discovered that the error for any hidden unit was the sum of the error for each output unit scaled by the connection weight between each output unit and the hidden unit. This summed error was then scaled by the derivative computed for the hidden unit's activation function. (For a more detailed introduction of this approach, see Dawson (2004).)

What the mathematical analysis determined was that the error for any hidden unit in a multiple-layer network could be considered as a signal that was sent to the hidden unit from the output units. The raw signal from each output unit was its error. As this raw signal was sent from an output unit to a hidden unit, it was scaled by the weight of the connection between the two units. The total error for a hidden unit was shown to be the sum of all of the weighted error signals that it received from the output units. Because this error term was essentially a signal being sent backwards from the output units to the hidden units, the learning rule that was developed by Rumelhart, Hinton, and Williams (1986a, 1986b) became known as the "error backpropagation" rule.

The general steps involved in training a network with the generalized delta rule can now be briefly described. One starts with a network that has small, randomly assigned connection weights. To train a network on one of the patterns in the training set, the pattern is presented to the network's input units, and (on the basis of its existing connection weights) the network generates a response to it. Early in training, this response will likely be incorrect. As a result, one can compute an error term for each output unit, where error is essentially the difference between the desired response of the output unit and its actual response. This error term can be used to modify the network's connections in such a way that the next time this pattern is presented to the network, the amount of error in the network's response will be smaller.

As we have just seen, when using the generalized delta rule, error is used to modify connection weights by sending it backwards through the network, in the opposite direction of the feedforward signal. Once the error term for each output unit has been calculated, an equation specifies how the connections directly attached to each output unit can have their weights changed. Once this is done, the output units send their error as a signal – to be scaled by the new connection weights – to the next layer of hidden units. Each hidden unit then computes its overall error. Once a hidden unit has computed its total error, it can alter all of the connections that are directly attached to it. This process can be repeated, if necessary, to send error signals to the next layer of hidden units, and stops once all of the connections in the network have been modified.

By repeating this procedure a large number of times for each pattern in the training set, the network's response errors for each pattern can be reduced to near zero. At the end of this training, the network will have a very specific pattern of connectivity (in comparison to its random start), and will have learned to perform a particular stimulus response pairing.

17.2.3   A generalized delta rule for value units

We have also already been using another variant of a gradient descent rule (Dawson & Schopflocher, 1992b) to train a perceptron that uses the Gaussian activation function in its output units. While this learning rule for value units can be used to train perceptrons, it was actually originally developed as a variant of the generalized delta rule for training multilayer perceptrons. In particular, it can be used for networks in which the output units and the hidden units are all value units (Dawson, 2004). The mathematics of the Dawson–Schopflocher rule for value unit networks are very similar to those of the generalized delta rule, because both rules belong to the same family of algorithms for training multilayer networks. The general steps of the algorithm for training a network of value units are identical to those that were described for the backpropagation of error training in the preceding section.

One interesting consequence of the learning rule for value units is that when it is sent to a hidden unit, error is merely a number. The hidden unit does not need to know anything else about the unit that is sending the error. For example, it does not matter if that processor is an integration device or a value unit. As a result, one can use backpropagation of error to train hybrid networks. In such a network, the output units might be value units and the hidden units might be integration devices. Given the existence of network by problem type interactions, this type of hybrid network can offer flexibility in training a network to solve a complex pattern recognition task (Dawson, 2004).

17.3   The Implications of the Generalized Delta Rule

The solution of the credit assignment problem has led to two general implications for connectionist contributions to cognitive science and psychology. On the one hand, researchers are now in possession of a tool that permits them to train powerful models to discover solutions to problems that are far beyond the capabilities of simpler networks. As a result, there has been an enormous revolution in the kinds of models that cognitive scientists have proposed for a diverse range of phenomena (Clark, 1989, 1993; Dawson, 1998).

On the other hand, in many cases after these networks have learned to solve a problem, a researcher may have little or no understanding of the internal workings of the simulation. Bonini's paradox occurs when a computer simulation is at least as difficult to understand as the phenomenon that it was supposed to illuminate (Dutton & Starbuck, 1971), and is particularly relevant for researchers who use connectionist networks. Connectionist researchers freely admit that in many cases it is extremely difficult to determine how their networks accomplish the tasks that they have been taught. "If the purpose of simulation modeling is to clarify existing theoretical constructs, connectionism looks like exactly the wrong way to go. Connectionist models do not clarify theoretical ideas, they obscure them" (Seidenberg, 1993, p. 229).

Difficulties in understanding how a particular connectionist network accomplishes the task that it has been trained to perform has raised serious doubts about the ability of connectionists to provide fruitful theories about cognitive processing. McCloskey (1991) warns: "connectionist networks should not be viewed as theories of human cognitive functions, or as simulations of theories, or even as demonstrations of specific theoretical points" (p. 387). In a nutshell, this dismissal was based largely on the view that connectionist networks are generally uninterpretable (see also Dawson & Shamanski, 1994). It is clear that the success of connectionist networks, or of any other type of model, to contribute to psychological theory depends heavily upon a researcher's ability to avoid Bonini's paradox.

The exercises that are provided in the chapters that follow explore both of these implications of the solution to the credit assignment problem. First we will be introduced to a program, called Rumelhart, which we will use to study multilayer perceptrons. We will then conduct a few simulations that demonstrate the power of multilayer networks. As we proceed further, we will investigate a variety of approaches for taking a network apart after it has been trained in order to extract some theory from the simulation. A connectionist approach in which networks are first constructed from a primitive set of building blocks, and then analyzed in order to make theoretical contributions to cognitive theory, has been described as one form of synthetic psychology (Dawson, 2004).

CHAPTER 18

The Rumelhart Program

18.1   Introduction

Rumelhart is a program written in Visual Basic 6.0 for the demonstration and exploration of multilayer perceptrons. It is designed for use on a computer running a Microsoft Windows operating system. A second program, RumelhartLite, is identical to Rumelhart with the exception that it does not include the capability to save network results in Microsoft Excel workbooks. A third program, RumelhartJava, is similar to RumelhartLite, but is written in Java in order to be run on platforms other than Windows. In this document, Rumelhart will be the only program referred to, as the user interface for it is identical to the interface for the other programs. All three programs are distributed as freeware from the website: http://www.bcp.psych.ualberta.ca/~mike/Book3/.

The purpose of the multilayer perceptron program is to learn a set of stimulus/response associations, which are usually interpreted in the context of pattern classification. This means that network responses are usually interpreted as representing names or categories that are applied to stimuli. The current program explores pattern classification with two main types of processing units: integration devices, which use the typical logistic activation function, and value units, which use a Gaussian activation function. These two processing units can be combined to create four different network types. The first is all integration devices. The second is all value units. The third uses value units as outputs, and integration devices as hidden units. The last uses integration devices as outputs, and value units as hidden units. Furthermore, the user always has the option of including direct connections from the input units to the output units. These variations of the multilayer perceptron are described in more detail in Dawson (2004, chapter 11).

18.2   Installing the Program

Rumelhart is distributed from the above website as a .zip file. The following steps will result in the program being installed on your computer:

1.   Download the file Rumelhart.zip to your computer by going to the website, click on the program icon, and save the file in any desired location on your computer.

2. Go to the saved Rumelhart.zip file on your computer, and unzip it with a program like WinZip. The result will be three different objects: setup.exe, setup.lst and Rumelhart.cab.

3. Run the setup.exe program. This will call an install program that will complete the installation of the program on your computer, which will include the installation of an "Examples" folder with a few sample training files.

18.3 Training a Multilayer Perceptron

18.3.1 Starting the program

The program can be started in two different ways. First, one can go into the directory in which the program was installed and double-click on the file "Rumelhart.exe". Second, one can go to the start button on the computer, choose programs, scroll to the program group BCPNet, and select the program Rumelhart.exe.

18.3.2 Loading a file to train a network

After the program is started, the first form that appears is used to select a file for training the multilayer perceptron (figure 18.1). By using the left mouse button and the drive selection tool located in the upper left of the form, one can choose a computer drive on which directories and files are located. The available directories on the selected drive are listed in the directory selection tool that is immediately below the drive selection tool. One opens a directory by double-clicking it with the left mouse button. If the directory contains any files that end with the extension .net, then these files will be displayed in the file selection box located in the upper middle of the form. The properties of .net files are described later in this book. These files have a particular format that the Rumelhart program is designed to read, and only files that end in this extension can be used to train the network.

One chooses a .net file by double-clicking one of the file names that is displayed in the file selection box. When this is done, the program reads the desired file, some of the file's properties are displayed, and another button appears on the form. In figure 18.1 the file "monk1.net" has been selected (and read). On the right of the form its general properties are displayed, and the button permitting the user to proceed to the next part of the program is displayed under the file selection box.

In this example, if "monk1.net" has been selected, but is not really the file that is desired, one can simply go back to the file selection tools and choose another file. When its file name is double-clicked, the new file will be read in, and will replace the properties of the previous (undesired) file.

Once the desired file has been selected, all that is required is to press the "Go To Next Page To Set Training Parameters" button with a left-click of the mouse. If instead one desires to close the program, then one can left-click the "Exit" button displayed on the bottom right of the form.

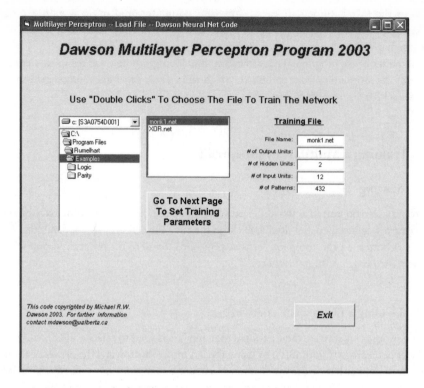

Figure 18.1   The form for loading a training file into the Rumelhart program

18.3.3   Setting the training parameters and training the network

When the program reads in the .net file, this only determines how many processing units are connected in the network, and defines the input and desired output patterns that are used in training. It is up to the user to define what learning rule to use, and to specify the value of the parameters to control (and stop) learning. The second form displayed by the program allows the user to choose these parameters (figure 18.2).

The second form consists of a number of different tools that can be used to quickly control the kind of learning that will be carried out by the multilayer perceptron. The first tool is used to choose which of four general architectures are going to be used to construct the multilayer perceptron. In essence, this tool determines the type of processor that will be used in the output units (integration device or value unit) as well as the type of processor that will be used in the hidden units (integration device or value unit). When a particular architecture is selected, default values for learning rates will also be set. These can be changed later by the user if desired. If all integration devices are used, then the learning rule that will be adopted is the gradient descent rule proposed by Rumelhart, Hinton, and Williams (1986a, 1986b). If all value units are used, then the learning rule will be the modification of the gradient descent rule proposed by Dawson and Schopflocher (1992). For the other two architectures, the learning rule that is applied will be defined by the choice of output unit.

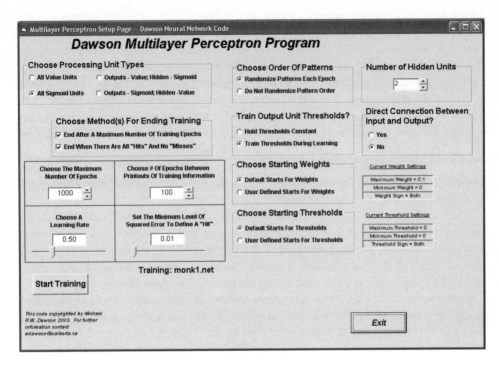

Figure 18.2   The form for setting parameters for the Rumelhart program

A second tool is used to choose a method for stopping training. In the first method, training stops after a maximum number of epochs (this value is set by the user). In the second method, training stops when there is a "hit" for every pattern and every output unit. This means that when each output is generating an acceptably accurate response for each pattern, training will stop. A left-click of the mouse is used to select either of these methods; when a method has been selected, a check mark appears in the tool. Importantly, the user can select both methods to be used in the same simulation. When this is done, then the simulation will stop as soon as one of the two conditions is met. This is the default situation, and it is recommended.

A third tool determines the order in which patterns will be trained. The program is epoch-based, which means that each epoch or "sweep" of training involves presenting every pattern once to the perceptron. When a pattern is presented, output unit error is used to modify the weight values. One can have the program present patterns in a random order each epoch, which is the recommended practice. However, if pattern order is being manipulated, you can turn this option off with a left-click of the mouse. When this is done, the patterns will always be presented in the order in which they are listed in the .net file that has been input.

A fourth tool determines whether unit thresholds (i.e., the logistic function's bias, or the value unit's mu) is to be trained. The default is to train this value, because this permits the output unit to "translate" its "cut" through pattern space. However, in some situations it may be required to hold this value constant, which can be done with a left-click of the mouse button.

A fifth tool is used to determine the starting values of the connection weights, which are randomly selected from a distribution. In the default situation, the maximum value of a weight is 0.1, the minimum value is 0, and the sign option is "both", which means that negative and positive weights are possible. These defaults are displayed to the right of the weight-start tool. With these default values, weights will be randomly selected from a rectangular distribution that ranges from −0.1 to +0.1. However, in some cases it may be desirable to explore different starting states. This can be accomplished by left-clicking the "User Defined Starts For Weights" option. When this option is selected, a new form appears (figure 18.3). This form is used to set the minimum (absolute) value for a weight, the maximum (absolute) value for a weight, and the desired sign for the weight (positive, negative, or either). When the desired settings have been selected, the "Use These Settings" button will select them, and close the form. If it is decided that the default settings are desired, then this can be accomplished by using the "Use Default Settings" button. Whatever settings have been selected will be updated on the right of the settings form.

A sixth tool is used to determine the starting values of the randomly selected thresholds for the output units. The default is to assign every output unit a threshold of 0, regardless of which activation function has been selected. If different randomly selected starts are desired, then a left-click of the "User Defined Starts For Thresholds" option will reveal a form similar to the form described above for manipulating the starting parameters for the weights.

A seventh tool allows the user to change the number of hidden units in the network, overriding the number of hidden units prescribed by the .net file that was read in. If the user wishes to alter the number of hidden units, then he or she can type in a new value in the text

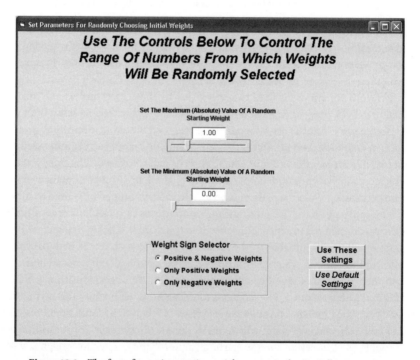

Figure 18.3   The form for setting starting weight ranges in the Rumelhart program

box, or manipulate the arrow tools with the mouse to increase or decrease the value. This manipulation will not change the .net file that was input. We use this tool to try and find the minimum number of hidden units required by a multilayer perceptron to solve a problem of interest.

An eighth tool permits the user to include direct connections between input and output units. The default situation does not include such connections, but they can be included by selecting the "Yes" value on this tool. This will increase the power of the network and, when selected, you might also consider reducing the number of hidden units used by the network.

The four remaining tools on the form are used to set numerical values that control training. The first is a tool for specifying the maximum number of training epochs by left-clicking either arrow beside the value's box. This will either increase or decrease the value of this parameter, depending upon which arrow is selected. The maximum number of training epochs can also be set directly by left-clicking the value box with the mouse, and typing in the desired value. Note that if the user chooses a value for this variable, then the "End After A Maximum Number Of Training Epochs" selection should also be selected. If this latter option does not have a check mark beside it, then the program will ignore this number when it is run. The default value (shown in figure 18.2) is 1,000.

The second is a tool for specifying the number of training epochs between printouts of training information. During training, the program will periodically print out information to tell the user how things are progressing. This includes information about what epoch has been reached, what the network SSE is, and the degree to which network SSE has changed since the last printout. The frequency of these printouts is controlled by the number displayed in this tool, which can be set in a fashion similar to that described for the previous tool. The default value (displayed in figure 18.2) is 100. If this value is selected, then every 100 epochs the user will receive updates about network learning. The value selected for this parameter also defines the spacing of the x-axis of the "SSE by Epochs" plot that can be created from a form described later.

The third is a tool for specifying the learning rate used in the learning rule. In setting the learning rate, two rules of thumb should be followed. First, if the learning rate is 0, then no learning will be accomplished. Second, it would not be typical to set learning rates greater than 1, although the user is free to explore the behavior of the network when this is done. The learning rate can be set in two different ways. One is to left-click on the arrow of the slider tool that is below the value box, hold the mouse button down, and use the mouse to slide the value of the learning rate up or down. The other is to select the box in which the learning rate is displayed, and to type in the desired learning rate.

The fourth is a tool for specifying the minimum level of error (that is, SSE) to define a "hit". The default value for this setting is 0.01. With this setting, this means that if the desired value of an output unit is 1.00, then if the unit generates activity of 0.9 or higher, a "hit" will have occurred. This is because $1.00 - 0.9 = 0.1$, and the square of 0.1 is 0.01. Similarly, if the unit generates activity of 0.1 or smaller for a desired output of 0.00, then a "hit" will have occurred. If a more conservative definition of "hit" is desired, then this tool should be used to make the minimum SSE value smaller. If a more liberal definition is required, then this value should be made larger. The smaller the value, the longer it will take for learning to occur. However,

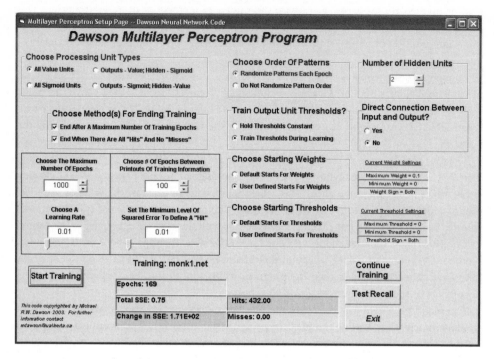

Figure 18.4   The parameter form after training has stopped

if this value is too large, learning will end quickly but the network's responses to stimuli will be less accurate.

Once these tools have been used to select the desired training parameters, associations (memories) can be stored in the network by pressing the "Start Training" button with a left-click of the mouse. When this is done, new boxes appear on the form to show the user how training is proceeding. When training stops, two new buttons appear on the form (see figure 18.4). By pressing the "Continue Training" button, more training occurs using the settings that have already been selected on this form. By pressing the "Test Recall" button, the user moves to a new form that can be used to explore the performance of the trained network. The details of this form are described below. Of course, pressing the "Exit" button terminates the program. Note that as training proceeds, information about the number of sweeps, the total network SSE, and the number of hits and misses is displayed. In figure 18.4, training stopped after 105 epochs because there were 432 hits and 0 misses on the training patterns for the monk1 problem.

18.4   Testing What the Network Has Learned

Once training has been completed, the perceptron has learned to classify a set of input patterns. With the press of the "Test Recall" button on the form that has just been described, the program presents a number of options for examining the ability of the network to retrieve the information that it has stored (figure 18.5). Some of these options involve the online examination of network responses, as well as the plotting of learning dynamics. Other options permit the user to save properties of the network in files that can be examined later. One of these file options enables the user to easily manipulate network data, or to easily move the data into another program (such as a statistical analysis tool) for more detailed analysis (e.g., factor analytic analysis of final connection weights).

The "Test Recall" causes the program to present a form to the user that permits him or her to do two general types of activities. The first is the study/saving of network properties, which is described in more detail below. The second is the ability to return to previous forms to either continue network training on the same problem, or to read in a new problem for training and study. For either of these two classes of activity, the user selects the specific activity to perform from either list that is illustrated in the figure. Double-clicking the list item with the left mouse button results in the activity being carried out. The sections that follow first describe the different activities that are possible by selecting any one of the actions laid out in the control box on the upper part of the form. Later sections then describe the result of double-clicking any one of the actions made available in the control box on the lower part of the form. Again, an "Exit Program" is also provided to allow the user to exit the program from this form.

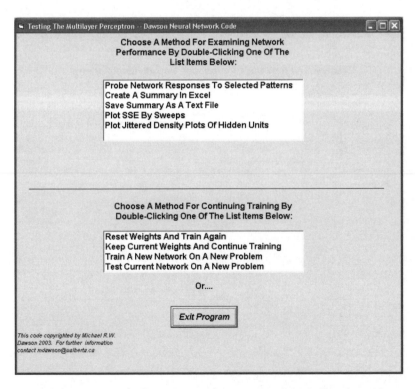

Figure 18.5   The form for testing a network created by the Rumelhart program

18.4.1   Testing responses to individual patterns

After the network has learned some classifications, it may be of interest to the user to examine the particular responses of the network to individual cue patterns in the training set. For instance, in cases where the network is not performing perfectly, it could be that it is responding correctly to some cues, but not to others. By double-clicking on the list item "Probe Network Responses To Selected Patterns", the user causes the program to provide a form that allows the network to be tested one cue pattern at a time.

The form that permits this is shown depicted in figure 18.6. The form provides a large window in which network behavior is printed. When the form is initially presented, this large window is blank. Left-button mouse clicks on the arrow controls at the top of the form are used to select the number of the pattern to be presented to the network. When the desired pattern number has been selected, the "Ok" button is pressed. The cue pattern is then presented to the network, and the network's response is displayed. The display provides details about the cue pattern, the actual network response, the desired network response, and the error of the network. For instance, in figure 18.6, Pattern 102 of the monk1 problem has just been presented to the network.

More than one pattern can be tested in this way. The new pattern information is always displayed on top of previous pattern information. One can use the two scroll bars on the window to examine all of the information that has been requested. At any point in time, one can send this information to the system's default printer by pressing the button for printing. Also, one

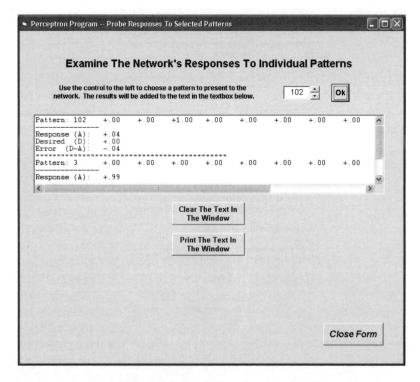

Figure 18.6   The form for presenting individual patterns to the network

can erase the window by pressing the button for clearing the display. When the "Close Form" button is pressed, this form closes, and the user is back to the "Test Recall" list options.

18.4.2 Plotting learning dynamics

A comparison of the three learning rules for the perceptron might require examining how network error changes as a function of epochs of training. If the user chooses the "Plot SSE By Sweeps" option from the list in the network testing form, then the program automatically plots this information using a bar chart (see figure 18.7). One can import this chart directly into a word processing document by simultaneously pressing the "Alt" and "Print Screen" keys on the keyboard (which copies the active window into the clipboard), going to the document, and pasting the clipboard into the document. One can print this chart on the default printer by left-clicking the mouse over the "Print The Graph" button. A left-click of the "Exit This Page" button closes the graph, and returns the user to the page that provides the options for testing network performance.

With respect to the graph produced in this form, the SSE axis is computed automatically, and the sampling of the bars across the Sweeps axis is determined by the choice of epochs between printouts made by the user on the program's second form. If the graph doesn't look quite right, then the user might consider re-running the simulation with a different choice for

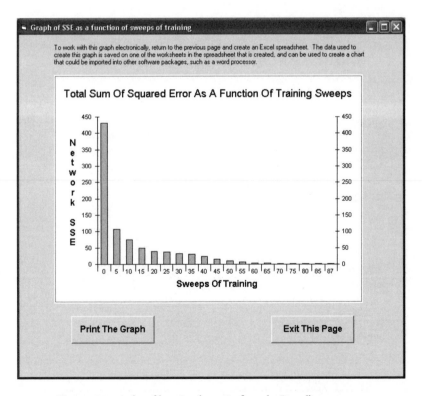

Figure 18.7 A plot of learning dynamics from the Rumelhart program

epochs between printouts. If a different kind of graph is desired, then the user might wish to save the network data to file. The data used to create this graph can be saved when this is done, and imported into a different software package that can be used to create graphs of different appearance.

18.4.3   Saving results in a text file

One of the options for storing information about network performance is to save network results as a text file. The form that permits this to be done, illustrated in figure 18.8, is accessed by choosing the list item "Save Summary As A Text File" from the form for testing the network.

There are two sets of controls on this form. The first is a set of drive, directory, and file control boxes that are very similar to those found on the very first form seen when the program starts to run. One uses the drive and directory controls to navigate to a folder in which network data is to be saved. If it is necessary to create a new folder, a left-click of the mouse on the "Create A New Directory" button creates a dialog that permits the new directory to be named and created. Once the desired directory has been opened, the existing text files (.txt) in it are displayed. This is because the network data will be saved in such a file. One can overwrite an existing file by double-clicking it with the left mouse button. If a new file needs to be created, the dialog for doing so is accessed by a left-click of the mouse on the "Create A New Filename" button.

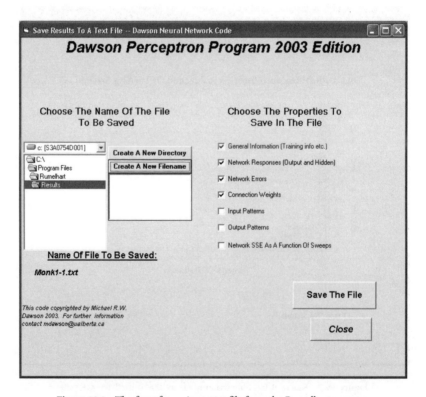

Figure 18.8   The form for saving a text file from the Rumelhart program

After choosing the location in which information is to be saved, the check boxes on the right of the form are set to determine what kinds of information will be saved. If a check box is not selected, then the corresponding information is simply not written to the file. To save the file, after the desired check boxes have been selected, the user left-clicks the "Save The File" button with the mouse. The form remains open after this is done, because in some instances the user might wish to save different versions of the network information in different locations. This form is closed by a left-mouse click on the "Close" button, which returns the user to the network testing form.

18.4.4   Saving results in an excel workbook

A second method for saving network performance is to save it in a structured Microsoft Excel workbook. This option is only available in the Rumelhart program, and has been removed from RumelhartLite. It should obviously only be selected by users who also have Microsoft Excel installed on their computer. It is selected by a double-click of the "Create A Summary In Excel" list item that is offered in the network testing form.

When this item is selected, a patience-requesting message is displayed on the "Test Network" form, and a number of different programming steps are taken to build an Excel workbook. When this is completed, the workbook is displayed as its own window, which will open on the user's computer in front of any of the Rumelhart program's windows. When the workbook has been created successfully, then the user should see something similar to the screen shot that is presented below in figure 18.9.

All of the possible information that could be saved in the text version of a saved network is saved on this spreadsheet. Each different class of information is saved on its own worksheet in this Excel workbook. One can view different elements of this information by using the mouse to select the desired worksheet's tab on the bottom of the worksheet. The worksheet in figure 18.9 opens with the "General Information" tab selected.

When this workbook is open, it is running in Excel as a standalone program that is separate from the Rumelhart software. One can select different tabs in the worksheet to examine network properties. For example, in figure 18.10, the "Hidden Unit Weights" tab has been selected. After examining the worksheet, the user might wish to save it to disk. This is done by using the Save File utilities from Excel.

One problem with having this information being displayed with a completely separate program is that it begins to use up memory resources on the computer that cannot be directly controlled by either program. For instance, it is possible to leave this workbook open, and to return to the Rumelhart program. This practice is not recommended. Instead, potential system crashes are likely to be avoided by closing the Excel workbook before returning to Rumelhart. When Rumelhart is returned to, the "test network" form will still be displayed.

If saving Excel files from Rumelhart causes system crashes, it is likely to be because of memory resource conflicts. The Excel options were built into Rumelhart because they provide a convenient format for working with network data after training has been accomplished. For instance, many of the results that are provided in chapters 11 and 12 of Dawson (2004) were created by selecting a table from an Excel worksheet, copying it, and pasting it directly into a Microsoft Word document. The Excel data can also be easily copied and pasted into statistical packages like Systat. However, the Excel capability is not required for the

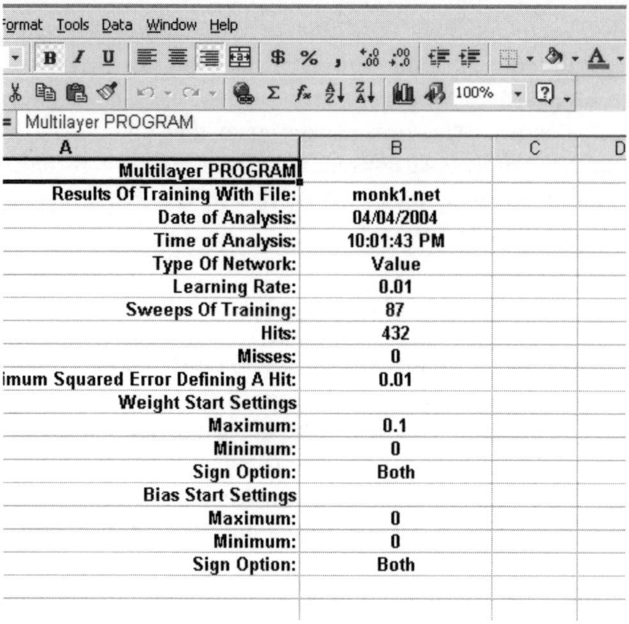
Format Tools Data Window Help
100%
Multilayer PROGRAM
A
B
C
D
Multilayer PROGRAM
Results Of Training With File: monk1.net
Date of Analysis: 04/04/2004
Time of Analysis: 10:01:43 PM
Type Of Network: Value
Learning Rate: 0.01
Sweeps Of Training: 87
Hits: 432
Misses: 0
imum Squared Error Defining A Hit: 0.01
Weight Start Settings
Maximum: 0.1
Minimum: 0
Sign Option: Both
Bias Start Settings
Maximum: 0
Minimum: 0
Sign Option: Both

Figure 18.9 An Excel spreadsheet open to the "General Information" tab

distributed associative memory software to be used productively. If Excel problems are encountered frequently on your computer, our recommendation is to use RumelhartLite instead, and save network performance as text files only.

18.4.5 Inspecting jittered density plots

When value units are used, one important characteristic they have is the banding of the jittered density plot of their hidden units. What this banding is, and its importance to network interpretation, is discussed in Dawson (2004). The Rumelhart program comes with a tool that lets the user quickly inspect the jittered density plots for each hidden unit, to determine whether banding exists. This might be an important consideration in deciding whether to save the results of a network for later analysis. You can access this tool choosing the list item "Plot Jittered Density Plots Of Hidden Units" from the network test page.

When this list item is selected, a mostly blank form appears. In the top right of this form is a number tool and an "Ok" button. Use the number tool to select a hidden unit. When the "Ok" button is pressed, the form is filled with a jittered density plot. This is illustrated in figure 18.11, where the plot for Hidden Unit 2 of the monk1 network has been created. This particular example indicates that several different bands have appeared in this unit.

In some instances, the bands may be faint, because there is a small number of patterns in the training set. To deal with this problem, one can press the "Artificially Darken The Bands Using Repeated Plotting" button. This causes the density plot to be plotted again, with different

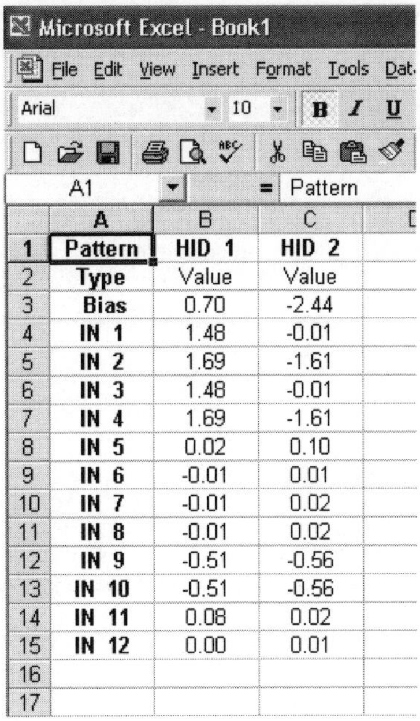

Microsoft Excel - Book1

File Edit View Insert Format Tools Dat.

Arial 10 B I U

A1 = Pattern

	A	B	C
1	**Pattern**	**HID 1**	**HID 2**
2	**Type**	Value	Value
3	**Bias**	0.70	-2.44
4	**IN 1**	1.48	-0.01
5	**IN 2**	1.69	-1.61
6	**IN 3**	1.48	-0.01
7	**IN 4**	1.69	-1.61
8	**IN 5**	0.02	0.10
9	**IN 6**	-0.01	0.01
10	**IN 7**	-0.01	0.02
11	**IN 8**	-0.01	0.02
12	**IN 9**	-0.51	-0.56
13	**IN 10**	-0.51	-0.56
14	**IN 11**	0.08	0.02
15	**IN 12**	0.00	0.01
16			
17			

Figure 18.10 An Excel spreadsheet open to the "Hidden Unit Weights" tab

random values, on the same plot. In the example in figure 18.12, the bands on the first plot (figure 18.11) have been darkened by pressing this button just once.

In using this tool, it should be cautioned that the bands that appear due to "artificial darkening" are not real. This tool is just a visualization aid. It is possible that this tool might suggest that some bands exist when they are not actually present. Whenever banding analysis is done on saved network data, it will only be performed on the actual network data – not on "artificially darkened" data.

18.4.6 Leaving the "Test Recall" network test form

Once the user has finished examining the performance of a trained network, the list at the bottom of the network test form provides different options for network training. If the "Reset Weights And Train Again" option is selected, then all of the connection weights are randomized, the network is readied to be trained on the same problem that it has just learned, and the user is returned to the form that permits training parameters to be selected. If the "Keep Current Weights And Train Again" option is selected, the network is trained on the same problem, but the weights created from the learning that was just completed are not erased. The user is returned to the form that permits training parameters to be selected. They must be set again if settings other than the default settings are desired. If the "Train A New Network On A New Problem" option is selected, then the user is returned to the program's first form to be able to read in a new problem for training. If the "Train The Current Network

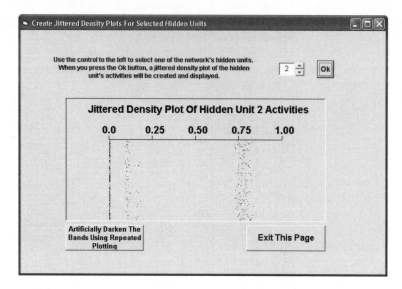

Figure 18.11   A jittered density plot created by the Rumelhart program

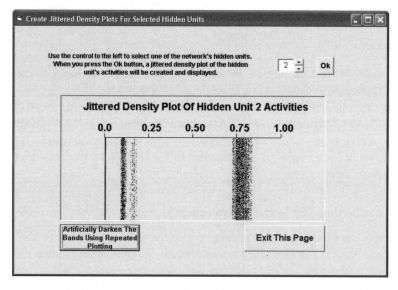

Figure 18.12   Jittered density plot with artificially darkened bands

On A New Problem" is selected, then the user can read in a new problem, but it will be presented to the network with the weights preserved from the previous training. This option can be used to study the effect of pretraining on learning a new problem, generalization of learning, or savings in learning. If none of these options are desired, then you can close the program by pressing the "Exit Program" button with a left-mouse click.

CHAPTER 19

Beyond the Perceptron's Limits

19.1 Introduction

In the history of connectionism research, the exclusive-or problem has often been at center stage. It is the prototypical example of a linearly nonseparable problem, and as a result it is often the first thing that comes to mind when one thinks of perceptron limitations and the death of old connectionism (Minsky & Papert, 1988). Pioneer connectionist Jack Cowan has recalled: "I knew from what we'd done with McCulloch that the exclusive-or was the key to neural computing in many ways" (Anderson & Rosenfeld, 1998, p. 107). Solving exclusive-or was one of the key motivators that drove researchers as they tried to find a way to train a multilayer network. David Rumelhart remembers: "In San Diego we were talking about the difficult problems, like solving the exclusive-or problem. Geoffrey [Hinton] said, 'OK, here's the problem. Here's a classic problem that the perceptrons don't work on.' I had read a little bit in Rosenblatt about his ideas on how to build multilayer systems. Of course, I'd read *Perceptrons*. And I thought, 'Well, somehow we have to figure out how to teach, how to train, a network that has more than one layer.' " (Anderson & Rosenfeld, 1998, p. 278).

Not surprisingly, one of the early examples of the capabilities of the generalized delta rule was training a network to solve the exclusive-or problem (Rumelhart, Hinton, & Williams, 1986b). "It is useful to begin with the exclusive-or problem since it is the classic problem requiring hidden units and since many other problems involve an XOR as a subproblem" (pp. 330–31). With their successful training of multilayer perceptrons on XOR and other classic, linearly nonseparable problems, they concluded "we have answered Minsky and Papert's challenge and *have* found a learning result sufficiently powerful to demonstrate that their pessimism about learning in multilayer machines was misplaced" (p. 361).

In the initial studies of training multilayer perceptrons to perform exclusive-or, two different architectures were explored. Both are illustrated in figure 19.1. In the first, two hidden units are used, and there are no direct connections between the input units and the output unit. In the second, only one hidden unit is used, but there are also direct connections between inputs and output. The first architecture can be described as solving exclusive-or by folding or transforming the pattern space, and the second architecture can be described as solving the problem by detecting a feature that increases the dimensionality of the pattern space (Dawson, 2004).

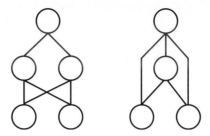

Figure 19.1   Two multilayer perceptrons for solving XOR: left, there are two hidden units, and no direct connections between the input units and the output unit; right, there is one hidden unit and direct connections between the input units and the output unit

19.2   The Generalized Delta Rule and Exclusive-Or

In the exercises below, we will continue the aforementioned tradition, and we will introduce the Rumelhart software package by training multilayer perceptrons to solve exclusive-or. We will first examine the 2-hidden unit architecture from the figure above, and will then turn to the 1-hidden unit network. In both types of networks, all of the hidden units and all of the output units will be integration devices.

19.2.1   Procedure for the 2-hidden unit network

Install the Rumelhart program from the website associated with this book, referring back to chapter 18 for instructions if necessary. Run the program and load the file "xor.net". This file defines the exclusive-or problem for a network that has two hidden units. On the setup page, for this problem, you can train the network using all of the default settings:

- Train with all sigmoid units
- End after a maximum number of training epochs
- End when there are all "hits" and no "misses"
- Randomize patterns each epoch
- Train thresholds during learning
- Default starts for weights
- Default starts for thresholds
- Maximum number of epochs = 1,000
- Number of epochs between printouts = 100
- Learning rate = 0.5
- Minimum level of squared error to define a "hit" = 0.01
- Number of hidden units = 2
- No direct connections between input and output units

Press the "Start Training" button to begin training. This particular problem can be tricky to solve. In some cases, the network will converge quickly, while in other cases the network will "stall" in a state where it only generates 2 hits. If the network does not converge after 1,000 epochs, press the "Continue Training" button. It is possible that this might have to be done more than once. If, after 4,000 or 5,000 sweeps of training, the network appears to be stalled, press the "Start Training" button again. This will reset the network, and begin training from scratch. Continue working with the buttons on this form until the network converges to a state in which it generates 4 hits and 0 misses. Then, have the program build an Excel spreadsheet to summarize the results. This spreadsheet will contain all of the information required to answer the following questions. If you are using a version of the Rumelhart program that does not use Excel, then save the results of training to a file that you can examine later to answer the questions.

Exercise 19.1

1. How many sweeps of training were required before the network converged?
2. What was the sum of squared error (SSE) for the network when it converged?
3. Remember that the hidden units and the output units use the logistic activation function, and that the bias of this function is analogous to the threshold of the step function. In the spreadsheet that you saved, examine all of the biases and connection weights in the trained network. Use this information to explain how the network uses its hidden units to solve this linearly separable problem. (Hint: an example of this approach to the network can be found in Dawson (2004).)

19.2.2   Procedure for the 1-hidden unit network

The second exercise is identical to the first, except that once the "xor.net" file has been loaded, a couple of tools on the setup page are used to alter the architecture so that it uses only one hidden unit, and so that it includes direct connections between the input units and the output unit. Run the Rumelhart program, and load the file "xor.net". On the setup page, for this problem, you can train the network using all of the default settings, with two exceptions. First, use the hidden unit tool on the setup page to reduce the number of hidden units from 2 to 1. Second, use the direct connections tool on the setup page to include direct connections between input and output units. After you do this, the following conditions should be true of the simulation:

- Train with all sigmoid units
- End after a maximum number of training epochs
- End when there are all "hits" and no "misses"
- Randomize patterns each epoch
- Train thresholds during learning
- Default starts for weights
- Default starts for thresholds
- Maximum number of epochs = 1,000

- Number of epochs between printouts = 100
- Learning rate = 0.5
- Minimum level of squared error to define a "hit" = 0.01
- *Number of hidden units = 1*
- *Direct connections between input and output units*

Press the "Start Training" button to begin training. This particular problem can be tricky to solve. In some cases, the network will converge quickly, while in other cases the network will "stall" in a state where it only generates two hits. If the network does not converge after 1,000 epochs, press the "Continue Training" button. It is possible that this might have to be done more than once. If, after 4,000 or 5,000 sweeps of training, the network appears to be stalled, press the "Start Training" button again. This will reset the network, and begin training from scratch. Continue working with the buttons on this form until the network converges to a state in which it generates 4 hits and 0 misses. Then, have the program build an Excel spreadsheet to summarize the results. This spreadsheet will contain all of the information required to answer the following questions. If you are using a version of the Rumelhart program that does not use Excel, then save the results of training to a file that you can examine later to answer the questions.

Exercise 19.2

1. How many sweeps of training were required before the network converged?
2. What was the sum of squared error (SSE) for the network when it converged?
3. You probably found in exercise 19.1 that when the 2-hidden unit was trained, it was temperamental, and as a result you might have had to restart training on more than one occasion. Is this also the case for the 1-hidden unit network, or was it better behaved? (To answer this question, you should conduct several different runs with the 1-hidden unit network.)
4. Remember that the hidden units and the output units use the logistic activation function, and that the bias of this function is analogous to the threshold of the step function. In the spreadsheet that you saved, examine all of the biases and connection weights in the trained network. Use this information to explain how the network uses its hidden units to solve this linearly separable problem. How does this solution compare to the one that you discovered in the 2-hidden unit network? (Hint: an example of this approach to the network can be found in Dawson (2004).)

CHAPTER 20

Symmetry as a Second Case Study

20.1 Background

Rumelhart, Hinton, and Williams (1986b) introduced the generalized delta rule by describing its performance when used to train multilayer perceptrons on simple benchmark problems. One of these problems was the symmetry problem. In a symmetry problem, a network is presented a set of binary inputs. If the input pattern is symmetric about its centre, then the single output unit is trained to turn on. The output unit is trained to turn off to any pattern that is not symmetric about its middle. "We used patterns of various lengths with various numbers of hidden units. To our surprise, we discovered that the problem could always be solved with only two hidden units" (p. 340).

In their chapter, Rumelhart, Hinton, and Williams (1986b) report the results of one of their simulations. It was a network trained to judge the symmetry of patterns represented using six input units. Their network converged to a solution in 1,208 epochs with a learning rate of 0.1. They do not report any details about starting states of weights, etc. Of particular interest to them was the structure of the final network. "For a given hidden unit, weights that are symmetric about the middle are equal in magnitude and opposite in sign. That means that if a symmetric pattern is on, both hidden units will receive a net input of zero from the input units, and, since the hidden units have a negative bias, both will be off" (p. 340). In this network, the output unit had a positive bias, and therefore would be on in this situation.

The size of the weights was also of interest to Rumelhart, Hinton, and Williams (1986b). The weights feeding into a hidden unit on one side of the midpoint of the string had a size ratio of 1:2:4. When net input is computed, "this assures that there is no pattern on the left that will exactly balance a non-mirror-image pattern on the right" (p. 341). Furthermore, "the two hidden units have identical patterns of weights from the input units except for sign. This insures that for every nonsymmetric pattern, at least one of the two hidden units will come on and turn off the output unit."

20.2 Solving Symmetry Problems With Multilayer Perceptrons

We will be exploring symmetry as well, using patterns defined by five input units instead of six. In the first exercise, we will be exploring how easy it is for a network of integration devices to solve the problem. We will then compare the structure of one of our solutions to the structure that Rumelhart, Hinton, and Williams (1986a, 1986b) reported for their 6-bit symmetry network. In the second exercise, we will use only one hidden unit, but will add direct connections between input and output units. In this case, we should frequently wind up in a local minimum. The point to take away from this is that such minima can be encountered – contrary to early claims about the generalized delta rule. But we also want to consider some of the properties of the local minima that we encounter.

20.2.1 Procedure for the 2-hidden unit network

Start the Rumelhart program and load the file "symmetry5.net". This file defines a five-input unit symmetry problem for a network that has two hidden units. On the setup page, for this problem, you can train the network using all of the default settings, with the exception that you should set the learning rate to be equal to 0.10, and the maximum number of epochs to 5,000:

- Train with all sigmoid units
- End after a maximum number of training epochs
- End when there are all "hits" and no "misses"
- Randomize patterns each epoch
- Train thresholds during learning
- Default starts for weights
- Default starts for thresholds
- *Maximum number of epochs* = 5,000
- Number of epochs between printouts = 100
- *Learning rate* = 0.10
- Minimum level of squared error to define a "hit" = 0.01
- Number of hidden units = 2
- No direct connections between input and output units

Press the "Start Training" button to begin training. Like exclusive-or, this particular problem can be tricky to solve. In some cases, the network will converge quickly, while in other cases the network will "stall". If the network does not converge after 5,000 epochs, press the "Continue Training" button. If it has not converged after 10,000 sweeps, press the "Start Training" button again. This will reset the network, and begin training from scratch. Continue working with the buttons on this form until the network converges to a state in which it generates 32 hits and 0 misses. Then, have the program build an Excel spreadsheet to summarize the results. This spreadsheet will contain all of the information required to answer the following questions. If you are using a version of the Rumelhart program that does not use Excel, then save the results of training to a file that you can examine later to answer the questions.

Exercise 20.1

1. For a network that was able to learn the problem, how many sweeps of training were required? When it converged, what was the network's SSE?
2. Examine the weights of this network, both for the hidden units and for the output units. How does the structure of your network compare to structure of the Rumelhart, Hinton, and Williams' network that was described above?
3. Is there anything puzzling or surprising about the structure of your network? (Hint: look at the weights from input unit 3 to either of the hidden units)
4. You likely encountered many "stalls" along the way. Is there any general characteristics of them (SSE, numbers of hits and misses) that you could use to identify them during training, and thus use these characteristics as a signal that you would have to reset the network and try to train it from scratch again?

20.2.2   Procedure for the 1-hidden unit network

The purpose of the second exercise is to explore local minima with the 5-bit symmetry problem. On the setup page, for this problem, you will have to make a number of changes, including changing the default starting values for the connection weights. Manipulate the setup page until the following properties are all true:

- Train with all sigmoid units
- End after a maximum number of training epochs
- End when there are all "hits" and no "misses"
- Randomize patterns each epoch
- Train thresholds during learning
- *Custom starts for weights. Set the weights to start in the range from −0.1 to +0.1 by setting the maximum weight to 0.1, the minimum weight to 0.0 and the sign value to "both"*
- Default starts for thresholds
- *Maximum number of epochs* = 5,000
- Number of epochs between printouts = 100
- *Learning rate* = 0.05
- Minimum level of squared error to define a "hit" = 0.01
- *Number of hidden units* = 1
- *Direct connections between input and output units*

Press the "Start Training" button to begin training. The "ideal" goal is to keep training this network until you get one that converges – you should find that this goal can be achieved, but not very frequently. To move towards this solution, you will have to decide when to press the "Continue Training" button and when to press the "Start Training" button (i.e., when to reset the network) by observing its performance. If you have not obtained convergence after

10,000 sweeps, then you should probably start over! What you are more likely to find is that error reduces to a frustratingly small level, but the network never converges. In fact, in most cases you should get 31 hits and 1 miss, with SSE just over 1.00. Train the network to produce two or three of these "solutions", saving each as a spreadsheet. Watch the performance of the network as it learns, because you will be asked about the dynamics that you observe. As well, as you become familiar with the dynamics of learning for both well-behaved and poorly behaved networks, you will be in a better position to decide when to change training parameters when tougher problems are encountered in later exercises.

Exercise 20.2

1. In very general terms, describe the dynamics of learning – give a brief description of whether SSE constantly decreased to the local minima value, or whether during different "periods" of learning, SSE changed at different rates. You could tell a similar story about changes in hits and misses over the course of training the network.
2. Take a look at one of your almost-converged networks. Why did it fail – is it generating fairly large errors to many patterns, or is it just having problems with one pattern? If it is having problems with one pattern, which pattern is it?
3. If you are fortunate enough to have a network converge to a solution to this problem, examine its connection weights and biases. How does it solve the symmetry problem? How does this solution relate to the one represented in a 2-hidden unit network?
4. On the basis of the simulations that you carried out in this chapter, which type of network has more difficulty with the symmetry problem (if any)? If you think that there is a difference between the two types of network, briefly speculate on why this difference might exist.

CHAPTER 21

How Many Hidden Units?

21.1 Background

We have already seen that the addition of hidden units permits the multilayer perceptron to represent solutions to problems that are beyond the capability of the perceptron. Imagine, then, that armed with this new power we proceed to train a multilayer network on some problem that we have never dealt with before. Immediately we are faced with a number of design decisions that we did not have to confront when using the perceptron: how many layers of hidden units should we use, and how many hidden units should be in this layer? We are going to have to come up with some procedure for making such decisions, so that at the very least we can justify the particular choices that we make. Otherwise, critics might claim that we used too many layers, or too many hidden units, for our simulations to be meaningful. We encountered this situation when we considered, in chapter 16, a network that was far too powerful for the training set with which it was presented (Delamater, Sosa, & Koch, 1999). This chapter provides some experience with an empirical approach to making a decision about these design issues.

21.1.1 How many layers of hidden units are required?

Cognitive scientists assume that cognition is a form of information processing, and their theories about the nature of cognition often take the form of proposals about information processing architectures (Dawson, 1998). One issue that such proposals must address is the computational power of the architecture. In general, if an architecture does not appear to be equivalent in power to a universal Turing machine, then cognitive scientists will rapidly lose interest in it (Bever, Fodor, & Garrett, 1968; Minsky & Papert, 1988).

One reason for modern interest in multilayer perceptrons is the fact that these networks have such computational power. Indeed, one of the earliest formal results in artificial neural networks was the proof that one could construct a universal Turing machine from a network of McCulloch–Pitts neurons (McCulloch & Pitts, 1943). For practical reasons, though, it is pertinent to ask questions about what kinds of resources are required to achieve this level of power. For instance, we know that in principle many layers provide such power. In practice, though, how many layers of hidden units will be required?

As we have seen, artificial neural networks are commonly used to classify patterns (Carpenter, 1989; Lippmann, 1987, 1989). The set of input activities for a particular stimulus define the location of a point in a multidimensional pattern space. The network "carves" this pattern space into different decision regions, which (potentially) can have different and complex shapes. The network classifies the input pattern by generating the "name" (i.e., a unique pattern of output unit activity) of the decision region in which the stimulus pattern point is located. When a network is described as a pattern classifier, claims about its computational power focus on what kinds of decision regions it can "carve", because this will define the complexity of the classifications that it can perform. How many additional layers of processors are required to partition the pattern space into arbitrary decision regions, and thus make a network capable of any desired classification? By considering the shape of decision regions created by each additional layer of monotonic processors, it has been shown that a network with only two layers of hidden units is capable of "carving" a pattern space into arbitrary decision regions (Lippmann, 1987). "No more than three layers are required in perceptron-like feed-forward nets" (p. 16).

Historically, PDP networks have been most frequently described as pattern classifiers. Recently, however, with the advent of so-called radial basis function (RBF) networks (Girosi & Poggio, 1990; Hartman, Keeler, & Kowalski, 1989; Poggio & Girosi, 1990; Poggio, Torre, & Koch, 1985; Renals, 1989), connectionist systems are now often described as function approximators. Imagine, for example, a mathematical "surface" defined in N-dimensional space. At each location in this space this surface has a definite height. A function approximating network with N input units and one output unit would take as input the coordinates of a location in this space, and would output the height of the surface at this location. How powerful a function approximator can a PDP network be? Rumelhart, Hinton, and Williams (1986b, p. 319) claimed "if we have the right connections from the input units to a large enough set of hidden units, we can always find a representation that will perform any mapping from input to output". More recently, researchers have attempted to analytically justify this bold claim, and have in fact proven that many different kinds of networks are universal approximators. That is, if there are no restrictions on the number of hidden units in the network and if there are no restrictions on the size of the connection weights, then in principle a network can be created to approximate – over a finite interval – any continuous mathematical function to an arbitrary degree of precision. This is true for networks with a single layer of hidden integration devices (Cotter, 1990; Cybenko, 1989; Funahashi, 1989), for networks with multiple layers of such hidden units (Hornik, Stinchcombe, & White, 1989), and for RBF networks (Hartman, Keeler, & Kowalski, 1989).

21.1.2   How many hidden units are needed in a layer?

The formal results that were sketched in the previous section indicate that only one or two layers of hidden units are required to achieve enormous computational power in a connectionist network. However, these results are mute with respect to a second crucial issue: how many individual hidden units are required in a layer in order for a network to be able to learn to solve some problem of interest? This is not a straightforward question to answer, and as a result a wide variety of different approaches to it can be found in the literature.

One approach, not to be recommended, is to adopt some rule of thumb that specifies how many hidden units to use. Many locations on the world wide web provide answers to frequently asked questions (FAQs) about neural networks (e.g., http://www.faqs.org/faqs/ai-faq/neural-nets/part3/). It provides examples of several different heuristics, which include making the number of hidden units somewhere between the number of inputs and the number of outputs, to set it equal to 2 * (number of inputs + number of outputs) / 3, to never use more than twice the number of input units, or to use as many as are required to capture 70% to 90% of the variance in the input data. The problem with all of these rules of thumb is that they ignore crucial issues such as how many training patterns are going to be presented to a network, or the complexity of the function that must be learned by the network. As a result, counterexamples to all of these rules of thumb can easily be produced, as one finds when the answers to the FAQs are read.

A second approach is to view a neural network as a statistical tool that has the purpose of capturing regularities in sample data that can be generalized; that is, that can be applied to new data. This view leads to an issue called the *bias–variance tradeoff* that is intrinsically related to the number of hidden units issue. The architecture of a network (the number of hidden units, the total number of connections) can be thought of as the resources for representing the regularities in a training set. On the one hand, if a network has too many resources, then it will overfit the training set. This means that it will not only represent the regularities in the training set, but will also represent the noise in the training set. The inclusion of noise representation introduces variance into the network's model of the data. On the other hand, if a network has too few resources, then it will not be able to capture important regularities in the data. The network will have a bias to represent some (but not all) of the important data features. The issue with the bias–variance tradeoff is to find the amount of network resources (including the number of hidden units) that offers an appropriate compromise between variance problems and bias problems. This has also been called the *three bears problem* because, like Goldilocks, a researcher must find the number of hidden units that is just right (Seidenberg & McClelland, 1989).

A large array of algorithms exists for allocating network resources in a fashion that optimizes the bias–variance tradeoff (Moody, 1998; Neuneier & Zimmermann, 1998; Orr & Muller, 1998; Ripley, 1996). In general, these methods involve modifying some aspect of the neural network architecture, and monitoring the effect of this modification on some statistical measure that is relevant to the bias–variance tradeoff. Some of these methods involve growing a network, in the sense that connection weights or hidden units are added to the network until the performance measure is optimized. Other methods involve starting with a network that has a large number of resources, and pruning it by removing connection weights or hidden units, again until the performance measure indicates that pruning should stop. The end result of any of these algorithms is that a researcher has a statistical justification that can be used to defend the choice of the number of hidden units in a network that has been trained to solve a particular problem.

A third approach is a compromise between the two that have been noted above. The advantage of algorithms for dealing with the bias–variance tradeoff is that they provide an empirical approach for determining the amount of resources to be included in a network. The disadvantage of these algorithms is that they require a particular interpretation of a network – that is, as a statistical predictor. If one wants to adopt different views of a network, then these approaches may not be completely appropriate. For instance, in my laboratory we are not as interested in the ability of networks to generalize to new instances as we are in interpreting how a particular network represents the regularities in a particular training set (Berkeley et al., 1995; Dawson, 1998, 2002, 2004; Dawson, Boechler & Valsangkar-Smyth, 2000; Dawson, Kremer, & Gannon, 1994; Dawson & Medler, 1996; Dawson, Medler, & Berkeley, 1997; Dawson, Medler, McCaughan, Willson, & Carbonaro, 2000; Dawson & Piercey, 2001; Leighton & Dawson, 2001; McCaughan, Medler, & Dawson, 1999; Medler, McCaughan, Dawson, & Willson, 1999; Piercey & Dawson, 1999). As a result, we generally do not use algorithms that optimize aspects of network performance that are related to generalization.

Instead, my students and I are usually interested in interpreting the network with the smallest number of hidden units that are still capable of representing the regularities in a training set. In other words, we adopt an empirical approach in which the number of hidden units is pruned until we find that if we remove any more from the network, then it will not be able to converge to a solution to the problem that the network is being presented. To adopt this approach on a completely new problem, we usually start with a rule of thumb, and include as many hidden units as there are input units. Then, we try to train the network on the problem. If the network learns the problem quickly, then we will reduce the number of hidden units, and train again. We will repeat this process until we find the smallest network that converges reliably. As was the case with the algorithms cited earlier in this section, the important point is that we have some empirical justification for examining a network with a particular number of hidden units at the end of this procedure.

The purpose of the exercises in this chapter is to provide some experience with this approach. As well, it will also demonstrate that in some instances if one explores other training parameters (e.g., learning rate, starting states of weights), one might alter one's conclusions about the minimum number of hidden units that are required to solve a problem.

21.2 How Many Hidden Value Units Are Required for 5-Bit Parity?

In several of the previous chapters we have explored the exclusive-or problem. This problem belongs to a set of very difficult problems called parity problems. In an odd parity problem, each input unit represents a "bit" in a string that can either be on or off. If an odd number of bits are on, then the output unit should turn on. If an even number is on, then the output unit should turn off. Exclusive-or is the smallest parity problem; we could also call it 2-bit parity.

In this chapter, we will be exploring a larger version of the parity problem, 5-bit parity. In this problem, there are five input units, a set of hidden units, and a single output unit. In our simulations, all of the hidden units and the output unit will be value units. In this problem, there are 32 different input patterns, created from the set of all possible binary numbers that can be represented with 5 bits. Half of these patterns are odd parity, while the other half are not.

In general, parity problems are extremely difficult because two patterns that are identical to each other except in one bit must be placed in different categories. The difficulty of the parity problem is reflected in the number of hidden units that are required to solve it. In a network of integration devices, if there are N input units, then no fewer than N hidden units are required to correctly carve the pattern space (Rumelhart, Hinton, & Williams, 1986b). For example, to solve the 5-bit parity problem that we will be studying in this chapter, five hidden integration devices are required. However, as N increases, using this minimum number of hidden units poses difficulties. While N hidden units are required in principle, in practice networks armed with this minimum number have difficulty converging to a solution (Tesauro & Janssens, 1988).

Value units are more powerful than integration devices in the sense that a single value unit carves up a pattern space in a more complicated fashion than does a single unit that uses the logistic activation function. As a result, it is usually the case that a network of value units requires fewer hidden units than does a network of integration devices, even when both networks are faced with the same problem (Dawson & Schopflocher, 1992b). How many hidden value units are required to represent a solution of the 5-bit parity problem? You should have a solid answer to this question when you finish the exercises in this chapter.

21.2.1 First procedure for 5-bit parity

Run the Rumelhart program, and load the "5par.net" file. Manipulate the setup page until the following properties are all true:

- *Train with all value units*
- End after a maximum number of training epochs
- End when there are all "hits" and no "misses"
- Randomize patterns each epoch
- Train thresholds during learning
- *Start the weights in the range −1 to +1 by selecting "User Defined Starts For Weights", and using the tool to set the maximum weight to 1, the minimum weight to 0, and to use positive and negative weights*
- Default starts for thresholds
- *Maximum number of epochs = 5,000*
- Number of epochs between printouts = 100
- Learning rate = 0.01
- Minimum level of squared error to define a "hit" = 0.01
- Number of hidden units = 5
- No direct connections between input and output units

Press the "Start Training" button to begin training. Let the network run for 5,000 sweeps (or fewer). If it converges to a solution (i.e., 32 hits and 0 misses), record the fact that it converged (see table 21.1), and record the number of epochs of training that were required for this to happen. If after 5,000 sweeps it has not converged, record the fact that it did not converge in the table, and use the value of 5,000 for the total sweeps. Then, repeat this process by pressing the "Start Training" button again. Repeat until five different simulations in this condition have been conducted.

At the end of this first set of simulations, you should have established that a network of hidden value units with 5 hidden units is able to solve the 5-bit parity problem. The next set of simulations will determine whether 4 hidden units will suffice. Use the "Hidden Unit" tool to reduce the number of hidden units from 5 to 4. Then repeat the procedure above until the

Table 21.1 *Results to be recorded for the first simulation*

Run number	Number of hidden units	Converged?	Total sweeps
1	5		
2	5		
3	5		
4	5		
5	5		
6	4		
7	4		
8	4		
9	4		
10	4		
11	3		
12	3		
13	3		
14	3		
15	3		
16	2		
17	2		
18	2		
19	2		
20	2		

next five rows in your table can be filled in. Once this has been completed, reduce the number of hidden units to three for the next five simulations, and then finally reduce the number of hidden units to two to complete the final five rows of your table 21.1. You will not need to save any network results in this exercise.

Exercise 21.1

1. On the basis of the results that you have recorded in your version of table 21.1, what would you conclude about the number of hidden value units that are required to solve this problem? What evidence would you use to defend this conclusion?
2. Examine the "sweeps to converge" column for the simulations that converged in table 21.1. Can you make any conclusions about what the effect of reducing the number of hidden units is on the amount of time that is required to learn the problem? If you believe that there is an effect, then why do you think this effect emerges?
3. Imagine that you wanted to determine how many hidden units are required to solve this problem without conducting an experiment like the one that you have just performed. Speculate about how you might predict the minimum number of hidden units that are required.

21.2.2   Second procedure for 5-bit parity

The purpose of the second exercise is to explore 5-bit parity a little further. In particular, we will manipulate some of the default settings to explore the possibility that with a little bit of luck, and a great deal of patience, we can solve this problem *using only two hidden units*.

Run the Rumelhart program, and load the "5par.net" file. Manipulate the setup page until the following properties are all true:

- *Train with all value units*
- End after a maximum number of training epochs
- End when there are all "hits" and no "misses"
- Randomize patterns each epoch
- Train thresholds during learning
- *Start the weights in the range −2 to +2 by selecting "User Defined Starts For Weights", and using the tool to set the maximum weight to 2, the minimum weight to 0, and to use positive and negative weights*
- Default starts for thresholds
- *Maximum number of epochs = 5,000*
- Number of epochs between printouts = 100
- *Learning rate = 0.001*
- Minimum level of squared error to define a "hit" = 0.01
- *Number of hidden units = 2*
- No direct connections between input and output units

Press the "Start Training" button to begin training. The goal is to keep training this network until you get one that converges – you should find that this goal is attainable, but not very frequently. To move towards this solution, you will have to decide when the press the "Continue Training" button and when to press the "Start Training" button (i.e., when to reset the network) by observing its performance. If you have not obtained convergence after 10,000 sweeps, then you should probably start over! What you are more likely to find is that error is reduced to a frustratingly small level, but then the network stalls.

As you train the network, keep a record of what you have done by filling out a table similar to table 21.2, which provides some real data that I collected when I worked through this

Table 21.2   *Some of this author's sample data for the second exercise*

Run number	Total sweeps	Converged?	SSE at end	Misses at end
1	10,000	No	0.74	3
2	10,000	No	0.86	5
3	5,000	No	3.99	17
4	5,000	No	3.69	17
5	15,000	No	3.69	16
6	10,000	No	5.63	23
7	**34,347**	**Yes!**	**0.03**	**0**
8	5,000	No	4.02	19
9	**7,605**	**Yes!**	**0.05**	**0**
10	10,000	No	3.69	15

exercise as I wrote the chapter. Eventually, you should be fortunate enough to have a network converge to a solution. When this occurs, press the "Test Recall" button, create an Excel spreadsheet, and save this spreadsheet to examine later. If you are using a version of the program that does not use Excel, then save the results of training as a text file instead. You will need to examine this information to answer the questions below.

Exercise 21.2

1. From your simulation records, what would you estimate to be the probability of having a network converge to a solution when these settings are used?
2. Can you explain why in the majority of runs the network fails to solve this problem, but in some cases a solution is found? What is the difference between runs that might affect whether the network will converge or not?
3. How many hidden value units would you now say are required to solve the 5-bit parity problem?
4. Assuming that you were able to train a network to solve the problem, examine its connection weights and biases, as well as the responses of the two hidden units to each pattern that was presented. Can you explain how this network is solving the parity problem? If you cannot come up with an explanation – and it might be difficult! – can you describe the source of the problem?

CHAPTER 22

Scaling Up With the Parity Problem

22.1 Overview of the Exercises

The purpose of these exercises is to use the Rumelhart program to explore how multilayer perceptrons learn a very difficult benchmark problem: parity. You will be exploring two different versions of the parity problem: 5-bit and 7-bit. You will be examining the performance of two different architectures on these problems – networks of value units, and networks of integration devices. One of the main purposes of this exploration is to re-visit the issue of what type of network might be selected to deal with a problem. We first saw this issue when we considered network by problem type interactions in chapter 14.

22.2 Background

Rumelhart, Hinton, and Williams (1986a, 1986b) introduced the generalized delta rule by describing its performance when used to train multilayer perceptrons on simple benchmark problems. One of these problems was the parity problem that was introduced in the previous chapter. "This is a very difficult problem because the most similar patterns (those which differ by a single bit) require different answers" (1986b, p. 340). They explored parity problems ranging in size from 2-bit (which is the XOR problem) to 8-bit. They report the results of one of their simulations. It was a network trained on the 4-bit parity problem. Their network converged to a solution in 2,825 epochs with a learning rate of 0.5. They do not report any details about momentum, starting states of weights, etc. They do note, however, that for any problem that has m input units, a network of integration devices will require m hidden units to solve the parity problem.

Rumelhart, Hinton, and Williams (1986a, 1986b) include the parity problem because it played a key role in an important critique of old connectionism (Minsky & Papert, 1988). They give the impression that while this is a difficult problem to solve, their learning algorithm finds an elegant solution to the problem in a straightforward manner. However, others would dispute this view of parity. Some researchers have found that parity is nearly impossible for standard networks to learn, particularly as the problem is scaled up in size

(Tesauro & Janssens, 1988). Other researchers have been frustrated in attempting to compare the performance of new architectures with the standard one, because the new architectures can learn parity easily, but "control condition" results are extremely difficult to obtain with networks of integration devices (Dawson & Schopflocher, 1992b).

22.3   Exploring the Parity Problem

You will be exploring two different sized parity problems, with two different architectures, and examining two different learning rates. As the networks attempt to learn the problems, you should pay attention to the dynamics of learning. Is the network well behaved? Or does network sum of squared error (SSE) or the number of hits change at different rates during different parts of learning? Can the networks solve the problems? Or are the networks subject to local minima problems of the type that were probably observed in the last chapter?

22.3.1   Procedure for value units and 5-bit parity

Run the Rumelhart program, and load the "5par.net" file. Manipulate the setup page until the following properties are all true:

- *Train with all value units*
- End after a maximum number of training epochs
- End when there are all "hits" and no "misses"
- Randomize patterns each epoch
- *Train thresholds during learning*
- *Start the weights in the range −1 to +1 by selecting "User defined starts for weights", and using the tool to set the maximum weight to 1, the minimum weight to 0, and to use positive and negative weights*
- Default starts for thresholds
- *Maximum number of epochs = 5,000*
- *Number of epochs between printouts = 500*
- Learning rate = 0.01
- Minimum level of squared error to define a "hit" = 0.01
- *Number of hidden units = 3*
- No direct connections between input and output units

Press the "Start Training" button to begin training. Let the network run for 5,000 sweeps (or fewer). If it converges to a solution (i.e., 32 hits and 0 misses), record the fact that it converged table 22.1, and record the number of epochs of training that were required for this to happen. If after 5,000 sweeps it has not converged, press the "Continue Training" button to see if it will converge. If it hasn't converged after 10,000 sweeps, then record the fact that it did not converge in your table, and use the value of 10,000 for the total sweeps. Then, repeat this process by pressing the "Start Training" button again. Repeat until five different simulations in this condition have been conducted and the results have been recorded.

Table 22.1 *Results to be recorded from the first simulation*

Run number	Learning rate	Total sweeps	Converged?	SSE at end	Misses at end
1	0.01				
2	0.01				
3	0.01				
4	0.01				
5	0.01				
6	0.001				
7	0.001				
8	0.001				
9	0.001				
10	0.001				

After the results of the first five simulations have been recorded, use the learning rate tool on the setup page to reduce the learning rate from 0.01 to 0.001. Then repeat the procedure above to obtain the results of another five simulations at this smaller learning rate, recording the results as indicated by table 22.1.

Exercise 22.1

1. From your observations of the network during training at the first learning rate, in a few sentences summarize the characteristics of the dynamics of learning this problem at these settings. For example, did learning proceed in a regular fashion, or did the network "plateau" at certain levels of hits and misses?
2. From your observations of the network during training at the second learning rate, in a few sentences summarize the characteristics of the dynamics of learning this problem at these settings.
3. In a sentence or two, and on the basis of the two sets of simulations that you have done, what would you say the effect of reducing the learning rate was on this problem for this architecture?

22.3.2 Procedure for value units and 7-bit parity

Run the Rumelhart program, and load the "7par.net" file. Manipulate the setup page until the settings that were used in Section 22.3.1 are true, with the exception that the number of hidden units should be set to 4. Then repeat the procedure that was used above. At the end of this procedure, you should have a record (following table 22.2) of the data from five different

Table 22.2   Results to be recorded from the second simulation

Run number	Learning rate	Total Sweeps	Converged?	SSE at end	Misses at end
1	0.01				
2	0.01				
3	0.01				
4	0.01				
5	0.01				
6	0.001				
7	0.001				
8	0.001				
9	0.001				
10	0.001				

attempts to train the network on 7-bit parity with a learning rate of 0.01, as well as the data from five different attempts to train with a learning rate of 0.001.

Exercise 22.2

1. From your observations of the network during training at the first learning rate, in a few sentences summarize the characteristics of the dynamics of learning this problem at these settings. For example, did learning proceed in a regular fashion, or did the network "plateau" at certain levels of hits and misses?

2. From your observations of the network during training at the second learning rate, in a few sentences summarize the characteristics of the dynamics of learning this problem at these settings.

3. In a sentence or two, and on the basis of the two sets of simulations that you have done, what would you say the effect of reducing the learning rate was on this problem for this architecture? How does this compare to what you found with the 5-parity problem?

22.3.3   Procedure for integration devices and 5-bit parity

Run the Rumelhart program, and load the "5par.net" file. Manipulate the setup page until the following properties are all true:

- *Train with all sigmoid units*
- End after a maximum number of training epochs
- End when there are all "hits" and no "misses"
- Randomize patterns each epoch

- Train thresholds during learning
- Default starts for weights
- Default starts for thresholds
- *Maximum number of epochs = 5,000*
- Number of epochs between printouts = 500
- *Learning rate = 0.1*
- Minimum level of squared error to define a "hit" = 0.01
- Number of hidden units = 5
- No direct connections between input and output units

Press the "Start Training" button to begin training. Let the network run for 5000 sweeps (or fewer). If it converges to a solution (i.e., 32 hits and 0 misses), record the fact that it converged following table 22.3, and record the number of epochs of training that were required for this to happen. If after 5,000 sweeps it has not converged, press the "Continue Training" button to see if it will converge. If it hasn't converged after 10,000 sweeps, then record the fact that it did not converge in your table, and use the value of 10,000 for the total sweeps. Then, repeat this process by pressing the "Start Training" button again. Repeat until five different simulations in this condition have been conducted and the results have been recorded.

After the results of the first five simulations have been recorded, use the learning rate tool on the setup page to change the learning rate to some value that you desire (e.g., one of the ones used in a previous exercise, or one larger than the one just used – however, making it too large (e.g., above 0.5) probably isn't a good idea!). Then repeat the procedure above to obtain the results of another five simulations at this new learning rate, recording the results (and the learning rate) as indicated in table 22.3.

Table 22.3   Results to be recorded from the third simulation

Run number	Learning rate	Total sweeps	Converged?	SSE at end	Misses at end
1	0.1				
2	0.1				
3	0.1				
4	0.1				
5	0.1				
6					
7					
8					
9					
10					

Exercise 22.3

1. From your observations of the network during training at the first learning rate, in a few sentences summarize the characteristics of the dynamics of learning this problem at these settings. For example, did learning proceed in a regular fashion, or did the network "plateau" at certain levels of hits and misses?
2. From your observations of the network during training at the second learning rate, in a few sentences summarize the characteristics of the dynamics of learning this problem at these settings.
3. In a sentence or two, and on the basis of the two sets of simulations that you have done, what would you say the effect of reducing the learning rate was on this problem for this architecture?
4. In general, from your experience with these simulations, what can you say in a couple of sentences about how the two different architectures (value units and integration devices) deal with this particular problem?
5. *Bonus question: Choose a learning rate of 0.1, and repeat the above exercise using the 7-bit parity problem, integration devices, and 7 hidden units. How well does a network of integration devices fare with this larger version of the same kind of problem? How does this compare to the value unit architecture?*

CHAPTER 23

Selectionism and Parity

23.1 Background

Since its birth in the mid-1950s, cognitive science has been guided by the digital computer metaphor, and has developed functionalist theories that have largely (and deliberately) ignored the neural bases of mental phenomena (Calvin, 1996a, 1996b; Clark, 1989, 1993; Edelman, 1987, 1988, 1989, 1992). More recently, a strong reaction against this practice has produced two biologically inspired theories of cognition, *instructionism* and *selectionism*. While both of these approaches have emerged as challengers to classical cognitive science, it is usually argued that instructionist and selectionist theories are mutually incompatible (Edelman, 1987; Piattelli-Palmarini, 1989).

Instructionist or epigenetic theories view cognition as the ultimate product of neuronal growth. In its most extreme form, the developing brain is viewed as initially being a *tabula rasa* (Pinker, 2002). Connectionist networks, such as multilayer perceptrons, can easily be cast as examples of instructionism. Prior to training, connections among processing units are essentially structureless, because initial connection weights are usually small, randomly selected values. During training, the network is presented a set of external stimuli that affect the connection weights in a manner prescribed by a procedure such as the generalized delta rule. As a result, specific connection weights grow in size, structure is "written" by the environment into the network, and eventually the network develops into a system capable of mapping a specific function between its input and output units.

In contrast to instructionism, selectionist theories of cognition deny the extreme epigenetic claim that the brain is a structureless *tabula rasa*. Instead, selectionists assume that the initial stages of brain development involve the generation of a large and varied amount of structure. This structure provides a preexisting repertoire of responses to be elicited by the environment. The interaction between the environment and preexisting structure selects some responses as being more appropriate than others, and this in turn modifies the underlying neural architecture. Rather than being neuronally inspired, selectionist theories are drawn from our understanding of biology (Cziko, 1995). In response to an infection, biological systems produce enormous amounts of antibodies. Any antibody can be considered as a specific three-dimensional label whose shape binds with the shape of an antigen. Once labeled in this fashion, the antigen becomes a target of other mechanisms that will destroy it. Importantly, antibodies can be produced to completely novel artificial substances. This suggests that there is no limit to the range of different antibodies than an organism can create. The issue in immunology became explaining this vast potential diversity in the immune response.

Jerne (1967) provided an alternative selectionist theory of the immune response. According to his theory, an animal initially possesses a relatively small number of individual antibodies, but within this small number there is an incredible diversity of different antibody types. Essentially, the animal starts with a repertoire of antibodies that is capable of dealing with any possible future infection. When a particular infection is encountered, a particular (pre-existing) antibody will bind to the antigen. When this binding occurs, the antibody produces a large number of copies of itself. Jerne also was the first to draw the link between selection in immunology and neural adaptation. "Looking back into the history of biology, it appears that wherever a phenomenon resembles learning, an instructive theory was first proposed to account for the underlying mechanisms. In every case, this was later replaced by a selective theory. [...] Antibody formation that was thought to be based on instruction by the antigen is now found to result from the selection of already existing patterns. It thus remains to be asked if learning by the central nervous system might not also be a selective process; i.e., perhaps learning is not learning either" (p. 204).

On the one hand, selectionist theories maintain a high degree of biological plausibility. Several researchers have observed that in the first year of human life there is a dramatic increase in both the number of neurons and in synaptic density, but that this is followed by a longer period of time in which both of these factors demonstrate substantial declines (Sporns & Tononi, 1994). This is predicted by selectionist theories in which early neuronal growth provides a large repertoire of neural circuits that is later pruned by environmental exposure. On the other hand, the strong biological nature of selectionist theories has worked against their formalization. While computer simulations have been used to study some selectionist predictions (e.g., Edelman, 1987, 1988, 1989, 1992), they have not successfully modeled some of the higher-order phenomena that PDP models have been used to study. As a result, selectionist theories have not had a strong impact on cognitive science in general. In their acknowledgement that selectionist theories have not taken advantage of possible modeling strategies, Changeux and Dehaene (1993) point out that "the crucial issue remains to find a learning rule coherent with such a Darwinian picture" (p. 384).

Dawson (2004) hypothesized that the learning rule being sought by selectionist researchers might in fact be the kind of rule that has already been established in instructionist models. Specifically, there is no reason in principle why procedures used to train PDP models, such as the generalized delta rule, cannot be used in a selectionist paradigm. For selectionism to work, systems must possess a great deal of initial structure that can be selected as needed by environmental pressures. If a connectionist network was a) provided many more hidden units than would ordinarily be required, and b) provided initial connection weights they were not near-zero, but instead were much larger, and exhibited high variability, then it might be possible to use a rule like the generalized delta rule to select useful, preexisting processing units from a pre-structured network.

In the exercises below, this hypothesis is explored by varying two different independent variables. One is the distribution from which connection weights were randomly sampled prior to the training of the network. This manipulation was used to insert initial structure into the PDP networks prior to training. In the control condition, all of the weights were initialized by randomly sampling values from a rectangular distribution that ranged from -1 to $+1$. Structure was added to initial weights by changing the variability (but not the mean) of this distribution. This was accomplished by inserting a "gap" in the distribution. For example, in one condition, weights are selected from the range -2 to -1, and $+1$ to $+2$, but *not* from the range -1 to $+1$.

The second independent variable is the number of hidden units available in the network prior to training. In one condition, there are as many hidden units as there were input units. In a second condition, there are twice as many hidden units as there were input units. In a third condition, there are three times as many hidden units as there were input units. The basic idea behind this manipulation is that as the number of hidden units is increased, so does the potential number of different internal responses to stimulus patterns. This is particularly true when this manipulation is combined with a condition in which the initial connection weights are highly structured.

If connectionism can be used to implement selectionism using these manipulations, then in networks in which initial connection weights were highly structured, and in which there is a large number of preexisting hidden units, there should be a dramatic increase in learning speed. However, this should only occur under the appropriate combination of the two independent variables. If a large number of hidden units are used, but not a high degree of structure, then learning should slow down. Similarly, learning should be slower with a high degree of structure that is not accompanied by a large number of hidden units. These expectations are explored in the exercises below.

23.2 From Connectionism to Selectionism

23.2.1 Procedure for 27-hidden unit condition

Run the Rumelhart program, and load the "9par.net" file. Manipulate the setup page until the following properties are all true:

- *Train with all value units*
- End after a maximum number of training epochs
- End when there are all "hits" and no "misses"
- Randomize patterns each epoch
- Train thresholds during learning
- *Choose value of weights according to table below!*
- Default starts for thresholds
- *Maximum number of epochs = 5,000*
- *Number of epochs between printouts = 500*
- *Learning rate = 0.01*
- Minimum level of squared error to define a "hit" = 0.01
- *Number of hidden units = 27*
- No direct connections between input and output units

Use the tool to change the settings for the weights to ensure that the weights will be set according to the table below. In the first condition (1, 0, Both) the weights will be selected from the range −1 to +1. In the second condition (2, 1, Both) the weights will be selected from the ranges −2 to −1 and +1 to +2. In the third condition (3, 2, Both) the weights will be selected from the ranges −3 to −2 and +2 to +3. Press the "Start Training" button, and let the network train for 5,000 or less sweeps. When training stops, record whether the network converged, and the number of sweeps (maximum = 5,000) in the format of table 23.1. Repeat this procedure until five runs with these settings have performed. Then change the starting configuration of the weights to the next condition, using the settings given in table 23.1. Collect the data from the training of five new networks in this condition, recording the data in your table. Once this is done, change the settings for initializing the weights to the third condition given in the table below, and collect the data from five more training runs to fill the last rows in your table.

23.2.2   Procedure for 18-hidden unit condition

Repeat the previous procedure, but *use 18 hidden units instead of 27 hidden units.* Use the same settings, starting the weights in the range from table 23.2. Collect all the data that is required to fill out your copy of table 23.2.

23.2.3   Procedure for 9-hidden unit condition

Repeat the previous procedure, but *use 9 hidden units instead of 18 or 27 hidden units.* Use the same settings, starting the weights in the range from table 23.3. Collect all the data that is required to fill out your copy of table 23.3.

Table 23.1   *Data to be recorded for the first simulation*

Run	Maximum weight	Minimum weight	Weight sign	Number of hidden units	Converged?	Sweeps to converge
1	1	0	Both	27		
2	1	0	Both	27		
3	1	0	Both	27		
4	1	0	Both	27		
5	1	0	Both	27		
1	2	1	Both	27		
2	2	1	Both	27		
3	2	1	Both	27		
4	2	1	Both	27		
5	2	1	Both	27		
1	3	2	Both	27		
2	3	2	Both	27		
3	3	2	Both	27		
4	3	2	Both	27		
5	3	2	Both	27		

(*Note:* For some readers, the 9-bit parity problem might be too much for their computer. If this is the case, then do this exercise using the smaller 7-bit parity problem instead. If this is done, use 21 hidden units instead of 27.)

Table 23.2 Data to be recorded for the second simulation

Run	Maximum weight	Minimum weight	Weight sign	Number of hidden units	Converged?	Sweeps to converge
1	1	0	Both	18		
2	1	0	Both	18		
3	1	0	Both	18		
4	1	0	Both	18		
5	1	0	Both	18		
1	2	1	Both	18		
2	2	1	Both	18		
3	2	1	Both	18		
4	2	1	Both	18		
5	2	1	Both	18		
1	3	2	Both	18		
2	3	2	Both	18		
3	3	2	Both	18		
4	3	2	Both	18		
5	3	2	Both	18		

(*Note:* For some readers, the 9-bit parity problem might be too much for their computer. If this is the case, then do this exercise using the smaller 7-bit parity problem instead. If this is done, use 14 hidden units instead of 18.)

Table 23.3 Data to be recorded for the third simulation

Run	Maximum weight	Minimum weight	Weight sign	Number of hidden units	Converged?	Sweeps to converge
1	1	0	Both	9		
2	1	0	Both	9		
3	1	0	Both	9		
4	1	0	Both	9		
5	1	0	Both	9		
1	2	1	Both	9		
2	2	1	Both	9		
3	2	1	Both	9		
4	2	1	Both	9		
5	2	1	Both	9		
1	3	2	Both	9		
2	3	2	Both	9		
3	3	2	Both	9		
4	3	2	Both	9		
5	3	2	Both	9		

(*Note:* For some readers, the 9-bit parity problem might be too much for their computer. If this is the case, then do this exercise using the smaller 7-bit parity problem instead. If this is done, use 7 hidden units instead of 9.)

Exercise 23.1

1. Examine the results that you have recorded in your tables. What are your general conclusions about how the manipulations of the starting states of the weights, and the number of hidden units, affect the ability to solve this problem?

2. In the exercises above, structure was manipulated in a fairly coarse manner, by varying the distribution from which connection weights were randomly initialized. Can you think of other ways in which structure could be inserted into a network prior to the start of training?

CHAPTER 24

Interpreting a Small Network

24.1 Background

In general, most cognitive scientists and psychologists approach research questions by using a form of reverse engineering. They start with an intact person, agent, or system and concern themselves with analyzing it into its components in order to determine the internal functions or mechanisms that are responsible for causing their subject's behavior (Cummins, 1983). Usually, this is a difficult task because researchers only have direct access to the behavior itself, and cannot directly observe the internal components that produce it. As a result, they must observe changes in the behavior that occur when changes are made in the stimulus environment in which the subject is embedded. By varying the environment, and by noting resulting changes in behavior, researchers hope to build up a strong case of evidence in support of their inferences about the internal nature of their subject. This has been called the analytic approach (Dawson, 2004).

Given the diversity of the research topics in cognitive science, it is not surprising that the analytic approach is not the only one that researchers have adopted. Many researchers are currently interested in exploring a synthetic approach to cognitive science (Pfeifer & Scheier, 1999). In the synthetic approach, researchers start with a set of internal components. They then put these components together – they synthesize a system – to observe the resulting behavior. The logic of this approach is that when a small set of components interact in some nonlinear fashion, and are furthermore parts of a system that is embedded in an environment that affects it nonlinearly, the result is an emergent set of behaviors that are far more complicated than one might have originally expected.

Some researchers have argued that because simple systems can produce surprising and complicated behavior, the synthetic approach will produce theories that are simpler than those that will arise from the analytic approach (Braitenberg, 1984). Braitenberg explicitly makes this point with his law of uphill analysis and downhill synthesis. His general point is that the analytic approach usually attributes more behavioral complexity to the internal workings of an agent than is necessary. Braitenberg believes that the analytic approach neglects the effect of the environment on the behavior of an organism. Because the synthetic approach begins by constructing an agent, and then observing its behavior when it is embedded in an environment, Braitenberg believes that it will develop theories that contain well understood and simple parts, and that are open to the explicit role of the environment. It is Braitenberg's view that by building behaving agents, cognitive science theories will be both simple and comprehendible.

One of the reasons that Braitenberg believes that the synthetic approach will produce theories that are easier to understand is because of his view that if one can construct an artifact, one must also understand what was constructed. At first glance, this view seems to make sense. For example, I would expect that the engineers who designed my car have a far better understanding of its workings than do I. However, with a more careful examination it is possible to realize that Braitenberg's view is not always going to be correct. For example, in cognitive science it is quite easy to construct a model that performs some task of interest, but which may also be enormously difficult to understand.

The connectionist models that we have been exploring in this book provide good examples of models that can be easily constructed, but which may not be easily understood. On one hand, it is fairly straightforward to design a set of input and output representations for a problem of interest, and to then use these representations to train the network to discover some mapping between stimulus and response. A general-purpose learning rule, such as the generalized delta rule, is completely capable of discovering this mapping even in circumstances where its nature is completely unknown to the original designer of the input and output representations. For this reason, it has been noted by some that no networks provide the opportunity for creating intelligence without requiring that intelligence be understood (Hillis, 1988).

On the other hand, after designing a training set, and after successfully training a network with it, it is quite likely that a researcher may have very little understanding of how the network represents the relationship between inputs and outputs. Leading connectionist researchers have freely admitted that one problem with artificial neural networks is the difficulty in interpreting their internal structure. "One thing that connectionist networks have in common with brains is that if you open them up and peer inside, all you can see is a big pile of goo" (Mozer & Smolensky, 1989). It has also been argued that the difficulty that connectionists have in describing their algorithms places a severe limit on connectionism's potential contributions to cognitive science (McCloskey, 1991).

It would appear that the law of uphill analysis and downhill synthesis does not universally apply. We can create networks easily, but this does not ensure that they are easy to understand. Alas, if connectionist networks are going to contribute to the theory of cognitive science, then researchers are going to have to face this difficulty, and are going to have to unravel the internal workings of the models that they have created.

Of course, connectionist cognitive scientists are acutely aware of this situation. There have been many techniques developed for extracting "programs" from the networks that have discovered them. For example, one strategy is to perform graphical or statistical analyses of connection weights in an attempt to define the structure of a trained network (Hanson & Burr, 1990; Hinton, 1986). A second approach is to analyze network behaviour in such a way that one can redescribe a network in more Classical, rule-like terms (Gallant, 1993; Omlin & Giles, 1996). A third approach is to map out the response characteristics of units within the network in an attempt to identify the features to which these processors are sensitive (Dawson, 2004; Dawson,

Boechler, & Valsangkar-Smyth, 2000; Dawson, Medler, & Berkeley, 1997; Dawson, Medler et al., 2000; Dawson & Piercey, 2001; Moorhead, Haig, & Clement, 1989).

The analysis of the internal structure of trained networks is a necessary component of connectionist cognitive science. Unfortunately, the fact that analysis is necessary does not mean that it is easy. The purpose of the exercise below is to acquaint the reader with this sad truth. The exercise will provide the reader with all of the details concerning a very small network trained to accomplish a very straightforward mapping between input and output. On the basis of this information, the reader is required to explain how this simple network actually works. Some of my students have found this particular exercise to be challenging, and very soon in this book we will explore some techniques for trying to make network interpretation a bit more straightforward. For the time being, take consolation in the fact that the network described below is presented for a particular historic reason. Many years ago, Don Schopflocher and I spent much of an afternoon interpreting this particular network. When we realized its simple and elegant nature, we spent the rest of the afternoon chiding each other about how dense we were. We then got to work on new techniques that would prevent us from wasting that kind of time in the future!

24.2   A Small Network

The network of interest to us in this exercise is a small system that has learned to solve the 4-bit parity problem. The network consists of four input units, each of which can either be turned off on or off. If an input unit is on, then it is given an activity of $+1$. If an input unit is off, then it is given an activity of -1. The four input units are all connected to two hidden value units; that is, processing units that use a Gaussian activation function. These two hidden units are then connected to a single output unit that is also a value unit. The network is trained to map a particular relationship between the input units and the output unit. If an even number of input units are turned on, then the output unit is trained to turn off (that is, to adopt an activity of 0). If an odd number of input units are turned on, then the output unit is trained to turn on (that is, to adopt an activity of 1). The relationship between the input units in the output unit for the 16 possible patterns that can be presented to this network can be seen in table 24.1.

The data provided in table 24.1 were used to train a network of value units to provide the desired stimulus/response mapping. After successfully learning to solve this problem, each hidden unit had been assigned a particular bias value (that is, the value of μ in the Gaussian equation), and the weight from each input unit to a hidden unit had also been assigned a definite value. The bias and weight values for each hidden unit are provided in table 24.2.

A second result of training was the assignment of values to the connections between the two hidden units and the output unit, as well as the assignment of a bias value to the output unit. The values that were assigned can be seen in table 24.3.

The pattern of connectivity that is given in tables 24.2 and 24.3 defines a network of value units that can solve the 4-bit parity problem that was defined earlier. Each input pattern in this problem produces particular levels of activity in the hidden units, which in turn produces

Table 24.1   *The relationship between inputs and outputs for one version of the 4-parity problem*

Pattern	Input 1	Input 2	Input 3	Input 4	Output
1	−1	−1	−1	−1	0
2	−1	−1	−1	+1	1
3	−1	−1	+1	−1	1
4	−1	−1	+1	+1	0
5	−1	+1	−1	−1	1
6	−1	+1	−1	+1	0
7	−1	+1	+1	−1	0
8	−1	+1	+1	+1	1
9	+1	−1	−1	−1	1
10	+1	−1	−1	+1	0
11	+1	−1	+1	−1	0
12	+1	−1	+1	+1	1
13	+1	+1	−1	−1	0
14	+1	+1	−1	+1	1
15	+1	+1	+1	−1	1
16	+1	+1	+1	+1	0

Table 24.2   *Hidden unit weights and biases for a network trained on the table 24.1 problem*

Input unit	Hidden 1	Hidden 2
1	0.58	0.63
2	0.59	0.58
3	0.57	0.64
4	0.59	0.62
Bias	−1.21	1.28

Table 24.3   *Output unit weights and bias for a network trained on the table 24.1 problem*

Hidden unit	Output
1	1.00
2	1.00
Bias	1.00

activity in the output unit. Table 24.4 provides the activity in the two hidden units and in the output unit that is produced by each of the 16 input patterns in the training set after the network has converged to a solution to the problem. If one compares the output unit activities in this table to the desired output activities that were provided earlier, then one will see that the network is generating responses that are acceptably accurate.

Table 24.4 *Responses of the hidden units and the output unit from a network that has learned the problem in table 24.1*

Pattern	Unit activity		
	Hidden 1	**Hidden 2**	**Output**
1	0.0192	0.0000	0.0482
2	0.9887	0.0000	0.9996
3	0.9987	0.0000	1.0000
4	0.0107	0.0085	0.0483
5	0.9887	0.0000	0.9996
6	0.0079	0.0032	0.0459
7	0.0107	0.0045	0.0471
8	0.0000	0.9847	0.9999
9	0.9950	0.0000	0.9999
10	0.0092	0.0073	0.0474
11	0.0124	0.0099	0.0492
12	0.0000	0.9972	0.9998
13	0.0092	0.0038	0.0464
14	0.0000	0.9748	0.9992
15	0.0000	0.9922	1.0000
16	0.0000	0.0115	0.0460

24.3 Interpreting This Small Network

When someone says that they have interpreted the internal structure of a network, what do they mean? Depending on the type of network that has been trained, the type of problem that the network has learned to solve, and the kinds of representations that the network has developed, there probably is no definitive answer to this question.

24.3.1 General instructions

For the present exercise, we can focus on one plausible answer to this question. The internal structure of the network above could be said to be interpreted if we provided an account of what feature the first hidden unit was detecting, an account of what feature a second hidden unit was detecting, and an account of how these two feature detectors were being combined to dictate the response of the network in its output unit activity. What kind of evidence would be required to provide these accounts? One source of evidence would be the pattern of connectivity in the network. A second source of evidence would be the activity produced in different components of the network by different input patterns. All of this information is provided in the tables above. Your task in the exercise below is to use this information to answer questions about the functional role of the different network components.

Exercise 24.1

1. What feature is being detected by Hidden Unit 1?
2. How do the connection weights and bias for Hidden Unit 1 permit it to detect this feature? (Remember that when an input unit is "off", it has an activation value of -1.)
3. What feature is being detected by Hidden Unit 2?
4. How do the connection weights and bias for Hidden Unit 2 permit it to detect this feature?
5. How are the features being detected by the two hidden units combined in order for the output unit to make the correct response to the 4-bit parity problem?

C**HAPTER** 25

Interpreting Networks of Value Units

25.1 Background

One of the main areas of interest in my own laboratory is the interpretation of PDP networks after they have been trained to perform some task of interest (e.g., Dawson, 2004). For the most part, my students and I have focused on interpreting networks of value units. The purpose of this chapter is to introduce the reader to some of the basics of interpreting this type of network.

25.1.1 Trigger features and neural networks

How do brain states represent the external world? One possible answer to this question comes from mapping the *receptive fields* of individual neurons in the visual system. For example, consider some of the pioneering work that involved studying the responses of cells in the frog's visual system (Lettvin, Maturana, McCulloch, & Pitts, 1959). Lettvin et al. began by assuming that the frog's eye is designed to detect visual patterns, and not just to detect levels of light. "If this should be the case, the laws found by using small spots of light on the retina may be true and yet, in a sense misleading" (p. 237). In consequence, "we should present the frog with as wide a range of visible stimuli as we could, not only spots of light but things he would be disposed to eat, other things from which he would flee, sundry geometrical figures, stationary and moving about, etc." (p. 237). When this approach was taken, they discovered a number of different receptive fields that corresponded to real-world stimuli important to a frog. For example, one type of receptive field that was found was called a convexity detector. A cell with this type of receptive field "responds best when a dark object, smaller than a receptive field, enters that field, stops, and moves about intermittently thereafter" (p. 254). For this reason, Lettvin et al. were tempted to call convexity detectors "bug perceivers".

Results like this from visual neuroscience eventually led to the so-called *neuron doctrine* for perceptual psychology (Barlow, 1972). According to that doctrine, "a description of that activity of a single nerve cell which is transmitted to and influences other nerve cells, and of a nerve cell's response to such influences from other cells, is a complete enough description for functional understanding of the nervous system" (p. 380). For sensory cells, this description requires identifying a neuron's receptive field, using techniques like those used by Lettvin et al. (1959).

A receptive field can be thought of as a neural representation of an ideal visual pattern. When a visual stimulus stimulates the receptive field of a neuron, and has an appearance that is an exact match to the receptive field's pattern, then it will produce maximum activity in the cell. In other words, the neuron will generate action potentials at its maximum frequency. In this case, the visual stimulus would be called the *trigger feature* for that cell. If the appearance of the visual stimulus differs from the pattern of the cell's receptive field, then the neuron will generate a weaker response (e.g., produce action potentials at a much lower frequency). The greater the difference between a stimulus and the receptive field, the smaller is the response of the neuron.

According to Barlow's (1972) neuron doctrine, if we could identify all of the trigger features of the neurons responsible for perception, then we would have a complete theory of perception. The validity of the neuron doctrine is a controversial issue. However, regardless of this controversy, it is possible that the neuron doctrine can be usefully applied to connectionist networks. In particular, one approach to interpreting the functional role of a hidden unit in a network would be to identify the trigger feature of that unit if such a feature existed.

25.1.2   Identifying trigger features for hidden integration devices

For some connectionist architectures, identifying the trigger feature for a hidden unit is quite straightforward. If the units in a network employ a monotonic activation function, such as the sigmoid-shaped function used in integration devices, then one can define the trigger feature by simply examining the connection weights that feed into the unit (Dawson, 2004). In order to produce maximum activity in the unit, the trigger feature must generate the highest possible net input. What pattern of input signals will do this? If the maximum net input is being produced, then this means that every positive connection feeding into a unit transmits a signal from an input unit that is generating its highest possible activity (i.e., the highest possible value for an input unit in the set of input patterns). Furthermore, if the maximum net input is being generated, then it must also be the case that every negative connection feeding into a unit carries a signal from an input unit that is generating its smallest possible activity (i.e., the lowest possible value for an input unit in the set of input patterns), Thus, the trigger feature is the one input pattern that has the highest possible input value assigned to each positive connection weight, and the lowest possible input value assigned to each negative weight, with these positive and negative weights all feeding into a single hidden integration device. This simple kind of technique has been successfully used to interpret the internal structure of a network that has been used to model some of the processes of early vision (Dawson, Kremer, & Gannon 1994).

25.1.3   Value units, trigger planes, and bands

Identifying the trigger features for hidden units in other kinds of connectionist architectures is not as straightforward. In particular, when the hidden unit is a value unit, it will not have a single trigger feature. Instead, there will be a family of patterns in which each member of the family will be able to generate the maximum activity in the hidden value unit. Identifying the trigger feature for the unit requires that all of the members of this family of patterns be determined. Unfortunately, it is difficult to do this just by inspecting connection weights.

Why do hidden value units have more than one trigger feature? Imagine a hidden value unit that has a bias of 0 (that is, that has $\mu = 0$ in the Gaussian equation for its activation function). A trigger feature is a pattern that will produce maximum activity in the unit. For this particular value unit, this will occur when the net input is equal to μ (i.e., equal to 0). However, the net input is simply the inner product between the vector representing the unit's weights and the vector representing the input pattern (see Dawson, 2004, chapter 9). When this inner product is equal to 0, then this means that the two vectors are orthogonal to one another. So, we can ask how many input patterns (in principle) are orthogonal to the vector of connection weights? The answer is (in principle) an infinite number of input patterns – because *any* input pattern whose vector falls in the plane that is perpendicular to the vector of connection weights will itself be orthogonal to the weight vector. In other words, for value units there is no such thing as a "trigger feature". Instead, there is a "trigger plane", and any pattern that lies in this plane will produce maximum activity in the unit.

In practice, of course, a training set is composed of a finite number of patterns. For a particular hidden unit, a subset of these patterns will lie in the "trigger plane", and all will produce maximum activity in the hidden unit. Another subset of these patterns is likely to be related, in the sense that the patterns all lie in a plane, but this plane is not orthogonal to the vector that represents the hidden unit's connection weights. Still another subset of patterns is likely to be related by falling into yet another nonorthogonal plane.

The first main practical implication of this geometric account of the relationship between subsets of patterns and the weights that feed into a hidden unit is that many different patterns will produce the same level of activity in the hidden unit. That is, if several different input patterns all lie in the same plane, then they all will produce the same level of activity in the hidden unit. If the plane that they fall into is the "trigger plane", then they will all produce activity of 1. If the plane that they fall into is some other plane, then they will all produce the same activity in the hidden unit, but this activity will be less than 1.

The second main practical implication of this geometric account is that in a finite set of training patterns, the patterns that are presented to the network will only fall into a small set of planes. What this means is that if one were to examine the different activations produced in a hidden unit by a finite set of patterns, one would expect to only see a small number of different activation values. For example, let us imagine that in a training set of 100 different patterns, all of the patterns could be classified as falling into one of three different planes (where the planes are being considered in terms of their orientation to a vector of hidden unit weights). We would predict in this case that we would only observe three different activation values being produced in a hidden unit (i.e., one for each plane), and that each of these values would be produced by more than one pattern (i.e., the different patterns that would fall into a plane).

Together, these two practical implications suggest one way in which a good deal of information about what a hidden unit is detecting could be revealed by plotting hidden unit responses in a particular format. A jittered density plot can be thought of as a one-dimensional scatterplot, and one can be created for each hidden unit in a network of value units. The x-axis of a jittered density plot will be used to represent activation values produced in a hidden unit by different stimulus patterns, and will therefore range from 0 to 1 for a value unit. In order to generate a jittered density plot, one takes a pattern (e.g., one of the patterns in the set used to train the network), and presents it to the network. The activity that this pattern generates in the hidden unit for which the graph is being created determines the x-position of a dot in the jittered density plot. The y-position of the dot is a random number, and as such is meaningless. This is done to prevent different dots associated with the same hidden unit activity from overlapping. Now that x- and y-coordinates have been determined for the input pattern, it is represented with a dot in the jittered density plot at that (x, y) position. This process can then be repeated for every remaining pattern in the training set. When the plot has been completed, there will be as many dots in the graph as there were training patterns.

In many respects, the creation of a jittered density plot is carried out by following a procedure that is analogous to that used by Lettvin et al. (1959) in their examination of the frog's visual system. A variety of stimuli are presented to the network, and the behavior of each hidden unit is recorded. The results of "wiretapping" the hidden unit are then represented graphically.

A jittered density plot for a standard processing unit (i.e., an integration device) is usually not very informative, because it is not very structured. Ordinarily it is just a smear of dots across the whole width of the graph. However, for value units, the jittered density plot is often highly structured, for the reasons that were outlined above. Instead of a smear of dots across the graph, the jittered density plot for a value unit is characteristically organized into tight bands, usually with a great deal of space separating one band from another. Of course, all of the input patterns that fall into the same plane produce the same activity in the unit, which results in a band of dots stacked one on top of each other in the plot. Different planes result in different bands being generated on the graph.

The bands that are revealed in the jittered density plots provide a method for identifying the kinds of features that are being detected by each unit in the network. For example, in some of our earliest work on interpreting value unit networks, we were able to determine that the input patterns that fell into the same band on a jittered density plot shared certain input features. In studying a training set in which a network learned to solve different logic problems, we were able to use these features to determine how the network was solving the logic problem, and to make an argument that connectionist networks might be more symbolic than was traditionally thought (Berkeley et al., 1995; Dawson, Medler, & Berkeley, 1997). More recently, we have developed a much stronger formal understanding of why banding occurs, and have used it to predict and discover banding for other problems and for other architectures (McCaughan et al., 1999). We have also developed more sophisticated interpretation techniques than the purely local ones that we reported in 1995 (Dawson, Boechler, & Valsang kar-Smyth, 2000; Dawson, Medler et al., 2000; Dawson & Piercey, 2001; Leighton & Dawson, 2001; Medler et al., 1999).

25.1.3 Bands and definite features

How does banding in a jittered density plot aid network interpretation? The bands reveal subsets of patterns that "belong together", in the sense that they produce similar activity in a hidden unit. Using this information, we can then proceed to ask *why* the patterns belong together. There must be some reason, some shared feature or set of features, that results in a subset of patterns lying in the same plane in our geometric account of the relationship between input patterns and connection weights. In order to identify what patterns that belong to the same band have in common, we need to identify definite features that are shared by those patterns (Berkeley et al., 1995).

A definite feature is an input property or feature that is shared by all of the patterns that have been identified as belonging to the same band in a jittered density plot. There are two types of definite features. The first is called a *definite unary feature*. When a definite unary feature exists, it means that an input unit has the same value for every pattern in the band. For example, imagine that every input pattern in a band shared the feature that input unit 2 always had a value of 1. This is a definite unary feature, and we could represent it by the expression **IN2 = 1**. The same patterns can have more than one definite unary feature. For instance, it could also be the case that input unit 1 always had a value of 0 for this set of patterns. This would mean that **IN1 = 0** is a second definite unary feature associated with this band.

Definite unary features can lead to straightforward interpretation, because the feature is always expressed in terms of the value of an input unit. We should be able to assign a meaning to such features, because we know – from building the training set in the first place – what each input feature represents. For example, in the network trained to do logic that we have studied in my lab (e.g., Dawson, Medler, & Berkeley, 1997), input units 1 and 2 were used to represent a variable in the first sentence of a logical argument. The possible values of this pair of input units (i.e., {0,0}, {0,1}, {1,0}, or {1,1}) were used to represent four possible variables (*A, B, C,* or *D*). So, imagine that a network trained on this problem had a band in which the following two definite features had been found: **IN1 = 0** and **IN2 = 1**. By knowing what these two input units represented, we could then provide a more meaningful interpretation of the feature: for all patterns falling into this band, the variable in the first sentence of the logical argument was "*B*".

The second type of definite feature is called a *definite binary feature*. With this kind of definite feature, an individual input unit is not constant within a band. However, its relationship to some other input unit is constant. For instance, imagine that for all of the patterns in a particular band, input unit 1 took on two different values (0 and 1). Input unit 1 is clearly not demonstrating a definite unary feature. However, let us further note that it is always the case that when input unit 1 has a value of 0, then input unit 9 has a value of 1, and that when input unit 1 has a value of 1, then input unit 9 has a value of 0. This is an example of a definite binary feature, because the relationship that holds in the band is that the value of input unit 1 is opposite to the value of input unit 2. We would represent this definite feature as **IN1 ≠ IN9**.

Again, the fact that definite binary features represent properties associated with input units permits us to provide a more meaningful interpretation to the feature, because we (as programmers) should already know what each input unit is used to represent. Pretend that we have trained a network on the logic problem, knowing that input units 1 and 2 represent a variable in the first sentence in a logical argument, and that input units 9 and 10 represent another variable in the second sentence of this argument. Imagine that we had a band in a jittered density plot in which we had identified the following two definite binary features: **IN1 = IN9** and **IN2 = IN10**. We could use these two features to support the more meaningful claim that the variable in the first sentence of the logical argument was the same as the variable in the second sentence of the logical argument. Using this sort of interpretative approach, Berkeley et al. (1995) were able to interpret the internal structure of a network trained to do the logic problem, and were able to show that the network had internalized rules of the sort that would be taught to philosophy students taking an introductory logic course.

25.1.4   Using descriptive statistics to identify definite features

In a large network of value units, there can be many different hidden units, and each of these hidden units can have several bands when jittered density plots are created for them. Clearly, it would be very useful if we could automate as much as possible the identification of definite features. Fortunately, once all of the patterns have been assigned to bands (which requires inspection of the jittered density plots), simple descriptive statistics can be used to identify definite features. In this section, I will briefly describe how this can be done to a single "band" of patterns, and then provide some ideas about how this approach can be applied to all of the bands in all of the hidden units in a network.

Imagine that we have identified a subset of training patterns as all belonging to the same band. We now want to examine this subset to identify any definite features that might exist. We do this by treating the input patterns as a set of psychological data, where each pattern is a subject, and each input unit value for a pattern is a variable that has been measured for that subject. For instance, in the problem that we will be working on later in this chapter, each stimulus is represented as a pattern of activity over 15 different input units. Imagine that there are 50 patterns in a band that we have identified. We would be applying descriptive statistics to a data matrix that consisted of 50 rows (one for each "subject") and 15 columns (one for each input "variable").

The first step is to apply descriptive statistics to each column of this data matrix. In particular, we need to calculate the mean and the standard deviation for each of the 15 input variables. We can use this information to identify definite unary features. If the standard deviation of a column is 0, then this means that there is no variation in the column, which indicates that the value of the variable is constant (and equal to the mean of the column) throughout the whole column. For example, imagine that for this band, we found that the standard deviation of the column for input unit 5 was 0, and that the mean of this column was 1. This information is sufficient for us to identify the definite unary feature **IN5** = **1**.

The second step is to use correlations to identify any definite binary features that might exist for this subset of patterns. This is accomplished by computing the Pearson product moment correlations between all of the columns in the data matrix. For our example, we will be producing a 15 × 15 matrix of correlations. Assume that the input unit activations are binary (i.e., either 0 or 1). In this case, a perfect correlation (that is, $r = +1.00$ or -1.00) represents the presence of a definite binary feature. Let us imagine that we found in this correlation matrix that the correlation between input units 2 and 7 was equal to $+1.00$. This would permit us to identify the definite binary feature **IN2** = **IN7**. Let us also imagine that we found a correlation of -1.00 between input units 1 and 5. This would permit us to claim that **IN1** ≠ **IN5**.

Clearly, to interpret an entire network, we would have to repeat these two steps for every band, in every hidden unit, in the network. The most straightforward way to do this is to copy the set of input patterns into a dataset to be analyzed by statistical software. In the problem that we will examine below, there are 432 input patterns, and each input pattern is defined by 15 input values, so we would begin by copying the input patterns as a 432 × 15 data matrix into a statistical package. We then would create one additional column to be added to this data, where each column corresponds to one of the hidden units in the trained network. In the problem that follows below, only two hidden value units are required, so we would be adding two columns to the database. A jittered density plot for the first hidden unit will frequently reveal three distinct bands, which we can call A, B, and C. We could label the first additional column "H1", for hidden unit 1. By inspection, we would determine which band in hidden unit 1 each of the 432 patterns belonged to. We would indicate band membership for each pattern by entering "A", "B", or "C" for this pattern in the H1 column. Similarly, it is usually the case for the problem that will be considering that the second hidden unit also reveals three distinct bands. We could label the second additional column "H2", and indicate band membership for each pattern by inspecting the jittered density plot, and entering "A", "B", or "C" to indicate which band each pattern fell into.

After the additional columns in the dataset have been filled out in this way, they can be used to select subsets of patterns for definite feature analysis. For example, we could tell the statistical package to only examine those patterns for which "H1 = A", and then compute the means, standard deviations, and the correlations, for the input unit values. This would provide all of the information required to analyze the definite features from Band A of Hidden Unit 1. We could then tell the statistical package to perform the same analyses, but only for those patterns for which "H1 = B", in order to analyze the definite features for the patterns that fall into the next band for that hidden unit. By repeating this procedure for all of the different labels in the additional columns that we have added to the dataset, we can quickly calculate all of the statistics required to interpret all of the bands for all of the hidden units in the network.

25.2 Banding in the First Monks Problem

In this section of the chapter, we will begin by training a network on a particular training set called the first monks problem. The purpose of training this network is to get some experience with identifying bands that can be found in jittered density plots obtained from each hidden unit in the network.

25.2.1 The first monks problem

The monks problems are a set of three different artificial training sets that have been used as a benchmark for comparing different algorithms for machine learning (Thrun et al., 1991). In this problem, each pattern represents a different monk, who is defined in terms of six different features: head shape, body shape, smiling, object held, jacket color, and presence of a tie. Table 25.1 indicates the possible values for each of these features, and shows how these features can be represented in a vector of 15 different input units. This particular representation is local, because each input unit stands for a particular feature value, and is turned on if the value is true, and is turned off if the value is false. For example, by using the key presented in the table, it can be confirmed that the input vector (1, 0, 0, 0, 1, 0, 1, 0, 0, 1, 0, 0, 0, 1, 0, 1) represents a monk with a round head, a square body, who smiles, holds a flag, has a green jacket, and wears a tie. Creating monks with all possible combinations of these features results in a complete training set that contains 432 different stimuli. The full datasets that define the monks problems can be obtained from the UCI Machine Learning Repository (Blake & Merz, 1998).

The different monks problems involve identifying a monk as belonging to a category (or not) on the basis of the features that they possess. We will be concerned with one of these

Table 25.1   *Local encoding scheme that uses 15 input units to represent the features that are required in the monks problems*

Head	Inputs 1–3	Body	Inputs 4–6	Smiles	Input 7	Holding	Inputs 8–10	Jacket	Inputs 11–14	Tie	Input 15
Round	100	Round	100	Yes	1	Sword	100	Red	1000	Yes	1
Square	010	Square	010	No	0	Balloon	010	Yellow	0100	No	0
Octagon	001	Octagon	001			Flag	001	Green	0010		
								Blue	0001		

tasks, called the first monks problem. In this problem, an input pattern belongs to the target category if it is consistent with the following rule: ((head shape = body shape) or (jacket color = red)). Of the 432 patterns, half of the stimuli belong to the target category, and half do not. We are interested in training a network, with fifteen input units, two hidden units, and one output unit, to correctly classify these patterns – that is, to learn to turn the output unit on to a pattern that is consistent with the rule, and to turn the output unit off to a pattern that is inconsistent with the rule. In this network, the output unit and the two hidden units are all value units. After training this network to solve the problem, we are particularly interested in examining the jittered density plots for the two hidden units.

25.2.2   General procedure

Start the Rumelhart program and load the file "monk15. net". This file defines a 15-input unit first monks problem for a network that has two hidden units. On the setup page, for this problem, you can train the network using all of the default settings after indicating to the program that you want to train will all value units:

- *Train with all value units*
- End after a maximum number of training epochs
- End when there are all "hits" and no "misses"
- Randomize patterns each epoch
- Train thresholds during learning
- Default starts for weights
- Default starts for thresholds
- Maximum number of epochs = 1,000
- Number of epochs between printouts = 100
- Learning rate = 0.01
- Minimum level of squared error to define a "hit" = 0.01
- Number of hidden units = 2
- No direct connections between input and output units

Press the "Start Training" button to begin training. The goal is to keep training this network until you get one that converges with a particular pattern to the jittered density plots for both hidden units. The network should converge to a solution fairly quickly – usually in less than 100 epochs. After the network converges, press the "Test Recall" button. Double-click the "Plot Jittered Density Plots Of Hidden Units" option in the top set of options. This will open a screen that will allow the jittered density plots for individual hidden units to be plotted to the screen. To see the jittered density plot for hidden unit 1, simply press the "Ok" button in this screen. A jittered density plot will be plotted on your computer. To see the jittered density plot for hidden unit 2, use the tool by the "Ok" button to change the hidden unit number from 1 to 2, and then press the "Ok" button to see a new plot.

The goal is to generate two plots that each can be described as having three bands, in order to obtain a solution similar to one that has been previously described (Dawson, 2004, chapter 12). Both jittered density plots will have roughly the same appearance: a very narrow band near 0, a broader, smeared band near 0.25 or 0.50 (sometimes this might actually look like two bands in this region), and a very narrow band near 1.00. Once this solution appears, inspect both plots to determine the range of activities on the axis that mark the start and the end of each band. (In a typical analysis, this information would be later used to label patterns in terms of what bands on the different units they belonged to, and record this information.) If this solution does not appear, exit the jittered density plot screen, and choose the option at the bottom of the screen to reset the weights and train the network again. Keep on training the network until the desired set of jittered density plots has been found. As you train different networks, pay attention to the appearance of the different jittered density plots. Do bands always appear? Are there other patterns of bands that are commonly seen? If you happen to get the desired set of jittered density plots on your first attempt, you should probably retrain the network several times in order to be able to make these sorts of observations!

Exercise 25.1

1. Consider hidden unit 1. What range of activities would a pattern require to fall into the first band? What range of activities would a pattern require to fall into the second band? What range of activities would a pattern require to fall into the third band?
2. Consider hidden unit 2. What range of activities would a pattern require to fall into the first band? What range of activities would a pattern require to fall into the second band? What range of activities would a pattern require to fall into the third band?
3. Are there any other common patterns of bands that are found when a network is trained on this problem? Describe the general characteristics of the two density plots for one other common pattern that differs from the one that you described above.
4. Did you ever find a solution that did not generate bands? If so, how frequently did this occur?
5. What are the implications of finding different patterns of bands for different networks that have been trained on the same problem?
6. How is it possible for different networks, trained on the same problem with the same settings, to arrive at different solutions to this problem?

25.3   Definite Features in the First Monks Problem

25.3.1   General instructions

After identifying banding in the hidden units of a value unit network, the next step would be to label each pattern in terms of which band it belonged to on each hidden unit. Statistics could then be applied to each band in order to identify definite features. Ordinarily, this type of analysis would be performed with some statistical software, as was described above.

For the final exercise in this chapter, this statistical analysis has already been performed for two of the bands that were found in the jittered density plot for hidden unit 1 in a previous example of this problem (Dawson, 2004). Table 25.2 presents the means and standard deviations for the 60 patterns that fell into the second band for this unit, and Table 25.3 provides the correlations among input values for this band. Table 25.4 gives the means and standard deviations for the 144 patterns that fell into the third band for this unit, and Table 25.5 lists the correlations among input values for this band.

The purpose of this exercise is to examine these tables in order to identify any definite features that are associated with these two example bands.

Table 25.2   *Descriptive statistics (means and standard deviations) for all of the input values of the 60 different patterns that fall into the second band of hidden unit 1*

	IN1	IN2	IN3	IN4	IN5	IN6	IN7	IN8	IN9	IN10	IN11	IN12	IN13	IN14	IN15
Mean	0.20	0.20	0.60	0.20	0.20	0.60	0.50	0.33	0.33	0.33	1.00	0.00	0.00	0.00	0.50
SD	0.40	0.40	0.49	0.40	0.40	0.49	0.50	0.48	0.48	0.48	0.00	0.00	0.00	0.00	0.50

Table 25.3   *Correlations between all of the input unit values for the 60 different patterns that fall into the second band of hidden unit 1*

	IN1	IN2	IN3	IN4	IN5	IN6	IN7	IN8	IN9	IN10	IN11	IN12	IN13	IN14	IN15
IN1	1.00														
IN2	−0.25	1.00													
IN3	−0.61	−0.61	1.00												
IN4	−0.25	−0.25	0.41	1.00											
IN5	−0.25	−0.25	0.41	−0.25	1.00										
IN6	−0.41	−0.41	−0.67	−0.61	−0.61	1.00									
IN7	0.00	0.00	0.00	0.00	0.00	0.00	1.00								
IN8	0.00	0.00	0.00	0.00	0.00	0.00	0.00	1.00							
IN9	0.00	0.00	0.00	0.00	0.00	0.00	0.00	−0.50	1.00						
IN10	0.00	0.00	0.00	0.00	0.00	0.00	0.00	−0.50	−0.50	1.00					
IN11	–	–	–	–	–	–	–	–	–	–	1.00				
IN12	–	–	–	–	–	–	–	–	–	–	–	1.00			
IN13	–	–	–	–	–	–	–	–	–	–	–	–	1.00		
IN14	–	–	–	–	–	–	–	–	–	–	–	–	–	1.00	
IN15	0.00	0.00	0.00	0.00	0.00	0.00	0.00	0.00	0.00	0.00	0.00	0.00	0.00	0.00	1.00

Table 25.4   *Descriptive statistics (means and standard deviations) for all of the input values of the 144 different patterns that fall into the third band of hidden unit 1*

	IN1	IN2	IN3	IN4	IN5	IN6	IN7	IN8	IN9	IN10	IN11	IN12	IN13	IN14	IN15
Mean	0.25	0.25	0.50	0.25	0.25	0.50	0.50	0.33	0.33	0.33	0.00	0.33	0.33	0.33	0.50
SD	0.44	0.44	0.50	0.44	0.44	0.50	0.50	0.47	0.47	0.47	0.00	0.47	0.47	0.47	0.50

Table 25.5   *Correlations between all of the input unit values for the 144 different patterns that fall into the third band of hidden unit 1*

	IN1	IN2	IN3	IN4	IN5	IN6	IN7	IN8	IN9	IN10	IN11	IN12	IN13	IN14	IN15
IN1	1.00														
IN2	−0.33	1.00													
IN3	−0.58	−0.58	1.00												
IN4	−0.33	−0.33	0.58	1.00											
IN5	−0.33	−0.33	0.58	−0.33	1.00										
IN6	−0.58	0.58	−1.00	−0.58	−0.58	1.00									
IN7	0.00	0.00	0.00	0.00	0.00	0.00	1.00								
IN8	0.00	0.00	0.00	0.00	0.00	0.00	0.00	1.00							
IN9	0.00	0.00	0.00	0.00	0.00	0.00	0.00	−0.50	1.00						
IN10	0.00	0.00	0.00	0.00	0.00	0.00	0.00	−0.50	−0.50	1.00					
IN11	–	–	–	–	–	–	–	–	–	–	1.00				
IN12	0.00	0.00	0.00	0.00	0.00	0.00	0.00	0.00	0.00	0.00	–	1.00			
IN13	0.00	0.00	0.00	0.00	0.00	0.00	0.00	0.00	0.00	0.00	–	−0.50	1.00		
IN14	0.00	0.00	0.00	0.00	0.00	0.00	0.00	0.00	0.00	0.00	–	−0.50	−0.50	1.00	
IN15	0.00	0.00	0.00	0.00	0.00	0.00	0.00	0.00	0.00	0.00	–	0.00	0.00	0.00	1.00

Exercise 25.2

1. Examine table 25.2. List any definite unary features revealed in this table.
2. If you found any definite unary features, what is their semantic interpretation, and what relevance does this interpretation have to the first monks problem?
3. Examine table 25.3. List any definite binary features revealed in this table.
4. If you found any definite binary features, what is their semantic interpretation, and what relevance does this interpretation have to the first monks problem?
5. Why are some of the cells in the lower triangle of the correlation matrix (table 25.3) blank, and why might this be important in terms of identifying the presence of definite *unary* features?
6. Examine table 25.4. List any definite unary features revealed in this table.
7. If you found any definite unary features, what is their semantic interpretation, and what relevance does this interpretation have to the first monks problem?
8. Examine table 25.5. List any definite binary features revealed in this table.
9. If you found any definite binary features, what is their semantic interpretation, and what relevance does this interpretation have to the first monks problem?

CHAPTER 26

Interpreting Distributed Representations

26.1 Background

In chapters 24 and 25, some successful steps were taken towards interpreting the internal structure of networks. However, in both of these chapters, most of the success was due to the fact that the hidden units could be interpreted locally. For example, in chapter 24, the two hidden units in the network that you interpreted were each detecting a particular feature. Similarly, in chapter 25, each band that you examined could also be interpreted as representing the presence of an individual feature. These representations were straightforward to interpret because they were local. This means that the interpretation just depended on local information (a single unit, a single band), and did not require considering information distributed across the network (e.g., represented in more than one unit, in more than one band on different units). It is important to realize, though, that even in value unit networks whose hidden units band nicely when plotted with jittered density plots, it is possible that local interpretations will not suffice. One of the interesting properties of PDP networks is that they can discover new, distributed, representations of problem solutions. The purpose of this chapter is to provide one approach for interpreting this kind of solution.

26.1.1 Subsymbolic representations in PDP networks

The potential difference between symbolic models and connectionist networks is a major issue in cognitive science (e.g., Dawson, 1998). For example, some have argued that while classical theories are symbolic in nature, connectionist networks are instead *subsymbolic* (Smolensky, 1988). To say that a network is subsymbolic is to say that the activation values of its individual hidden units do not represent interpretable features that could be represented as individual symbols. Instead, each hidden unit is viewed as indicating the presence of a *microfeature*. Individually, a microfeature is unintelligible, because its "interpretation" depends crucially upon its context (i.e., the set of other microfeatures which are simultaneously present (Clark, 1993)). However, a collection of microfeatures represented by a number of different hidden units can represent a concept that could be represented by a symbol in a classical model. In other words, according to this view, a symbolic interpretation of a PDP network is not localized to individual units, but is instead distributed across the microfeatures represented by several different hidden units at the same time.

The possibility that connectionist networks develop subsymbolic representations poses an interesting challenge for network interpretation. First, these sorts of representations are highly unlikely to produce interpretable local features of the type that we have been dealing with over the last two chapters. As a result, the techniques that we have explored to this point are not likely to succeed. Second, these sorts of representations require us to seek regularities that govern relationships between activities in different hidden units. As a result, we need to find a new technique that looks at hidden unit activities in such a way that these distributed regularities can be revealed. The next section briefly describes one plausible statistical analysis, called cluster analysis.

26.1.2   Cluster analysis and distributed features

Cluster analysis is a method for dividing a set of n observations into g groups (Ripley, 1996). For example, k-means is the name of a statistical method that separates data points into a prespecified (k) number of groups by minimizing the sum of squared distances from each data point to the center of its assigned cluster (Aldenderfer & Blashfield, 1984). In other words, when clustering is performed by k-means, stimuli that are assigned to the same cluster are nearer to each other than they are to stimuli that are assigned to different clusters.

How would we use cluster analysis to seek out interpretable distributed representations? Through much of this book, we have represented input patterns as vectors of input unit activities. However, other representations are possible. After a network has been trained, the activities produced in hidden units when an input pattern is presented can be thought of as a transformation of the input vector (see Dawson, 2004, pp. 214–15). So an alternative representation for an input pattern could be as vectors of hidden unit activations.

If input patterns were represented as the vectors of hidden unit activations that they produce, then cluster analysis would appear to be an ideal approach for grouping these vectors into meaningful groups. All of the patterns that are assigned to the same group would be related in the sense that they produced similar patterns of activation across a group of hidden units. In other words, they would be similar because they produced similar distributed patterns of activity. After patterns were assigned to groups on this basis, we could search for definite features amongst all of the patterns that belonged to the same cluster. This would provide a method for discovering features that were distributed across hidden units.

26.1.3   Cluster analysis, neural networks, and the number of clusters

Given that the primary goal of cluster analysis is to assign data to groups, an obvious question to ask is "How many groups should be used?" Unfortunately, no single method for determining the optimal number of clusters in a dataset has been agreed upon (Aldenderfer & Blashfield, 1984; Everitt, 1980; Gorsuch, 1983). This is reflected in the fact that many different methods exist for dealing with this issue.

While researchers have failed to develop a *general* solution to the number of clusters problem, this does not rule out the possibility for identifying a solution to this problem that can be usefully applied to a *specific* domain. Fortunately for us, the hidden unit activities of a trained connectionist network represent one specific domain for which the number of clusters problem can be solved.

Consider a network that has been successfully trained to map each member of a stimulus set to the correct member of a response set. We could then use this network to produce the vector of hidden unit activities for each stimulus presented to the network. We could then analyze this set of vectors with k-means cluster analysis in order to reduce this potentially large number of vectors into a much smaller number of clusters. Our hope is that these clusters will be interpretable – by examining the properties of each cluster, one should be able to determine how the trained network actually translated input features into an output response.

How many clusters should the set of hidden unit activity vectors be assigned to? The answer to this question depends upon one crucial piece of information that we have about the domain that is being clustered: there is a correct mapping from hidden unit activity vectors to output responses. We know this, because if the network has correctly learned the task that it was presented, then the network itself has discovered one such mapping. This knowledge can be used as follows: *we should extract the smallest number of clusters in which all the vectors assigned to the same cluster produce the same output response in the network.* In other words, every pattern that is assigned to the same cluster should produce the same output response in the network if all of the patterns in the cluster truly belong together. We should find the smallest number of clusters for which this property is true.

26.1.4   An example: choosing the number of clusters for a parity network

To illustrate this rule in action, let us consider a value unit network that has been trained to solve the 5-parity problem. This network uses two hidden units to solve this problem. It was trained using the Rumelhart program, with a learning rate of 0.001, connection weights starting in the range from -1 to $+1$, and all other settings at the default values. It converged to a solution to the problem after 5,566 epochs.

After training the network, each of the 32 input patterns could be represented as a vector of activities produced in the two hidden units. In order to seek out distributed interpretations for this trained network, k-means cluster analysis was applied to these hidden unit vectors. Of interest in this section is the basis for deciding how many clusters to assign the data to.

In my first pass at the data, I decided to assign the 32 hidden unit vectors to four different clusters. After this cluster analysis was completed, I used it to create a two-way frequency table for the data. This table records the number of instances in each cluster that correspond to each possible output vector for the network. For example, in the parity network, this table would indicate how many patterns that fell into cluster x were even parity patterns (desired output $= 0$) and how many patterns that fell into cluster x were odd parity patterns (desired output $= 0$). Table 26.1 provides the results of this frequency analysis:

By examining table 26.1, it can be determined whether another k-means analysis is required (an analysis involving partitioning the data into a larger number of clusters). If the cluster analysis is incomplete, then there will be more than one non-zero entry in at least one of its rows, indicating that members of the same cluster map onto two (or more) different network responses. In this case, another cluster analysis should be performed, with patterns being assigned to at least one additional cluster. An examination of table 26.1 indicates that the cluster analysis is not complete. Only one cluster (cluster 2) is "pure" in the sense that all of its members map onto the same output response. The other three clusters are mixed in the sense that some of their members map onto one response, while other members map onto the other. Because of this, a second cluster analysis, with $k = 5$, was performed. The frequency table for this second cluster analysis is presented in table 26.2.

This second cluster analysis is much better, for our purposes, than was the first. Four of the clusters are pure, with all cluster members mapping onto the same network response. However, one of the clusters (cluster 4) was still mixed. As a result, more cluster analysis is still required. The frequency table for the third cluster analysis, with $k = 6$, is given in table 26.3.

In this final frequency table, it can be seen that in all of the clusters every cluster member maps onto the same output response. As a result, we can conclude that the optimal cluster analysis of this 5-parity network is one in which k-means cluster analysis is used to assign the hidden unit vectors to six different clusters.

26.1.5   Interpreting clusters

After the hidden unit activities have been clustered, there are a number of different approaches that could be taken to interpreting the network's representations. One approach

Table 26.1   *Frequency table for the $k = 4$ cluster solution*

Cluster	Output		Total
	0	**1**	
1	7	14	21
2	3	0	3
3	4	1	5
4	2	1	3
Total	16	16	32

Table 26.2   *Frequency table for the $k = 5$ cluster solution*

Cluster	Output		Total
	0	**1**	
1	0	15	15
2	3	0	3
3	4	0	4
4	2	1	3
5	7	0	7
Total	16	16	32

Table 26.3   *Frequency table for the k = 6 cluster solution*

Cluster	Output		Total
	0	1	
1	0	15	15
2	3	0	3
3	4	0	4
4	2	0	2
5	7	0	7
6	0	1	1
Total	16	16	32

would be to consider input patterns once again as vectors of input unit values. However, now we also know that each input pattern can also be thought of as belonging to a particular cluster. Armed with this knowledge, we can treat each cluster in exactly the same way that we treated the hidden unit bands in chapter 25. That is, using the subset of input patterns that fall into a particular cluster, we can compute means, standard deviations, and correlations for all of the input values in an attempt to identify definite unary and binary features. The idea here is that these features are the symbolic interpretations that are supported by patterns of (uninterpretable) microfeatures that are distributed across the set of hidden units. For an example of this kind of network interpretation, see the analysis of the zoo network in Dawson (2004, chapter 12).

However, for some networks, this approach may not work particularly well. For instance, consider the parity problem. In this particular task, the meaning of a particular input unit (i.e., its effect on the network's output) depends crucially on whether other input units are on or off. Parity (the notion of an odd number of input units being active) is an intrinsically distributed notion! For this reason, definite features may not provide the best insight into how the network functions. Instead, a researcher may have to develop different measures that reflect the nature of the input units; measures which themselves might be determining how the network functions, but which may not be evident as definite features. In the parity problem, for example, one kind of measure that is important to consider is the total number of input units that are on (i.e., the sum of the input values), because whether this sum is odd or even determines the response of the network.

26.2   Interpreting a 5-Parity Network

We now turn to some exercises to give you the experience of interpreting a parity network. The network that we will focus on is the 5-parity network that was described earlier. We will consider two different approaches to interpreting the network, both of which will rely on the cluster analysis of hidden unit activations.

Exercise 26.1

After training the 5-parity network using the procedure described earlier, we discovered that the optimal *k*-means analysis of the hidden unit activities assigned hidden unit vectors to six different clusters. Table 26.4 presents a good deal of information about each individual pattern: the pattern name, the values of its five input units, the sum of its five input units, the activities that it produces in the two hidden units, the activity that it produces in the output unit, and the cluster to which the pattern belongs. The table is sorted in terms of cluster membership. In the first exercise, your task is to examine the data in this table in order to gain some insight into how this particular network is using its two hidden units to solve this version of the parity problem.

Table 26.4 Characteristics of the patterns that fall into each of the six identified clusters

Pattern	Input unit					Input sum	Hidden unit		Output	Cluster
	1	2	3	4	5		1	2		
2	0.00	0.00	0.00	0.00	1.00	1.00	0.48	0.01	1.00	1
3	0.00	0.00	0.00	1.00	0.00	1.00	0.48	0.01	1.00	1
5	0.00	0.00	1.00	0.00	0.00	1.00	0.38	0.09	1.00	1
8	0.00	0.00	1.00	1.00	1.00	3.00	0.42	0.00	1.00	1
9	0.00	1.00	0.00	0.00	0.00	1.00	0.33	0.17	1.00	1
12	0.00	1.00	0.00	1.00	1.00	3.00	0.48	0.01	1.00	1
14	0.00	1.00	1.00	0.00	1.00	3.00	0.39	0.09	1.00	1
15	0.00	1.00	1.00	1.00	0.00	3.00	0.39	0.09	1.00	1
17	1.00	0.00	0.00	0.00	0.00	1.00	0.38	0.09	1.00	1
20	1.00	0.00	0.00	1.00	1.00	3.00	0.42	0.00	1.00	1
22	1.00	0.00	1.00	0.00	1.00	3.00	0.44	0.00	1.00	1
23	1.00	0.00	1.00	1.00	0.00	3.00	0.44	0.00	1.00	1
26	1.00	1.00	0.00	0.00	1.00	3.00	0.39	0.09	1.00	1
27	1.00	1.00	0.00	1.00	0.00	3.00	0.39	0.09	1.00	1
32	1.00	1.00	1.00	1.00	1.00	5.00	0.44	0.00	1.00	1
1	0.00	0.00	0.00	0.00	0.00	0.00	0.99	0.82	0.00	2
10	0.00	1.00	0.00	0.00	1.00	2.00	0.99	0.80	0.00	2
11	0.00	1.00	0.00	1.00	0.00	2.00	0.99	0.80	0.00	2
4	0.00	0.00	0.00	1.00	1.00	2.00	0.04	0.00	0.00	3
21	1.00	0.00	1.00	0.00	0.00	2.00	0.03	0.00	0.00	3
30	1.00	1.00	1.00	0.00	1.00	4.00	0.03	0.00	0.00	3
31	1.00	1.00	1.00	1.00	0.00	4.00	0.03	0.00	0.00	3
13	0.00	1.00	1.00	0.00	0.00	2.00	0.02	0.95	0.00	4
25	1.00	1.00	0.00	0.00	0.00	2.00	0.02	0.95	0.00	4
6	0.00	0.00	1.00	0.00	1.00	2.00	1.00	0.00	0.00	5
7	0.00	0.00	1.00	1.00	0.00	2.00	1.00	0.00	0.00	5
16	0.00	1.00	1.00	1.00	1.00	4.00	1.00	0.00	0.00	5
18	1.00	0.00	0.00	0.00	1.00	2.00	1.00	0.00	0.00	5
19	1.00	0.00	0.00	1.00	0.00	2.00	1.00	0.00	0.00	5
24	1.00	0.00	1.00	1.00	1.00	4.00	1.00	0.00	0.00	5
28	1.00	1.00	0.00	1.00	1.00	4.00	1.00	0.00	0.00	5
29	1.00	1.00	1.00	0.00	0.00	3.00	0.00	0.48	1.00	6

1. Consider all the patterns that belong to cluster 1. In general terms, what hidden unit activities characterize these patterns? Inspect the input unit values for these patterns. Do there appear to be any definite features? If so, list these features out. Inspect the input unit sums for these patterns. Is there any regularity to these sums?

2. Consider all the patterns that belong to cluster 2. In general terms, what hidden unit activities characterize these patterns? Inspect the input unit values for these patterns. Do there appear to be any definite features? If so, list these features out. Inspect the input unit sums for these patterns. Is there any regularity to these sums?

3. Consider all the patterns that belong to cluster 3. In general terms, what hidden unit activities characterize these patterns? Inspect the input unit values for these patterns. Do there appear to be any definite features? If so, list these features out. Inspect the input unit sums for these patterns. Is there any regularity to these sums?

4. Consider all the patterns that belong to cluster 4. In general terms, what hidden unit activities characterize these patterns? Inspect the input unit values for these patterns. Do there appear to be any definite features? If so, list these features out. Inspect the input unit sums for these patterns. Is there any regularity to these sums?

5. Consider all the patterns that belong to cluster 5. In general terms, what hidden unit activities characterize these patterns? Inspect the input unit values for these patterns. Do there appear to be any definite features? If so, list these features out. Inspect the input unit sums for these patterns. Is there any regularity to these sums?

6. Inspect the single pattern that belongs to cluster 6. Characterize it in the general terms that you have been using for the other clusters. Can you see any reason for this pattern belonging to its own cluster, and not belonging to cluster 1?

7. On the basis of the answers that you have generated for the questions above, can you provide a very general description of how the network solves this parity problem?

Exercise 26.2

In the preceding exercise, we tried to understand the parity network by using a table to look at the properties of individual patterns that belong to different clusters. Another approach to interpreting the network would be to plot the input patterns in terms of their hidden unit activities in order to arrive at some sort of geometric understanding. Figure 26.1 presents a plot of the individual patterns on two axes, where each axis represents activation in one of the hidden units. The solid circles represent odd parity patterns, and the unfilled circles represent even parity patterns.

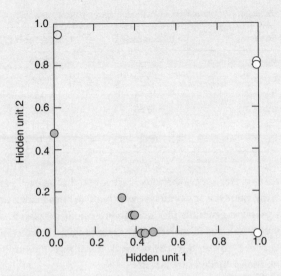

Figure 26.1 The 16 patterns plotted in the space defined by the activity that they produce in the two hidden units

1. Relate figure 26.1 to table 26.4 as follows: examine the hidden unit activities for each cluster in that table. Use this information to circle the data points that belong to each cluster on the figure.
2. Using the smallest number of straight lines possible, draw decision regions in the figure above that separate the odd parity problems from the even parity problems.
3. Remembering that the output unit of this network is a value unit, provide a general, qualitative account of how the two hidden units rearrange the input pattern space in such a way that the network solves this problem.
4. Can you find any relationship between your answer to question 3 above and your answer to question 7 in exercise 26.1?

Exercise 26.3

A final approach to understanding how this particular network solves the parity problem would be to consider the pattern of connectivity in the network. Often times this sort of examination makes much more sense only after performing the sorts of analyses that we have already conducted in this chapter. For the particular network that we have been studying, the output unit had $\mu = -0.93$. The weight of the connection from hidden unit 1 to this output unit was -2.02, and the weight of the connection from hidden unit 2 to this output unit was -1.89. In terms of the pattern of connectivity from input units to hidden units, this information is provided below in table 26.5.

Table 26.5   *Connections to hidden units in the parity network*

Source	Hidden unit 1	Hidden unit 2
Bias (μ)	0.06	−0.25
Input 1	−0.50	0.62
Input 2	−0.54	−1.01
Input 3	−0.50	0.62
Input 4	0.54	1.02
Input 5	0.54	1.02

1. In the previous two exercises, you should have found that an even parity pattern produces an extreme value (i.e., extremely low or high) in both hidden units. In contrast, an odd parity problem generally produces an intermediate value in one hidden unit, and an extremely low value in the other. By examining the connection weights in the table above, can you explain how the network transforms the notion of parity into this simpler notion of hidden unit activity?

2. By examining the connection weights above, can you come up with any account of why the one odd parity problem that falls into cluster 6 differs from all of the other patterns that fall into cluster 1?

CHAPTER 27

Creating Your Own Training Sets

27.1 Background

In using the software to do the exercises in this book, you have been working on training sets that I have provided you. Of course, the most interesting connectionist research to conduct is to train networks on problems that are of particular interest to you. This can easily be done, by creating your own training sets in a format that can be read by the software that you have been using. This final chapter describes the general properties of the .net files that are used to train a network. We then describe the steps that the user can take to define their own training sets for further study.

27.2 Designing and Building a Training Set

27.2.1 Design issues

The typical way for a student to start in my lab is for him or her, motivated by some curiosity about neural networks, to drop by my office. Usually, the student has some interest in a core topic in cognition or perception, and they want to explore that topic using connectionism. At some point in our first meeting they will ask me whether it is possible for a PDP network to learn to do x, where x is the core topic of interest to them. Now, it is well known that the PDP networks have the same in-principle power as a universal Turing machine (Dawson, 1998). So, the easy, and short, in-principle answer to their question is always "yes". Of course, the student is more interested in the longer, and harder, practical answer to his or her question. This answer involves actually creating a network, which is often the topic of a thesis. To create a network, a number of different design decisions must be explored.

The first design issue requires making a decision about what specific task will be learned by a network. For example, one of my former students was interested in studying the Wason card selection task with a neural network (Leighton & Dawson, 2001). When human subjects perform this task, they are presented four different cards and a logical rule. They have to decide which cards to turn over in order to test the validity of the rule. How could we get a neural network to perform an analogous task? We decided that we would present some representation of cards and a rule to a network, and that we would train the network to show with its output units which of the four cards it would turn over if it could. In general, in order to get a neural network to do some task of interest, you have to translate the task into some sort of pattern classification problem. This is particularly true for a network of value units, because for such a network the output units need to be trained to turn on or off, and cannot be trained easily to generate intermediate values.

This leads immediately to the second design issue. How does one represent network inputs and outputs? Consider one network that was trained to solve Piaget's balance scale problem (Dawson & Zimmerman, 2003). When children are presented this task, they see a real balance scale that has pegs equally spaced along the top of its arms. Different numbers of disks can be placed on the pegs. Children must decide whether the balance scale will tip to the left, tip to the right, or balance. How can this task be converted into a pattern classification problem, and encoded for a network? We decided to represent the balance scale configurations using 20 input units. The first five units represented left weight and were *thermometer coded*. In thermometer coding, a unit was turned on for every weight that was placed on a peg. So, if two weights were on a peg, the first two input units were activated; if four weights were on a peg, then the first four input units were activated. The second set of five units represented left distance and were unary coded. With this coding, only one unit is turned on to represent which peg the weights were placed on. For example, if the third peg were to be used, then only the third input unit in this group would be activated. The same encoding was repeated for the remaining ten input units to represent right weight (with five units) and right distance (with the remaining five units). Of course, other input schemes could be used. We could use thermometer coding for distance as well. We could use unitary coding for the number of pegs. We could use some completely different coding scheme for both properties. One of the important things to remember about representing inputs is that there will always be a variety of different encodings, and some might be easier to use or might generate more interesting results then others.

In terms of the output response for the balance scale network, two output units were used (Dawson & Zimmerman, 2003). If the left output unit was turned on, then this meant that the balance scale would tip to the left. If the right output unit was turned on, then this indicated that the balance scale would tip to the right. Problems in which the scale balanced were represented by zero values on both output units. Again, other output encodings are possible. For instance, we could have used three output units instead of two, where the third output unit would have been used indicate that the scale balanced.

A third, and perhaps subtle, design issue concerns what responses will be made by a network to its stimuli when training is over. For example, consider the Wason card selection network (Leighton & Dawson, 2001). In one version of this network, we trained it to make responses that were logically correct. However, this task is of interest to cognitive psychologists because human subjects usually make systematic errors. In other versions of this network, we trained it to make the responses that humans would make instead of training it to respond correctly. By examining these other versions of the network, we were able to gain some insight into how humans deal with the card selection problem.

A fourth design issue concerns the pattern of connectivity in a network. In particular, how many hidden units should be used? Furthermore, should there be direct connections between the input units and the output units? Sometimes these questions will be answered by having a particular theory about how the network should solve the problem. However, it's usually the case that these questions are answered empirically. Because network interpretation is usually the primary focus of research in my lab, we usually decide to explore a problem to find the smallest number of hidden units that can be used to reliably learn a stimulus–response mapping (Berkeley et al., 1995). In order to do this, you have to start out with an educated guess about the number of hidden units. For problem of moderate size, I might start out with the same number of hidden units as there are input units, or perhaps a slightly smaller number of hidden units. I would then train the network. If it learned the problem quickly, then I would reduce the number of hidden units and train it again. I would keep on doing this until I found a number of hidden units such that if I went below this number the network would not converge, but if I used this number of hidden units the network would converge. Unfortunately, there is no principled way to choose the correct number of hidden units before hand.

27.2.2   Format for a training set file

After deciding on a representation for the inputs and outputs of a training set, and after deciding about some issues concerning network connectivity, you are in a position to create a training set that can be read by the software packages that you have been using while going through this book. The training set is simply a text file that provides a little bit of information about network connectivity, that provides the set of input patterns, and that provides the set of output responses. This file can be created with any word processor, and then saved as a text file. After the file has been saved, it needs to be renamed to have the extension .net. The software that you have been using will only read files that have this extension.

All of the files that can be read by the software are organized in the same fashion. The first four lines in the file provide the number of output units, the number of hidden units, the number of input units, and the total number of training patterns. For architectures that do not use hidden units, the number zero must be in that spot in the file. The next set of lines present each of the input patterns in the training set. Each row represents one input pattern. Each number in the row represents a value for an input unit. Importantly, within a row different input values are separated by a single space. The remaining lines in the file represent the desired network response to each input pattern. The first line in this part of the file represents the network's response to the first input pattern, the second line represents the response to the second input pattern, and so on. Within a line, each value represents the desired value for an output unit, and again adjacent values are separated by a single space.

The numbers below provide an example file for the 3-parity problem. In this example, we see that the network will have one output unit, two hidden units, three input units, and there will be eight training patterns in total. The next eight lines present the eight input patterns. Notice that each line has three values in it, one for each input unit. The final eight lines represent the responses to each of the input patterns. Note that because there is only one input unit there is only one response value per line.

```
1
2
3
8
0        0        0
0        0        1
0        1        0
0        1        1
1        0        0
1        0        1
1        1        0
1        1        1
0
1
1
0
1
0
0
1
```

All readers need to do to create their own training set for the software used in this book is to create a text file that has the same general characteristics as those that were just described. The steps for doing this are:

1. Decide on a set of input pattern/output pattern pairs of interest.
2. Open a word processor (e.g., the Microsoft Notepad program) to create the file.
3. On separate lines, enter the number of output units, hidden units, input units, and training patterns.
4. On separate rows, enter each input pattern. Remember to separate each value with a space.
5. On separate rows, enter each output pattern. Remember to separate each value with a space.
6. Save the file as a text file.
7. In Windows, rename the file to end with the extension .net instead of the extension .txt. Remember that the software will only read in files that have the .net extension.
8. Your file can now be read in by one of the three programs that you have been using, and you can use the software to train a network to solve a problem that you are interested in.

Exercise 27.1

To complete this exercise, you will need to define a problem that could be presented to a network. You will have to say exactly how this problem would be represented. *However, you do not have to build the training set for the problem*. You only need to describe what it would look like if you did build it. If you wanted to take the next step and build the training set to present to one of my programs, then you could build your training set using the instructions that were given above.

1. In a short paragraph, describe the general nature of the problem that you would like translate into some form that could be presented to one of the networks that we have dealt with in this book.
2. If you were to build this training set, how many output units would you need?
3. What would each output unit in your network represent (i.e., what representation would you use to encode network outputs)?
4. If you were to build this training set, how many input units would you need?
5. What would each input unit represent (i.e., describe your input encoding)?
6. How many patterns would be in your training set?
7. In a short paragraph, answer the following question. If you were to build this training set, what architecture would you present it to, and why would you choose this architecture?

References

Aldenderfer, M. S. & Blashfield, R. K. (1984). *Cluster Analysis*, vol. 07–044. Beverly Hills, CA: Sage Publications.

Anderson, J. A. & Rosenfeld, E. (1998). *Talking Nets: An Oral History of Neural Networks*. Cambridge, MA: MIT Press.

Ballard, D. (1986). Cortical structures and parallel processing: Structure and function. *The Behavioral And Brain Sciences*, 9, 67–120.

Barlow, H. B. (1972). Single units and sensation: A neuron doctrine for perceptual psychology? *Perception*. 1, 371–94.

Berkeley, I. S. N., Dawson, M. R. W., Medler, D. A., Schopflocher, D. P., & Hornsby, L. (1995). Density plots of hidden value unit activations reveal interpretable bands. *Connection Science*, 7, 167–86.

Bever, T. G., Fodor, J. A., & Garrett, M. (1968). A formal limitation of associationism. In T. R. Dixon & D. L. Horton (eds), *Verbal Behavior and General Behavior Theory* (pp. 582–5). Englewood Cliffs, NJ: Prentice Hall.

Blake, C. L. & Merz, C. J. (1998). *UCI Repository of machine learning databases*. Irvine, CA: University of California, Department of Information and Computer Science. Available: [http://www.ics.uci.edu/~mlearn/MLRepository.html].

Blyth, T. S. & Robertson, E. F. (1986). *Matrices and Vector Spaces*, vol. 2. London: Chapman and Hall.

Boole, G. (1854). *An investigation of the laws of thought, on which are founded the mathematical theories of logic and probabilities*. London: Walton and Maberley.

Boole, G. (1952). *Studies in logic and probability*: Watts.

Braitenberg, V. (1984). *Vehicles: Explorations In Synthetic Psychology*. Cambridge, MA: MIT Press.

Brown, T. H. (1990). Hebbian synapses: Biophysical mechanisms and algorithms. *Annual Review of Neuroscience*, 13, 475–511.

Calkins, M. W. (1894). Association. *Psychological Review*, 1, 476–83.

Calvin, W. H. (1996a). *The Cerebral Code*. Cambridge, MA: MIT Press.

Calvin, W. H. (1996b). *How Brains Think*. New York, NY: Basic Books.

Carpenter, G. A. (1989). Neural network models for pattern recognition and associative memory. *Neural Networks*, 2, 243–57.

Caudill, M. & Butler, B. (1992a). *Understanding neural networks*, vol. 1. Cambridge, MA: MIT Press.

Caudill, M. & Butler, B. (1992b). *Understanding neural networks*, vol. 2. Cambridge, MA: MIT Press.

Changeux, J.-P. & Dehaene, S. (1993). Neuronal models of cognitive functions. In M. H. Johnson (ed.), *Cognition and Brain Development: A reader* (pp. 363–402). Oxford: Blackwell.

Clark, A. (1989). *Microcognition*. Cambridge, MA: MIT Press.

Clark, A. (1993). *Associative engines*. Cambridge, MA: MIT Press.

Cotman, C. W., Monaghan, D. T., & Ganong, A. H. (1988). Excitatory amino acid neurotransmission: NMDA receptors and Hebb-type synaptic plasticity. *Annual Review of Neuroscience*, 11, 61–80.

Cotter, N. E. (1990). The Stone–Weierstrass theorem and its application to neural networks. *IEEE Transactions on Neural Networks*, 1, 290–5.

Cummins, R. (1983). *The Nature of Psychological Explanation*. Cambridge, MA.: MIT Press.

Cybenko, G. (1989). Approximation by superpositions of a sigmoidal function. *Mathematics of Control, Signals, and Systems*, 2, 303–314.

Cziko, G. (1995). *Without Miracles: Universal Selection Theory and the Second Darwinian Revolution*. Cambridge, MA: MIT Press.

Dallett, K. M. (1966). Effects of within-list and between-list acoustic similarity on the learning and retention of paired associates. *Journal of Experimental Psychology*, 72(5), 667–77.

Dawson, M. R. W. (1991). The how and why of what went where in apparent motion: Modeling solutions to the motion correspondence process. *Psychological Review*, 98, 569–603.

Dawson, M. R. W. (1998). *Understanding Cognitive Science*. Oxford, UK: Blackwell.

Dawson, M. R. W. (2002). From embodied cognitive science to synthetic psychology. In Wang, Y., Johnston, R. H. & Smith, M. R. (eds) *Proceedings of the First IEEE International Conference on Cognitive Informatics (ICCI'02)*. IEEE Computer Society: Los Alamitos, CA, (pp. 13–22)

Dawson, M. R. W. (2004). *Minds And Machines: Connectionism and Psychological Modeling*. Malden, MA: Blackwell Publishing.

Dawson, M. R. W., Boechler, P. M., & Valsangkar-Smyth, M. (2000). Representing space in a PDP network: Coarse allocentric coding can mediate metric and nonmetric spatial judgements. *Spatial Cognition and Computation*, 2, 181–218.

Dawson, M. R. W., Kremer, S. & Gannon, T. (1994). Identifying the trigger features for hidden units in a PDP model of the early visual pathway. In R. Elio (ed.), *Tenth Canadian Conference On Artificial Intelligence* (pp. 115–19). San Francisco, CA: Morgan Kaufmann.

Dawson, M. R. W. & Medler, D. A. (1996). Of mushrooms and machine learning: Identifying algorithms in a PDP network. *Canadian Artificial Intelligence*, 38, 14–17.

Dawson, M. R. W., Medler, D. A., & Berkeley, I. S. N. (1997). PDP networks can provide models that are not mere implementations of classical theories. *Philosophical Psychology*, 10, 25–40.

Dawson, M. R. W., Medler, D. A., McCaughan, D. B., Willson, L., & Carbonaro, M. (2000). Using extra output learning to insert a symbolic theory into a connectionist network. *Minds and Machines*, 10, 171–201.

Dawson, M. R. W. & Piercey, C. D. (2001). On the subsymbolic nature of a PDP architecture that uses a nonmonotonic activation function. *Minds and Machines*, 11, 197–218.

Dawson, M. R. W. & Pylyshyn, Z. W. (1988). Natural constraints on apparent motion. In Z. W. Pylyshyn (ed.), *Computational Processes in Human Vision: An Interdisciplinary Perspective* (pp. 99–120). Norwood, NJ: Ablex.

Dawson, M. R. W. & Schopflocher, D. P. (1992a). Autonomous processing in PDP networks. *Philosophical Psychology*, 5, 199–219.

Dawson, M. R. W. & Schopflocher, D. P. (1992b). Modifying the generalized delta rule to train networks of nonmonotonic processors for pattern classification. *Connection Science*, 4, 19–31.

Dawson, M. R. W. & Shamanski, K. S. (1994). Connectionism, confusion and cognitive science. *Journal of Intelligent Systems*, 4, 215–62.

Dawson, M. R. W. & Zimmerman, C. (2003). Interpreting the internal structure of a connectionist model of the balance scale task. *Brain and Mind*, 4, 129–49.

De Wilde, P. (1997). *Neural Network Models*, 2nd edn. London: Springer.

Deese, J. & Hulse, S. H. (1967). *The Psychology Of Learning*, 3rd edn. New York, NY: McGraw-Hill.

Delamater, A. R., Sosa, W., & Koch, M. (1999). Elemental and configural processes in patterning discrimination learning. *The Quarterly Journal Of Experimental Psychology*, 52B, 97–124.

Duch, W. & Jankowski, N. (1999). Survey of neural transfer functions. *Neural Computing Surveys*, 2, 163–212.

Dutton, J. M. & Starbuck, W. H. (1971). *Computer simulation of human behavior*. New York: John Wiley & Sons.

Edelman, G. M. (1987). *Neural Darwinism*. New York: Basic Books.

Edelman, G. M. (1988). *Topobiology*. New York: Basic Books.

Edelman, G. M. (1989). *The Remembered Present*. New York: Basic Books.

Edelman, G. M. (1992). *Bright Air, Brilliant Fire*. New York: Basic Books.

Eich, J. M. (1982). A composite holographic associative recall model. *Psychological Review*, 89, 627–61.

Eichenbaum, H. (1992). The Hippocampal System and Declarative Memory in Animals. *Journal of Cognitive Neuroscience*, 4(3), 217–31.

Eichenbaum, H. (2000). A cortical-hippocampal system for declarative memory. *Nature Reviews Neuroscience*, 1(1), 41–50.

Eichenbaum, H., Dudchenko, P., Wood, E., Shapiro, M., & Tanila, H. (1999). The hippocampus, memory, and place cells: Is it spatial memory or a memory space? *Neuron*, 23(2), 209–26.

Everitt, B. (1980). *Cluster Analysis*. New York: Halsted.

Fodor, J. A. & Pylyshyn, Z. W. (1988). Connectionism and cognitive architecture. *Cognition*, 28, 3–71.

Freeman, J. A. (1994). *Simulating Neural Networks With Mathematica*. Reading, MA: Addison-Wesley.

Funahashi, K. (1989). On the approximate realization of continuous mappings by neural networks. *Neural Networks*, 2, 183–92.

Furumoto, L. (1980). Mary Whiton Calkins (1863–1930). *Psychology of Women Quarterly*, 5, 55–68.

Gallant, S. I. (1993). *Neural network learning and expert systems*. Cambridge, MA: MIT Press.

Gallistel, C. R. (1990). *The Organization of Learning*. Cambridge, MA: MIT Press.

Girosi, F. & Poggio, T. (1990). Networks and the best approximation property. *Biological Cybernetics*, 63, 169–76.

Gorsuch, R. L. (1983). *Factor Analysis*, 2nd edn. Hillsdale, NJ: Lawrence Erlbaum Associates.

Hanson, S. J. & Burr, D. J. (1990). What connectionist models learn: Learning and representation in connectionist networks. *Behavioral and Brain Sciences*, 13, 471–518.

Hartman, E., Keeler, J. D., & Kowalski, J. M. (1989). Layered neural networks with Gaussian hidden units as universal approximation. *Neural Computation*, 2, 210–15.

Hawkins, R. D. B. & Bower, G. H. (1989). *Computational models of learning in simple neural systems*. San Diego: Academic Press.

Hebb, D. O. (1949). *The Organization Of Behavior*. New York: John Wiley & Sons.

Hertz, J., Krogh, A., & Palmer, R. G. (1991). *Introduction to the Theory of Neural Computation*. Redwood City, CA: Addison-Wesley.

Hillis, W. D. (1988). Intelligence as emergent behavior, or, the songs of Eden. In S. R. Graubard (ed.), *The Artificial Intelligence Debate* (pp. 175–89). Cambridge, MA: MIT Press.

Hinton, G. E. (1986). Learning distributed representations of concepts. Paper presented at the 8th Annual Meeting of the Cognitive Science Society, Ann Arbor, MI.

Hinton, G. E. & Anderson, J. A. (1981). *Parallel Models Of Associative Memory*. Hillsdale, NJ: Lawrence Erlbaum Associates.

Honda, M., Barrett, G., Yoshimura, N., Sadato, N., Yonekura, Y., & Shibasaki, H. (1998). Comparative study of event-related potentials and positron emission tomography activation during a paired-associate memory paradigm. *Experimental Brain Research*, 119(1), 103–15.

Hornik, M., Stinchcombe, M., & White, H. (1989). Multilayer feedforward networks are universal approximators. *Neural Networks*, 2, 359–66.

Hunt, R. G. (1959). Meaningfulness and articulation of stimulus and response in paired-associate learning and stimulus recall. *Journal of Experimental Psychology*, 57(4), 262–7.

James, W. (1890). *The Principles Of Psychology, Volume One*. New York, NY: Dover Publications.

Jerne, N. K. (1967). Antibodies and learning: Selection versus instruction. In G. C. Quarton, T. Melnechuk & F. O. Schmitt (eds), *The Neurosciences: A study program* (pp. 200–208). New York: Rockefeller University Press.

Jevons, W. S. (1971). *Pure logic, and other minor works*. B. Franklin.

Kahana, M. J. (2002). Associative symmetry and memory theory. *Memory & Cognition*, 30(6), 823–40.

Kasabov, N. K. (1996). *Foundations of Neural Networks, Fuzzy Systems, and Knowledge Engineering*. Cambridge, MA: MIT Press.

Kehoe, E. J. (1988). A layered network model of associative learning: Learning to learn and configuration. *Psychological Review*, 95, 411–33.

Kintsch, W. (1970). *Learning, Memory, and Conceptual Processes*. New York, NY: John Wiley & Sons.

Kruschke, J. K. (1992). ALCOVE: An exemplar-based connectionist model of category learning. *Psychological Review*, 99, 22–44.

Kruschke, J. K. (1993). Human category learning: Implications for backpropagation models. *Connection Science*, 5, 3–36.

Leighton, J. P. & Dawson, M. R. W. (2001). A parallel distributed processing model of Wason's selection task. *Cognitive Systems Research*, 2, 207–31.

Lettvin, J. Y., Maturana, H. R., McCulloch, W. S., & Pitts, W. H. (1959). What the frog's eye tells the frog's brain. *Proceedings of the IRE*, 47(11), 1940–51.

Levitan, I. B. & Kaczmarek, L. K. (1991). *The Neuron: Cell and Molecular Biology*. New York: Oxford University Press.

Lewis, C. I. & Langford, C. H. (1959). *Symbolic logic*, 2nd edn. New York: The Century Co.

Lippmann, R. P. (1987). An introduction to computing with neural nets. *IEEE ASSP Magazine*, April, 4–22.

Lippmann, R. P. (1989). Pattern classification using neural networks. *IEEE Communications Magazine*, November, 47–64.

Long, J. M., Mellem, J. E., & Kesner, R. P. (1998). The effects of parietal cortex lesions on an object spatial location paired-associate task in rats. *Psychobiology*, 26(2), 128–33.

Martinez, J. L. & Derrick, B. E. (1996). Long-term potentiation and learning. *Annual Review of Psychology*, 47, 173–203.

McCaughan, D. B., Medler, D. A., & Dawson, M. R. W. (1999). Internal representation in networks of nonmonotonic processing units. Paper presented at the International Joint Conference on Neural Networks, Washington, DC.

McClelland, J. L. (1986). Resource requirements of standard and programmable nets. In D. Rumelhart, J. McClelland and the PDP Group (eds), *Parallel Distributed Processing* (vol. 1, pp. 460–87). Cambridge, MA: MIT Press.

McClelland, J. L. & Rumelhart, D. E. (1986). *Parallel Distributed Processing*, vol. 2. Cambridge, MA: MIT Press.

McClelland, J. L. & Rumelhart, D. E. (1988). *Explorations In Parallel Distributed Processing*. Cambridge, MA: MIT Press.

McCloskey, M. (1991). Networks and theories: The place of connectionism in cognitive science. *Psychological Science*, 2, 387–95.

McCulloch, W. S. (1988). Agathy tyche of nervous nets – the lucky reckoners. In W. S. McCulloch (ed.), *Embodiments of Mind*. Cambridge, MA: MIT Press.

McCulloch, W. S. & Pitts, W. H. (1943). A logical calculus of the ideas immanent in nervous activity. *Bulletin of Mathematical Biophysics*, 5, 115–33.

McCulloch, W. S. & Pitts, W. H. (1988). A logical calculus of the ideas immanent in nervous activity. In W. S. McCulloch (ed.), *Embodiments Of Mind* (pp. 19–39). Cambridge, MA: MIT Press.

Medler, D. A. (1998). A brief history of connectionism. *Neural Computing Surveys*, 1, 18–72.

Medler, D. A., McCaughan, D. B., Dawson, M. R. W., & Willson, L. (1999). When local isn't enough: Extracting distributed rules from networks. Paper presented at the International Joint Conference On Neural Networks, Washington, D.C.

Mendelson, E. (1970). *Schaum's outline of theory and problems of Boolean algebra and switching circuits*. New York: McGraw-Hill.

Minsky, M. (1963). Steps toward artificial intelligence. In E. A. Feigenbaum & J. Feldman (eds), *Computers and Thought* (pp. 406–50). New York, NY: McGraw-Hill.

Minsky, M. & Papert, S. (1988). *Perceptrons*, 3rd edn. Cambridge, MA: MIT Press.

Moody, J. (1998). Forecasting the economy with neural nets: A survey of challenges and solutions. In G. Orr & K. Muller (eds), *Neural Networks: tricks of the trade* (pp. 347–72). Berlin; New York: Springer.

Moorhead, I. R., Haig, N. D., & Clement, R. A. (1989). An investigation of trained neural networks from a neurophysiological perspective. *Perception*, 18, 793–803.

Mozer, M. C. & Smolensky, P. (1989). Using relevance to reduce network size automatically. *Connection Science*, 1, 3–16.

Murdock, B. B. (1982). A theory for the storage and retrieval of item and associative information. *Psychological Review*, 89, 609–26.

Murdock, B. B. (1997). Context and mediators in a theory of distributed associative memory (TODAM2). *Psychological Review*, 104, 839–62.

Neuneier, R. & Zimmermann, H. G. (1998). How to train neural networks. In G. Orr & K. Muller (eds), *Neural Networks: tricks of the trade* (pp. 373–423). Berlin; New York: Springer.

O'Keefe, J. & Dostrovsky, J. (1971). The hippocampus as a spatial map: preliminary evidence from unit activity in the freely moving rat. *Brain Research*, 34, 171–5.

O'Keefe, J. & Nadel, L. (1978). *The Hippocampus As A Cognitive Map*. Oxford: Clarendon Press.

Omlin, C. W. & Giles, C. L. (1996). Extraction of rules from discrete-time recurrent neural networks. *Neural Networks*, 9, 41–52.

Orr, G. & Muller, K. (1998). *Neural Networks: tricks of the trade*. Berlin; New York: Springer.

Pao, Y.-H. (1989). *Adaptive Pattern Recognition and Neural Networks*. Reading, MA: Addison-Wesley.

Papert, S. (1988). One Ai or Many? *Daedalus*, 117(1), 1–14.

Pearce, J. M. (1997). *Animal Learning and Cognition: An Introduction*. East Sussex: Psychology Press.

Pearce, J. M. & Bouton, M. E. (2001). Theories of associative learning in animals. *Annual Review of Psychology*, 52, 111–39.

Pfeifer, R. & Scheier, C. (1999). *Understanding Intelligence*. Cambridge, MA: MIT Press.

Piattelli-Palmarini, M. (1989). Evolution, selection and cognition: From "learning" to parameter setting in biology and in the study of language. *Cognition*, 31, 1–44.

Piercey, C. D. & Dawson, M. R. W. (1999). Coarse coding in value units: Subsymbolic implications of nonmonotonic processing units. In M. Hahn & S. C. Stoness (eds), *Proceedings of the Twenty First Annual Conference of the Cognitive Science Society* (pp. 537–42). Malwah, NJ: Lawrence Erlbaum Associates.

Pike, R. (1984). Comparison of convolution and matrix distributed memory systems for associative recall and recognition. *Psychological Review*, 91, 281–94.

Pinker, S. (2002). *The Blank Slate*. New York, NY: Viking.

Poggio, T. & Girosi, F. (1990). Regularization algorithms for learning that are equivalent to multilayer networks. *Science*, 247, 978–82.

Poggio, T., Torre, V., & Koch, C. (1985). Computational vision and regularization theory. *Nature*, 317, 314–19.

Poldrack, R. A., Clark, J., Pare-Blagoev, E. J., Shohamy, D., Moyano, J. C., Myers, C., & Gluck, M. A. (2001). Interactive memory systems in the human brain. *Nature*, 414(6863), 546–50.

Pylyshyn, Z. W. (1991). The role of cognitive architectures in theories of cognition. In K. VanLehn (ed.), *Architectures For Intelligence* (pp. 189–223). Hillsdale, NJ: Lawrence Erlbaum Associates.

Renals, S. (1989). Radial basis function network for speech pattern classification. *Electronics Letters*, 25, 437–9.

Ripley, B. D. (1996). *Pattern Recognition and Neural Networks*. Cambridge, UK: Cambridge University Press.

Rizzuto, D. S. & Kahana, M. J. (2001). An autoassociative neural network model of paired-associate learning. *Neural Computation*, 13(9), 2075–92.

Rojas, R. (1996). *Neural Networks: A Systematic Exploration*. Berlin: Springer.

Rosenblatt, F. (1962). *Principles of Neurodynamics*. Washington: Spartan Books.

Rumelhart, D. E., Hinton, G. E., & Williams, R. J. (1986a). Learning internal representations by back-propagating errors. *Nature*, 323, 533–6.

Rumelhart, D. E., Hinton, G. E., & Williams, R. J. (1986b). Learning internal representations by error backpropagation. In D. Rumelhart, J. McClelland and the PDP Group (eds), *Parallel Distributed Processing* (vol. 1. pp. 318–62) Cambridge, MA: MIT Press.

Rumelhart, D. E. & McClelland, J. L. (1986). *Parallel Distributed Processing*, vol. 1. Cambridge, MA: MIT Press.

Seidenberg, M. (1993). Connectionist models and cognitive theory. *Psychological Science*, 4, 228–35.

Seidenberg, M. & McClelland, J. (1989). A distributed, developmental model of word recognition and naming. *Psychological Review*, 97, 447–52.

Selfridge, O. G. (1956). Pattern recognition and learning. In C. Cherry (ed.), *Information Theory* (pp. 345–53). London: Butterworth Scientific Publications.

Shanks, D. R. (1995). *The Psychology of Associative Learning*. Cambridge, UK: Cambridge University Press.

Shannon, C. E. (1938). A symbolic analysis of relay and switching circuits. *Transactions of the American Institute of Electrical Engineers*, 57, 713–23.

Shannon, C. E. (1949). The synthesis of two-terminal switching circuits. *Bell System Technical Journal*, 28, 59–98.

Shepherd, A. J. (1997). *Second-Order Methods For Neural Networks*. London: Springer.

Smolensky, P. (1988). On the proper treatment of connectionism. *Behavioral and Brain Sciences*, 11, 1–74.

Sporns, O. & Tononi, G. (1994). *Selectionism and the Brain*. San Diego, CA: Academic Press.

Steinbuch, K. (1961). *Die lernmatrix. Kybernetik*, 1, 36–45.

Sutton, R. S. & Barto, A. G. (1981). Toward a modern theory of adaptive networks: Expectation and prediction. *Psychological Review*, 88(2), 135–70.

Sutton, R. S. & Barto, A. G. (1998). *Reinforcement Learning*. Cambridge, MA: MIT Press.

Taylor, W. K. (1956). Electrical simulation of some nervous system functional activities. In C. Cherry (ed.), *Information Theory* (pp. 314–28). London: Butterworth Scientific Publications.

Tesauro, G. & Janssens, B. (1988). Scaling relationships in backpropagation learning. *Complex Systems*, 2, 39–44.

Thrun, S. B., Bala, J., Bloedorn, E., Bratko, I., Cestnik, B., Cheng, J., De Jong, K., Dzeroski, S., Fahlman, S. E., Fisher, D., Hamann, R., Kaufman, K., Keller, S., Kononenko, I., Kreuziger, J., Michalski, R. S., Mitchell, T., Pachowicz, P., Reich, Y., Vafaie, H., Van de Welde, W., Wenzel, W., Wnek, J., & Zhang, J. (1991). *The MONK's Problems – A Performance Comparison of Different Learning Algorithms* (Technical Report CS-CMU-91-197). Pittsburgh: Carnegie Mellon University.

Underwood, B. J. (1957). Interference and forgetting. *Psychological Review*, 64(1), 49–60.

Underwood, B. J. (1966). *Experimental Psychology*, 2nd edn. New York, NY: Appleton-Century-Crofts.

Underwood, B. J., Runquist, R. N. & Schulz, R. W. (1959). Response learning in paired-associate lists as a function of intralist similarity. *Journal of Experimental Psychology*, 58(1), 70–78.

Widrow, B. & Hoff, M. E. (1960). Adaptive switching circuits. *Institute of Radio Engineers, Wester Electronic Show and Convention, Convention Record, Part 4*, 96–104.

Wimer, C. C. & Lambert, W. E. (1959). The differential effects of word and object stimuli on the learning of paired associates. *Journal of Experimental Psychology*, 57(1), 31–6.

Zurada, J. M. (1992). *Introduction To Artificial Neural Systems*. St. Paul, MN: West.

Index of Names

Subject Index